PRENTICE-HALL FOUNDATIONS OF FINANCE SERIES

John C. Burton

The Management of Working Capital

Alan Coleman

Financial Management of Financial Institutions

Herbert E. Dougall

Capital Markets and Institutions, 2nd ed.

Robert K. Jaedicke and Robert T. Sprouse

Accounting Flows: Income, Funds, and Cash

James T. S. Porterfield

Investment Decisions and Capital Costs

Alexander A. Robichek and Stewart C. Myers

Optimal Financing Decisions

Ezra Solomon and Jaime C. Laya

Measuring Profitability

James C. Van Horne

The Function and Analysis of Capital Market Rates

J. Fred Weston

The Scope and Methodology of Finance

PRENTICE-HALL FOUNDATIONS OF FINANCE SERIES

Ezra Solomon, *Editor*

The Function and Analysis of Capital Market Rates

James C. Van Horne

Stanford University

PRENTICE-HALL, INC., Englewood Cliffs, New Jersey

P 13–331934–2
C 13–331942–3

Library of Congress Catalog Card No. 73–99453
Printed in the United States of America

Current printing (last digit) :
10 9 8 7 6 5 4 3 2 1

PRENTICE-HALL INTERNATIONAL, INC., *London*
PRENTICE-HALL OF AUSTRALIA, PTY. LTD., *Sydney*
PRENTICE-HALL OF CANADA, LTD., *Toronto*
PRENTICE-HALL OF INDIA PRIVATE LIMITED, *New Delhi*
PRENTICE-HALL OF JAPAN, INC., *Tokyo*

Editor's Note

The subject matter of financial management is in the process of rapid change. A growing analytical content, virtually nonexistent ten years ago, has displaced the earlier descriptive treatment as the center of emphasis in the field.

These developments have created problems for both teachers and students. On the one hand, recent and current thinking, which is addressed to basic questions that cut across traditional divisions of the subject matter, do not fit neatly into the older structure of academic courses and texts in corporate finance. On the other hand, the new developments have not yet stabilized and as a result have not yet reached the degree of certainty, lucidity, and freedom from controversy that would permit all of them to be captured within a single, straightforward treatment at the textbook level. Indeed, given the present rate of change, it will be years before such a development can be expected.

One solution to the problem, which the present Foundations of Finance Series tries to provide, is to cover the major components of the subject through short independent studies. These individual essays provide a vehicle through which the writer can concentrate on a single sequence of ideas and thus communicate some of the excitement of current thinking and controversy. For the teacher and student, the separate self-contained books provide a flexible up-to-date survey of current thinking on each subarea covered and at the same time permit maximum flexibility in course and curriculum design.

Ezra Solomon

Preface

This book is designed primarily for use as a supplement for courses in money and banking, money and capital markets, and monetary policy. It is comprised of two parts. The first deals with the role of interest rates in channeling savings in an economy to investment opportunities in that economy. We consider such issues as why financial instruments exist in an economy, the efficiency of financial markets in channeling savings, the measurement of savings flows, and the way in which interest rates bring about equilibrium in financial markets. An asset choice model is developed for explaining the equilibrating process.

In the second part of the book, we are concerned with explaining differences in observed yields for various financial instruments. Here the effects that maturity (the term structure of interest rates), default risk, marketability, callability, and taxability have on yields are investigated. Our focus is on the theoretical foundations for yield differentials as well as on various "real world" conditions which affect these differentials. In the last chapter, we extend our analysis to consider common stocks and convertible securities. Because of the special nature of these instruments, we analyze their returns separately from those for fixed-income securities.

In the book, a conceptual framework is developed for analyzing interest rates under conditions of uncertainty. Hopefully, this framework will enable the reader to better understand both absolute and relative movements in interest rates. With the exception of its effect through interest-rate expectations, no attempt is made to analyze the effect of monetary policy on interest rates. This exclusion was dictated by the extensive treatment of the topic elsewhere and by the limited scope of the present study.

In writing this book, I have a number of debts of gratitude. Professors Alan Kraus and Ezra Solomon read the manuscript and offered many helpful comments. Professor Robert Wilson provided helpful suggestions for structuring the appendix to Chapter 3. I have profited much from numerous discussions with Gert von der Linde, a former colleague, on finanical markets. The book has been influenced also by the works of a number of scholars who are cited in the references. Finally, I am grateful to my wife, Mimi, who both typed and read the manuscript.

JAMES C. VAN HORNE

Contents

The Function and Analysis
of Capital Market Rates

111111111111111111111111111111111111111111111111111111111111111111111111111111111111111
111111111111111111111111111111111111111111111111111111111111111111111111111111111111111
111111111111111111111111111111111111111111   111111111111111111111111111111111111111111
111111111111111111111111111111111111111111   111111111111111111111111111111111111111111
111111111111111111111111111111111111111111   111111111111111111111111111111111111111111
111111111111111111111111111111111111111111   111111111111111111111111111111111111111111
111111111111111111111111111111111111111111   111111111111111111111111111111111111111111
111111111111111111111111111111111111111111   111111111111111111111111111111111111111111
111111111111111111111111111111111111111111   111111111111111111111111111111111111111111
111111111111111111111111111111111111111111   111111111111111111111111111111111111111111
111111111111111111111111111111111111111111   111111111111111111111111111111111111111111
111111111111111111111111111111111111111111   111111111111111111111111111111111111111111
111111111111111111111111111111111111111111111111111111111111111111111111111111111111111
111111111111111111111111111111111111111111111111111111111111111111111111111111111111111

The Function of Financial Markets

IN this book, the underlying structure of financial markets is examined, as is the price mechanism, which brings about a balance between supply and demand. Our purpose is not to describe specific money or capital markets or the institutions involved in these markets, and it is not to provide data on financial flows; this information is available elsewhere.[1] Rather, this book provides a basis for understanding and analyzing interest rates and funds movements in financial markets. The instruments studied are financial assets. Unlike real, or tangible, assets, a *financial* asset is a claim on some other economic unit. It does not provide its owner with the physical services that a real asset does. Instead, financial assets are held as a store of value and for the return that they are expected to provide. The holding of these assets, with the exception of equity securities, indicates neither direct nor indirect ownership of real assets in the economy.

---

[1] See Herbert E. Dougall, *Capital Markets and Institutions* (Englewood Cliffs, N.J.: Prentice-Hall, Inc., 1965); Roland I. Robinson, *Money and Capital Markets* (New York: McGraw-Hill Book Company, 1964); G. Walter Woodworth, *The Money Market and Monetary Management* (New York: Harper & Row, Publishers, 1965); and Raymond W. Goldsmith, *The Flow of Capital Funds in the Postwar Economy* (New York: National Bureau of Economic Research, 1965).

Savings-Investment Foundation

Financial assets exist in an economy because the savings of various economic units (current income less current expenditures) during a period of time differ from their investment in real assets. In this regard, an economic unit can be (1) a household or partnership, (2) a nonprofit organization, (3) a corporation (financial or nonfinancial), or (4) a government (federal, state, or local). Assume for the moment a closed economy in which there are no foreign transactions. If savings equal investment for all economic units in that economy over all periods of time, there would be no external financing and no financial assets. In other words, each economic unit would be self-sufficient; current expenditures and investment in real assets would be paid for out of current income. A financial asset is created only when the investment of an economic unit in real assets exceeds its savings, and it finances this excess by borrowing, issuing equity securities, or issuing money (if the economic unit happens to be a monetary institution).[2] For an economic unit to finance, of course, another economic unit or other units in the economy must be willing to lend. This interaction of the borrower with the lender determines interest rates. For identification, economic units whose current savings exceed their investment in real assets are called *savings-surplus units*. Economic units whose investment in real assets exceeds their current savings are labeled *savings-deficit units*.[3] In the economy as a whole, funds are provided by savings-surplus units to the savings-deficit units. This exchange of funds is evidenced by pieces of paper representing financial assets to the holders and financial liabilities to the issuers.

If an economic unit holds existing financial assets, it is able to cover the excess of its investment in real assets over savings by means other than issuing financial liabilities. It simply can sell some of the financial assets it holds. Thus, as long as an economic unit holds financial assets, it does not have to increase its financial liabilities by an amount equal to its excess of investment over savings. The purchase and sale of existing financial assets occur in the *secondary market*. Transactions in this market do not increase the total stock of financial assets outstanding. It is possible, although unlikely, for a substantial number of savings-deficit units to exist in an economy over a period of time and for little change to occur in total financial assets outstanding. For this to happen, however, savings-deficit units must have sufficient financial assets to cover the excess of their investment in real assets over savings and, of course, must be willing to sell these assets.

---

[2] A financial asset may be created for the purpose of financing consumption in excess of current income. Although it is possible for investment in real assets for a period to be zero, that investment still would exceed the negative savings of the economic unit.

[3] These labels correspond to those given by Goldsmith, *The Flow of Capital Funds in the Postwar Economy*.

Efficiency of Financial Markets

The purpose of financial markets is to allocate savings efficiently in an economy to ultimate users, either for investment in real assets or for consumption. In this section, we regard financial markets in a broad sense as including all institutions and procedures for bringing buyers and sellers of financial instruments together, no matter what the nature of the financial instrument. If those economic units which saved were the same as those which engaged in capital formation, an economy could prosper without financial markets. In modern economies, however, the economic units most responsible for capital formation—nonfinancial corporations—invest in real assets in an amount in excess of their total savings. Households, on the other hand, have total savings in excess of total investment. Therefore, a balance is not achieved. The more diverse the patterns of desired savings and investment among economic units, the greater the need for efficient financial markets to channel savings to ultimate users. Their job is to allocate savings from savings-surplus economic units to savings-deficit units so that the highest level of want satisfaction can be achieved. These parties should be brought together, either directly or indirectly, at the least possible cost and with the least inconvenience.

Efficient financial markets are absolutely essential to assure adequate capital formation and economic growth in a modern economy.[4] For example, if there were no financial assets other than paper money, each economic unit could invest in real assets only to the extent that it saved.[5] Without financial assets, then, an economic unit would be constrained greatly in its investment behavior. If it wanted to invest in real assets, it would have to save to do so. If the amount required for investment in a real asset were large in relation to current savings, an economic unit simply would have to postpone investment until it had accumulated sufficient savings. Moreover, these savings would have to be accumulated as money balances, there being no alternatives. Because of the absence of financing, many worthwhile investment opportunities would have to be postponed or abandoned by economic units lacking sufficient savings.[6]

---

[4] Capital formation represents net additions to the stock of real assets within the country and the stock of claims on foreign countries. Real assets are taken to include productive assets, dwellings, and consumer durables. This definition differs from that of Kuznets, who excludes the latter category. See Simon Kuznets, *Capital in the Postwar Economy* (New York: National Bureau of Economic Research, 1961), p. 16.

[5] In a barter economy, without money or financial assets, each economic unit must be in balance with respect to savings and investment. It must invest in real assets in an amount equal to its savings. No economic unit could invest more than it saved.

[6] The development of this section draws on John G. Gurley and Edward S. Shaw, *Money in a Theory of Finance* (Washington, D.C.: The Brookings Institution, 1960); and John G. Gurley, "The Savings-Investment Process and the Market for Loanable Funds," reprinted in Lawrence S. Ritter, ed., *Money and Economic Activity* (Boston: Houghton Mifflin Company, 1967), pp. 50–55.

In such a system, savings in the economy would not be channeled to the most promising investment opportunities; and accordingly, capital would be less than optimally allocated. Those economic units which lacked promising investment opportunities would have no alternative except to accumulate money balances. Likewise, economic units with very promising opportunities might not be able to accumulate sufficient savings rapidly enough to undertake the projects. Consequently, inferior investments might be undertaken by some economic units, while very promising investment opportunities would be postponed or abandoned by others. Capital is misallocated in such a system, and total investment tends to be low relative to what it might be with financial assets. In this situation, growth in the economy is restrained, if not stagnant, and the level of want satisfaction is far from optimal. An important resource—namely, capital—is allocated inefficiently with an adverse effect upon national income and the standard of living for individuals in that economy. For want of a better system, financial assets must come into being.

The discussion above has been confined to the private sector of the economy. With paper money, however, the federal government is able to finance its purchases of goods and services by issuing money. If the federal government increases the supply of money, in keeping with increases in the demand for money by other economic units, purchases of goods and services by the government increase.[7] To the extent that the federal government centralizes investment and channels it into promising opportunities, capital formation in the economy is efficient. In underdeveloped countries, much of the capital formation for productive assets is brought about by the federal government. The private sector simply does not have the financial markets necessary for allocating savings with any degree of efficiency.

We turn now to the situation where there are financial assets as well as paper money in the economy, but no financial institutions. With financial assets, investment in real assets by an economic unit is no longer constrained by the amount of its savings. If it wants to invest more than it saves, it can do so by reducing the amount of its money balances, by selling financial assets, or by increasing its financial liabilities. When an economic unit increases its financial liabilities, it issues a *primary security*. For this to be done, however, another economic unit or other units in the economy must be willing to purchase it. In a developing economy, these transactions between borrower and lender usually take the form of direct loans. The ability of economic units to finance an excess of investment over savings improves greatly the allocation of savings in a society. Many of the problems cited earlier are eliminated. Individual economic units no longer need to postpone promising investment opportunities for lack of accumulated savings. Moreover, savings-surplus units have an outlet for their savings other than money balances—an outlet that provides an expected return.

[7]Gurley, "The Savings-Investment Process and the Market for Loanable Funds," p. 51.

With financial assets in the form of direct loans, the overall level of want satisfaction in the economy is higher than it would be otherwise. Still, there are degrees of efficiency. A system of direct loans may not be sufficient to assemble and "package" large blocks of savings for investment in large projects. To the extent that a single savings-surplus economic unit cannot service the capital needs of a savings-deficit unit, the latter must turn to additional savings-surplus units. If the need for funds is large, the user may have considerable difficulty in locating pockets of available savings and in negotiating multiple loans. For one thing, his communication network is limited. Consequently, there is a need to bring together ultimate savers and investors in a more efficient manner than through direct loans between the two parties.

To service this need, various loan brokers may come into existence to find savers and bring them together with economic units needing funds. Because a broker is a specialist who is continually in the business of matching the need for funds with the supply, usually he is able to do it more efficiently and at a lower cost than are individual economic units themselves. One improvement is that he is able to divide a primary security of a certain amount into smaller amounts more compatible with the preferences of savings-surplus economic units. As a result, savers are able to hold their savings in a diversified portfolio of primary securities; this feature encourages savers to invest in financial assets. The resulting increased attractiveness of primary securities improves the flow of savings from savers to users of funds. In addition to performing the brokerage function involved in selling securities, investment bankers may underwrite an issue of primary securities. By underwriting, the investment banker bears the risk of selling the issue. He buys the primary securities from the borrower and resells them to savers. Since he pays the borrower for the security issue, the latter does not bear the risk of not being able to sell the securities. This guaranteed purchase makes it easier than otherwise for savings-deficit economic units to finance their excess of investment in real assets over savings.

Another innovation that enhances the efficiency of the flow of savings in an economy is the development of *secondary markets*, where existing securities can be either bought or sold. With a viable secondary market, a savings-surplus economic unit achieves flexibility when it purchases a primary security. Should it need to sell the security in the future, it will be able to do so because the security is marketable. The existence of secondary markets encourages more risk-taking on the part of savings-surplus economic units. If, in the future, they want to invest more than they save, they know that they will be able to sell financial assets as one means of covering the excess. This flexibility encourages savings-surplus economic units to make their savings available to others rather than to hold them as money balances. All the innovations discussed contribute to the efficiency of the flow of savings from ultimate savers to ultimate users through primary securities. As a result, capital allocation is more efficient: Savings are more readily channeled to the most promising investments.

Up to now, we have considered only the direct flow of savings from savers to users. However, the flow can be indirect if there are financial intermediaries in the economy. Financial intermediaries include such institutions as commercial banks, savings banks, savings and loan associations, life insurance companies, and pension and profit-sharing funds. These intermediaries purchase primary securities and, in turn, issue their own securities. Thus, they come between ultimate borrowers and ultimate lenders. In essence, they transform direct claims—primary securities—into indirect claims—called *indirect securities*—which differ in form from direct claims. For example, the primary security that a savings and loan association purchases is a mortgage; the indirect claim issued is a savings account or certificate of deposit. A life insurance company, on the other hand, purchases mortgages and bonds and issues life insurance policies.

Financial intermediaries transform funds in such a way as to make them more attractive.[8] On one hand, the indirect security issued to ultimate lenders is more attractive than is a direct, or primary, security. In particular, these indirect claims are well suited to the small saver. On the other hand, the ultimate borrower is able to sell its primary securities to a financial intermediary on more attractive terms than it could if the securities were sold directly to ultimate lenders. Financial intermediaries provide a variety of services and economies that make the transformation of claims attractive.

1. Economies of scale. Because financial intermediaries continually are in the business of purchasing primary securities, economies of scale not available to the borrower or to the individual saver are possible.
2. Divisibility and flexibility. A financial intermediary is able to pool the savings of many individual savers to purchase primary securities of varying sizes. In particular, it is able to tap small pockets of savings for ultimate investment in real assets. The offering of indirect securities of varying size contributes significantly to the attractiveness of financial intermediaries to the saver. The borrower achieves flexibility in dealing with a financial intermediary as opposed to a large number of lenders. He is able to obtain terms tailored to his needs more readily.
3. Diversification and risk. By purchasing a number of different primary securities, the financial intermediary is able to spread risk. If these securities are less than perfectly correlated with each other, the intermediary is able to reduce the risk associated with fluctuations in value of principal. The benefits of reduced risk are passed on to the indirect security holders. As a result, the indirect security provides a higher degree of liquidity to the saver than does a like commitment to a single primary security.

---

[8] See Raymond W. Goldsmith, *Financial Institutions* (New York: Random House, Inc., 1968), pp. 22–33.

4. Maturity. A financial intermediary is able to transform a primary security of a certain maturity into indirect securities of different maturities. As a result, the maturities on the primary and the indirect securities may be more attractive to the ultimate borrower and lender than they would be if the loan were direct.

5. Expertise and convenience. The financial intermediary is an expert in making purchases of primary securities and in so doing eliminates the inconvenience to the saver of making direct purchases. For example, not many individuals are familiar with the intricacies of making a mortgage loan; they have neither the time nor the inclination to learn. For the most part, they are happy to let savings and loan associations, commercial banks, savings banks, and life insurance companies engage in this type of lending and to purchase the indirect securities of these intermediaries. The financial intermediary is also an expert in dealing with ultimate savers—an expertise lacking in most borrowers.

Financial intermediaries tailor the denomination and type of indirect securities they issue to the desires of savers. Their purpose, of course, is to make a profit by purchasing primary securities yielding more than the return they must pay on the indirect securities issued and on operations. In so doing, they must channel funds from the ultimate lender to the ultimate borrower at a lower cost or with more convenience or both than is possible through a direct purchase of primary securities by the ultimate lender. Otherwise, they have no reason to exist.

To illustrate this notion, consider again a savings and loan association. Suppose that the current rate on a prime mortgage is 8 per cent, whereas the rate on a savings account is 5 per cent. The 3 per cent spread should cover expenses and provide some profit for the savings and loan association. Suppose further that without financial intermediaries of the type that purchase mortgages, the equilibrium rate on prime mortgages is 11 per cent. Obviously, the ultimate borrower is better off with financial intermediaries in the economy, for he pays less interest on his mortgage. However, the ultimate lender also must be better off. To understand his preference for an indirect security over a direct one, consider the expense and inconvenience of making a direct loan and the added risk in purchasing the mortgage as opposed to the indirect security of the savings and loan association. Suppose that for a $15,000 mortgage on a house, five dentists are willing to band together to make the loan out of their collective savings. (Actually, the formation of this group of savers to make a direct purchase represents an innovation of sorts.) By their coming together in a syndicate, their small savings are pooled into an amount sufficient to purchase a primary security, which is somewhat "lumpy." Of course, there is an inconvenience in having to meet and make joint arrangements.

Assume that we are able to measure the expense of making the loan, administering the mortgage, and incurring inconvenience. Assume also that, in total, these amount to 4 per cent of the loan on an annual basis. Moreover, suppose that the added risk to the purchasers of the primary security, as opposed to the indirect securities of the savings and loan association, can be measured and that the risk premium involved is 3 per cent. If so, the net yield to the dentists on a direct loan, adjusted to a basis equivalent to the indirect security, is as follows.

Rate on primary security without financial intermediaries		11 per cent
Less:		
Marginal expenses and cost of inconvenience	4 per cent	
Risk premium above indirect security	3 per cent	7 per cent
Net yield on equivalent loan		4 per cent

We see in this hypothetical example that the ultimate lenders receive less on the direct purchase of the mortgage—4 per cent on an adjusted basis—than they do on the purchase of the indirect security—5 per cent. As a result, the presence of financial intermediaries is beneficial both to ultimate borrowers and to ultimate lenders.

Thus, financial intermediaries tend to make financial markets more efficient. By transforming primary securities into indirect securities, they lower the cost to the ultimate borrower and provide a security better suited to the ultimate lender. The yield differential, as represented by the difference in yield on the primary security and the net yield to the saver on an equivalent loan, is narrowed by their presence. In our example, it is narrowed from an 11–4 per cent spread to an 8–5 per cent spread. One of the marks of efficient financial markets is that when opportunities for profit exist or arise, financial intermediaries and other financial innovations come into being to exploit the opportunity. By entering the market, they tend to narrow the differential, as defined above. Thus, they facilitate the movement of savings from ultimate savers to ultimate borrowers at a lower cost and with less inconvenience. The result is a higher level of want satisfaction in the economy.

With the introduction of financial intermediaries, we have four main sectors in an economy: households, nonfinancial business firms, governments, and financial institutions. These four sectors form a matrix of claims against one another. This matrix is illustrated in Fig. 1-1, which shows hypothetical balance sheets for each sector. Financial assets of each sector include money as well as primary securities. Households, of course, are the ultimate owners of all business enterprises, whether they be nonfinancial corporations or private financial institutions. The figure illustrates the distinct role of financial intermediaries. Their assets are predominantly financial assets; they hold a relatively small amount of real assets. On the right-hand side of the balance sheet, financial liabilities

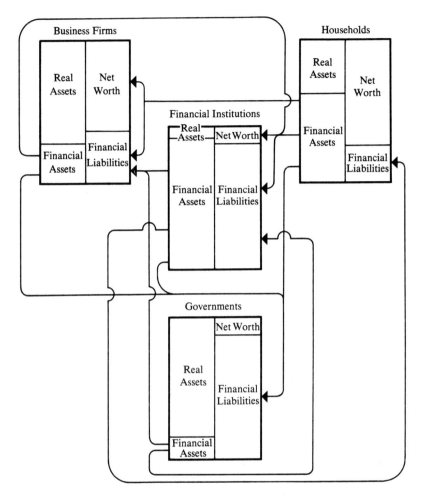

Fig. 1-1. Relationship of claims.

are predominant. Financial institutions, then, are engaged in transforming direct claims into indirect claims that have a wider appeal. The relationship of financial to real assets and of financial liabilities to net worth distinguishes them from other economic units.[9]

The more varied the vehicles by which savings can flow from ultimate savers to ultimate users of funds, usually the more efficient the financial markets of an economy. With efficient financial markets, there can be sharp differences between the pattern of savings and the pattern of

---

[9] For an analysis of the sources and uses of funds of financial intermediaries, see Goldsmith, *Financial Institutions*, Chapter 3.

investment for economic units in the economy. The result is a higher level of capital formation, growth, and want satisfaction. Individual economic units are not confined either to holding their savings in money balances or to investing them in real assets. Their alternatives are many; each contributes to the efficient channeling of funds from ultimate savers to users.

The Implication of Savings

Having outlined the reason for financial assets in an economy and traced through the efficiency of financial markets, we consider now the implications of savings, individually and collectively, for economic units. Recall that savings represent current income less current consumption.

For the *individual*, savings represent expenditures foregone out of current income, and they may be the result of a number of acts. One of the most familiar is spending less than one's discretionary income, with the difference going into a savings account. The build-up in a savings account, in itself, does not represent an act of savings but, rather, is the result of it. Other aspects of savings for the individual are less familiar. For example, savings may be the result of repayment of principal in a mortgage payment. Another means by which net worth may be increased is through contributions, either voluntary or involuntary, to a pension or profit-sharing plan or both. In addition, an individual may save through the payment of a premium on a life insurance policy.

For the *corporation*, *net* savings represent earnings retained during the period being studied—that is, profits after taxes and after the payment of dividends on preferred and common stock. *Gross* savings for corporations include capital-consumption allowances (mainly depreciation) in addition to retained earnings. Finally, savings for a *government* unit represent a budget surplus, and dissavings a budget deficit.

For a given period of time, the total uses of funds by an economic unit must equal its total sources. Thus,[10]

$$RA + MT + L + E = S + D + IM + B + IE \qquad (1\text{-}1)$$

where RA = gross change in real assets
MT = change in money held
L = lending (change in fixed-income securities held)
E = equity investment (change in equity securities held)
S = net savings
D = capital-consumption allowance
IM = issuance of money
B = borrowing
IE = issuance of equity securities

---

[10]This equation is a modification of an equation developed by Goldsmith, *The Flow of Capital Funds in the Postwar Economy*, p. 59. For simplicity, we assume a closed economy with no foreign transactions.

All the symbols represent net flows over a period of time, and they can be positive or negative. Depending upon the type of economic unit involved, however, some of the variables may not be applicable. As only monetary institutions can issue money, IM is applicable only to the central bank and commercial banks. Similarly, only corporations can issue equity securities, so IE applies only to them. For the economic unit, the total uses of funds on the left side of the equation must equal total sources on the right side.

For purposes of financial-market analysis, net savings for the economic unit usually are defined as[11]

$$S = (MT + L + E) - (IM + B + IE) + (RA - D) \qquad (1\text{-}2)$$

gross savings through financial assets	financing	net savings through real assets

net savings through financial assets

For the economy as a whole, *ex post* savings for a given period of time must equal *ex post* investment in real assets for that period. Consequently,

$$\sum_j S = \sum_j (RA - D) \qquad (1\text{-}3)$$

where j is the jth economic unit in the economy. Thus, changes in financial assets for a period cancel out when summed for all economic units in the economy.

$$\sum_j (MT + L + E) - \sum_J (IM + B + IE) = 0 \qquad (1\text{-}4)$$

As a result, savings for the economy as a whole must correspond to the increase in net real assets in that economy. There is no such thing as savings through financial assets for the economy as a whole. However, individual economic units can save through financial assets, and this is the process we wish to study. The fact that financial assets wash out when they are totaled for all economic units in the economy is a recognizable identity. It is the interaction between the issuers of financial claims and the potential holders of those claims that is important.

Liquidity and Financial Markets

All financial instruments have a common denominator in that they are expressed in terms of money—the accepted medium of exchange. Thus,

---

[11]Again, this equation is a modification of Goldsmith, *The Flow of Capital Funds in the Postwar Economy.*

financial flows occur in terms of money. Money, the most liquid of assets, is the measure against which various types of financial instruments are compared as to their degree of substitution. In this regard, *liquidity* may be defined as the ability to realize value in money. As such, it has two dimensions: (1) the length of time and transaction cost required to convert the asset into money, and (2) the certainty of the price realized.[12] The latter represents the stability of the ratio of exchange between the asset and money—in other words, the degree of fluctuation in market price. The two factors are interrelated. If an asset must be converted into money in a very short period of time, there may be more uncertainty as to the price realized than if there were a reasonable time period in which to sell the asset.

Financial markets tend to be efficient relative to other markets. As the good involved is a claim, evidenced by a piece of paper, it is transportable at little cost and is not subject to physical deterioration. Moreover, it can be defined and classified easily. For most financial markets, information is available readily, and geographical boundaries are not a great problem. By their very nature, then, financial markets are fairly efficient when compared with the full spectrum of markets.

Frequently, these markets are classified according to the final maturity of the particular instrument involved. On one hand, *money* markets usually are regarded as including financial assets that are short term, are highly marketable, and, accordingly, possess low risk and a high degree of liquidity. These assets are traded in highly impersonal markets, where funds move on the basis of price and risk alone. Thus, a short-term loan negotiated between a corporation and a bank is not considered a money-market instrument. Examples of money markets include the markets for short-term government securities, bankers' acceptances, and commercial paper. *Capital* markets, on the other hand, include instruments with longer terms to maturity. These markets are somewhat more diverse than money markets. Examples include markets for government, corporate, and municipal bonds; corporate stocks; and mortgages. The maturity boundary that divides the money and capital markets is rather arbitrary. Some regard it as one year, while others maintain that it is five years. Because the foundation for their existence is the same, we have not concerned ourselves in this chapter with the breakdown between the two markets.

Financial Flows and Interest Rates

In studying financial markets, we are interested in the flow of savings from ultimate savers to ultimate users. These flows can be analyzed with *flow-of-funds* data. Flow of funds is a system of social accounting that

---

[12] James C. Van Horne and David A. Bowers, "The Liquidity Impact of Debt Management," *Southern Economic Journal*, XXXIV (April, 1968), 527.

enables one to evaluate savings flows between various sectors in the economy. This system and its usefulness are examined in Chapter 2. The actual allocation, or channeling, of savings in an economy is accomplished primarily through interest rates. Presumably, economic units with the most promising investment opportunities will pay more for the use of funds than will those with inferior opportunities. To the extent that the former bid funds away from the latter, savings tend to be channeled to the most efficient uses. Interest rates adjust continually to bring changing supply and demand in each market into balance. The movement toward equilibrium occurs not only in an individual financial market but also across financial markets. The role of interest rates in the equilibrating process is studied in Chapter 3.

The remainder of the book is devoted to an analysis of relative yields for various financial instruments. In Chapters 4, 5, and 6, we investigate reasons for differences in the level of interest rates among fixed-income securities. These differences are called *yield differentials*. In Chapters 4 and 5, we examine the effects of length of time to maturity, default risk, and marketability on interest rates. In Chapter 6, we investigate the effect of the call feature and taxability on interest rates as well as the structure of long-term market rates for fixed-income securities. Finally, Chapter 7 covers the market for equity securities. Because of the special nature of equity securities, we consider returns in this market separately from those for fixed-income securities.

Summary

A financial asset is a claim against some economic unit in an economy. It is held for the return it provides and as a store of value—reasons that differentiate it from a real asset. Financial assets and markets exist because, during a period of time, some economic units save more than they invest in real assets, while other economic units invest more than they save. To cover an excess of investment over savings for a period, an economic unit can reduce its holdings of existing financial assets, increase its financial liabilities, or undertake some combination of the two. When it increases its financial liabilities, a new financial instrument is created in the economy. The existence of financial markets permits investment for economic units to differ from their savings.

The purpose of financial markets is to allocate efficiently savings in an economy to ultimate users of funds. For the economy as a whole, *ex post* investment must equal *ex post* savings. However, this is not true for individual economic units; they can have considerable divergence between savings and investment for a particular period of time. The more vibrant the financial markets in an economy, the more efficient the allocation of savings to the most promising investment opportunities, and the greater the capital formation in that economy. A number of innovations make financial markets efficient. Among the most important are financial intermediaries. A financial intermediary transforms the direct claim of the ultimate borrower into an indirect claim, which is sold to ultimate lenders. Intermediaries channel savings from ultimate savers to ultimate borrowers at a lower cost and with less inconvenience than is possible on a direct basis.

All financial flows occur in terms of money—the most liquid of assets. Liquidity may be defined as the ability to realize value in money. Generally, financial markets are efficient relative to other markets. In the chapters that follow, we shall investigate, in depth, both the flow of savings and the price mechanism—namely, interest rates— which brings about a balance between supply and demand in the various financial markets. Our concern is with both the level of interest rates and the differentials between interest rates for different financial instruments.

Selected References

Commission on Money and Credit, *Private Capital Markets*. Englewood Cliffs, N.J.: Prentice-Hall, Inc., 1964.

Dougall, Herbert E., *Capital Markets and Institutions*. Englewood Cliffs, N.J.: Prentice-Hall, Inc., 1965.

Goldsmith, Raymond W., *Financial Institutions*. New York: Random House, Inc., 1968.

———, *Financial Intermediaries in the American Economy Since 1900*. Princeton, N.J.: National Bureau of Economic Research, 1958.

———, *The Flow of Capital Funds in the Postwar Economy*, Chapter 1. New York: National Bureau of Economic Research, 1965.

———, *A Study of Saving in the United States*, 3 vols. Princeton, N.J.: National Bureau of Economic Research, 1955.

Gurley, John G., "The Savings-Investment Process and the Market for Loanable Funds," reprinted in Lawrence S. Ritter, ed., *Money and Economic Activity*, pp. 50–55. Boston: Houghton Mifflin Company, 1967.

———, and Edward S. Shaw, *Money in a Theory of Finance*. Washington, D.C.: The Brookings Institution, 1960.

———, "Financial Intermediaries and the Saving-Investment Process," *Journal of Finance*, XI (May, 1956), 257–66.

Moore, Basil J., *An Introduction to the Theory of Finance*, Chapters 1, 3, and 4. New York: The Free Press, 1968.

Robinson, Roland I., *Money and Capital Markets*. New York: McGraw-Hill Book Company, 1964.

Woodworth, G. Walter, *The Money Market and Monetary Management*. New York: Harper & Row, Publishers, 1965.

Flow-of-Funds Analysis

An indispensable tool of the financial-market analyst is the flow-of-funds framework. This framework enables him to analyze the movement of savings through the economy in a highly structured, consistent, and comprehensive manner. He is able not only to evaluate the complex interdependence of financial claims throughout the economy but also to identify various pressure points in the system. The insight gained from studying these pressure points is invaluable when it comes to analyzing market rates of interest. In addition, the flow-of-funds framework makes possible an analysis of the interaction between the financial and the real segments of the economy. Such analysis was not possible before flow-of-funds data were available.

The flow of funds itself is a system of social accounting developed only in recent years. Its foundation was Morris A. Copeland's celebrated work in 1952.[1] The Board of Governors of the Federal Reserve System first began to publish data on the flow of funds in 1955[2] and published a

---

[1] *A Study of Moneyflows in the United States* (New York: National Bureau of Economic Research, 1955).

[2] *Flow of Funds in the United States, 1939–1953* (Washington, D.C.: Board of Governors of the Federal Reserve System, 1955).

revised and quarterly presentation of data in 1959.[3] Since 1959, quarterly data have been published regularly in the *Federal Reserve Bulletin*. Whereas the national-income accounting system deals with goods and services, flow-of-funds data provide information on the financial segment of the economy, thereby complementing the information provided in the national-income accounts. For example, national-income accounts provide data on the amount of savings, but they give no information on how savings are used. The process by which funds flow from savings to investment is omitted. One must turn to flow-of-funds data to obtain this information. In this chapter, we discuss the structure of the flow-of-funds accounting system, examine the interrelationship of sources and uses of funds for various sectors in the economy, and finally, investigate the uses of this information.

Structure of System

Flow-of-funds data for an economy are derived for a specific period of time by (1) preparing source- and use-of-funds statements for each sector in the economy, (2) totaling the sources and uses for all sectors, and (3) presenting the information in a flow-of-funds matrix for the entire economy.[4] The time span studied usually is either a quarter or a full year. The starting point in any flow-of-funds accounting system is the division of the economy into a workable number of sectors. The idea is to lump together those economic units with similar behavior. Because funds movements through sectors are being analyzed, economic units in a sector must be relatively homogeneous decision-making units if the analysis is to be meaningful.

For this reason, sectors are defined along institutional lines according to the similarity of their asset and liability structures. The number of sectors used depends upon the purpose of the analysis, the availability of data, and the cost involved in collecting these data. The maximum possible number of sectors, of course, is the total number of economic units in the economy; in the United States, this would be over 70 million. The minimum number is two, for there can be no flow of funds with only one sector—the economy as a whole. If there are too few sectors, significant relationships among various groups of economic units are likely to be hidden. On the other hand, if there are too many sectors, the analysis of the interaction among sectors becomes very cumbersome. Here, the problem is that important relationships, although not hidden, may be overlooked. Needless to say, the number of sectors finally employed usually represents a compromise. In the sectoring of the economy,

---

[3]See "A Quarterly Presentation of Flow of Funds and Savings," *Federal Reserve Bulletin*, 45 (August, 1959), 828–59.

[4]See Lawrence S. Ritter, *The Flow of Funds Accounts: A Framework for Financial Analysis* (New York: Institute of Finance, New York University, 1968), for an exposition on the preparation of a flow-of-funds system of social accounting.

it is absolutely necessary that all economic units be included. Moreover, if foreign transactions are considered, a sector must be included for the rest of the world. The four main sectors used in the United States flow-of-funds system are households, governments, business enterprises, and financial institutions. For reporting purposes, the Federal Reserve has subdivided some of these sectors, breaking them down into ten categories:[5]

1. Consumers and nonprofit organizations. This sector includes all households, personal trusts, and nonprofit organizations. It is one of the largest sectors and usually is labeled *households*.
2. Farm business.
3. Nonfarm, unincorporated, nonfinancial, business enterprises. This sector includes such economic units as trade associations and farm cooperatives. This sector often is combined with sector 2 for presentation.
4. Corporate business.
5. Federal government.
6. State and local governments.
7. Commercial banks, Federal Reserve System, and treasury monetary funds.
8. Savings institutions, including mutual savings banks, savings and loan associations, and credit unions.
9. Insurance companies and private pension plans.
10. Financial institutions not otherwise classified, including finance companies, open-end investment companies, and security brokers and dealers.

In addition, the Federal Reserve has a rest-of-the-world sector, comprising all residents and governments of countries outside the United States. As the Federal Reserve is the principal source of flow-of-funds data for the economy, the analyst must settle for this breakdown of the economy.

Once the economy has been divided into sectors, the next step is to prepare a source- and use-of-funds statement for each sector.[6] The starting point here is a balance sheet for each sector at the beginning of the period being studied:

Sector A
January 1, 19___

Assets		*Liabilities and Net Worth*	
Money		Financial liabilities	
Other financial assets			
Real assets	_____	Net worth	_____
Total assets	======	Total liabilities and new worth	======

Most of the assets in the above balance sheet are reported at their market values. The problems involved in valuation will be taken up later

---

[5] "A Quarterly Presentation of Flow of Funds and Savings," pp. 831, 846–48.

[6] The development of the immediate presentation draws upon Ritter, *The Flow of Funds Accounts*.

in this chapter, after our examination of how the data are prepared. It is important to recognize that the presence of financial assets on the balance sheet for one sector means that financial liabilities of the same amount appear on the balance sheets of other sectors in the economy. Also, financial assets and liabilities among economic units in a particular sector are netted out. The financial-asset figure for the sector includes only claims against economic units in other sectors. By the same token, the financial-liability figure includes only claims held by economic units in other sectors against economic units in the sector being studied. As long as at least one economic unit in a sector holds a financial claim against another economic unit in that sector, the financial-asset figure and the financial-liability figure shown on the balance sheet for the sector will be less than the sum of financial assets and the sum of financial liabilities for all economic units in that sector. This statement does not hold for real assets, however. Because a real asset appears on the balance sheet only of the economic unit which owns it, the real-asset figure shown on the balance sheet for a sector is the sum of real assets for all economic units in the sector.

By definition, a balance sheet shows the stocks of assets, liabilities, and net worth of a sector at a moment in time. By taking the change which occurs in stocks between two balance sheets at different points in time, we obtain the net flows for the sector over the time span. These net flows can be expressed in a source- and use-of-funds statement for the sector:

Sector A
Source and Uses of Funds 19____

Uses	Sources	
Δ Money	Δ Financial liabilities	
Δ Other financial assets	Δ Net worth	_____
Δ Real assets _____		
Δ Total assets _____	Δ Total liabilities and new worth	_____

For the period, the net change in total assets for a sector must equal the net change in total liabilities and net worth. The change in net worth represents savings for the period—that is, the difference between current income and current expenditures. Positive savings imply an increase in total assets, a decrease in total liabilities, or both. A savings-deficit sector, with investment in real assets greater than its savings, must reduce its money holdings, sell other financial assets, increase its liabilities, or perform some combination of these actions. Conversely, a savings-surplus sector must show an increase in its holdings of financial assets (including money), a reduction in its financial liabilities, or some combination.

Once source- and use-of-funds statements have been prepared for all sectors, these statements can be combined into a matrix for the entire economy. A hypothetical example of such a matrix is shown in Table 2-1.

TABLE 2-1   Matrix of Flow of Funds of Entire Economy 19__

	Households		Business Firms		Financial Institutions		Governments		All Sectors	
	U	S	U	S	U	S	U	S	U	S
Net worth (savings)		101		77		4		-3		179
Real assets (investment)	82		96		1				179	
Money	2		2			5	1		5	5
Other financial assets	37		18		60		17		132	
Financial liabilities		20		39		52		21		132
	121	121	116	116	61	61	18	18	316	316

In the table, a closed economy consisting of four sectors—households, business firms, financial institutions, and governments—is assumed. We see that the matrix forms an interlocking system of flows of funds for the period. For each sector, the total uses of funds equal the total sources. Because the system is self-contained, the total uses of funds for all sectors must equal the total sources for these sectors. More important, total savings for all sectors during the period must equal the total increase in real assets for that period. Likewise, the total change in financial assets, including money, must equal the total change in financial liabilities. Again, we see that financial assets and financial liabilities cancel out for the economy as a whole.

The value of the matrix is that it allows analysis of the flow of funds through various sectors of the economy in a manner similar to that of an input-output analysis. For the individual sector, savings need not equal investment in real assets, and the change in financial assets need not equal the change in financial liabilities. For example, business firms represent a savings-deficit sector in Table 2-1. For this sector, the excess of investment in real assets over savings was financed by an increase in financial liabilities in excess of the increase in financial assets. The existence of this rather large savings-deficit sector means that there must be one or more savings-surplus sectors in the economy for the period being studied. When we analyze the matrix, we see that households, the sector primarily responsible for financing the business sector on a net basis, is the largest savings-surplus sector. In addition, however, financial institutions are a savings-surplus sector, although the excess of savings over investment for this sector is small. This sector acts almost entirely as a financial intermediary; it increases its financial assets by issuing financial liabilities to finance the increase in financial assets. Because the sector contains commercial banks and the monetary authorities, it "provides" money to other sectors in the economy. The $5 source of money for this sector represents an increase in demand deposits and currency held by the public and governments as claims against commercial banks and the monetary authorities. Therefore, the total increase in money held by households, business firms, and governments must equal the increase in money-balance claims against the financial-institutions sector.

The last sector in our example, governments, is a savings-deficit sector. As a whole, federal, state, and local governments ran a budget deficit for the period. Although governments made substantial expenditures for real assets, their expenditures are not shown because of the lack of reliable estimates. Unfortunately, then, this rather important effect must be omitted from any analysis. A budget deficit for the governments sector must be financed by an increase in financial liabilities in excess of the increase in financial assets. The matrix in Table 2-1 illustrates the fundamental aspects of flow of funds in an economy over a period of time. The example is kept purposely simple, with only four sectors in the economy. This sectoring, of course, limits the analysis of the interlocking claims among economic units in the economy. Later in this chapter, however, a more extensive flow-of-funds matrix prepared by the Federal Reserve is illustrated. In addition, the use of flow-of-funds data is evaluated in relation to specific financial markets. First, however, we must consider certain problems inherent in the preparation of flow-of-funds data.

Limitations

Aggregation and Netting

In the preparation of the flow-of-funds data, certain information is "destroyed" in the final presentation of the results. As mentioned earlier, the change in financial assets and liabilities for a sector reflects changes that occur only with other sectors. No information is given about financial transactions among economic units in a given sector. Financial claims among these economic units simply cancel out. As a result, we do not know how much net financing occurs within the sector. The need for this information decreases, of course, as the number of sectors used in the flow-of-funds system increases. With aggregation of economic units into a sector, no information is given about the distribution of investment-savings behavior for economic units in that sector. Only the total for all economic units is reported.

Another problem is that the flow of funds for a period represents the net rather than the gross flow between two points in time. For example, the change in financial assets for a sector is simply beginning financial assets less ending financial assets. During the period, there may have been numerous changes in claims against economic units in other sectors. However, no information is given about the magnitude of these changes. For example, financial institutions may purchase $30 billion in mortgages over the period, while principal payments on existing mortgages held and the sale of existing mortgages amount to $25 billion. The net change in mortgages reported in flow-of-funds data for the financial institutions sector is $5 billion. Although it may be revealing to know the gross funds flow over time, we are constrained to the information available—namely, the net flow between the two dates. This problem, however, occurs in any source- and use-of-funds analysis.[7] Although all flows are netted, financial assets and liabilities for single transaction categories are not netted out. For example, a household may borrow to purchase a house. In this case, the asset and liability are not netted; both are shown.[8]

Valuation

The valuation principle most frequently used in the flow-of-funds accounting system is the *current market value* of the asset or a close approximation thereof. Thus, most flow-of-funds data are based upon differences in current market values between two points in time. The obvious problem is that the flow of funds between the two dates reflects not one but two factors: the "new" flow of funds for the period and the capital gain or loss. For common stocks in particular, the difference between asset levels at two moments in time may be largely the result of capital gains or losses. If savings for a sector are, for flow-of-funds purposes, the residual of changes in real and financial assets less changes in financial liabilities, savings for the period also will be affected by capital gains and losses. As a result, savings, as derived for flow-of-funds purposes by the above method, may not approximate very closely the actual difference between current income and current consumption.[9] Many analysts are interested in the separate influences of "new" flow of funds, or net infusions, and "flows" which are the result of changes in the market values of existing assets. However, this information is not provided, and we are not able to adjust accurately the data for fluctuations in market price. This problem, perhaps, is the most serious shortcoming in the flow-of-funds data. For nonmarketable assets, valuation usually is on the basis of the *book value* of the asset. Because of differences in accounting treatment, however, it is possible for the holder of a financial asset to carry it at a book value different from that carried by the economic unit which issues the claim. These differences lead to discrepancies when financial assets and liabilities are totaled for the economy as a whole.

In this section we have pointed out some of the shortcomings involved with the use of flow-of-funds data. These shortcomings, together with the problem of appropriate sectoring of the economy discussed previously, should be recognized when interpreting the published data. In certain cases, they may have an important influence upon the conclusions reached.

---

[7] See James C. Van Horne, *Financial Management and Policy* (Englewood Cliffs, N.J.: Prentice-Hall, Inc., 1968), p. 530.

[8] "A Quarterly Presentation of Flow of Funds and Savings," p. 832.

[9] See Roland I. Robinson, "Discussion of the Flow of Funds Accounts," *Journal of Finance*, XVIII (May, 1963), 262–63.

Although a detailed analysis of the technical aspects of measuring flows is beyond the scope of this book, and probably beyond the interest of most readers, a familiarity with the problems is important.[10]

Federal Reserve Flow-of-Funds Matrix

The Federal Reserve publishes in the *Federal Reserve Bulletin* a matrix of the flow of funds for each quarter, seasonally adjusted to annual rates. An example of such a matrix is shown in Table 2-2 for the second quarter of 1968 on a seasonally adjusted, annual basis. We see that the presentation differs somewhat from that in our example in Table 2-1; however, the principles taken up also underlie this more complex presentation. In total, eight sectors are shown in Table 2-2: households, business, two governmental sectors, three financial sectors, and a rest-of-the-world account. Because of foreign transactions, the latter sector is necessary. In this sector all foreign economic units are lumped together. The sector records transactions only between economic units in foreign countries and economic units in the United States. A transaction between a business firm in France and one in Germany would not be shown. We note also in Table 2-2 that state and local governments are treated as a private sector, separate from the federal government.

The analysis of Table 2-2 is much the same as that of Table 2-1, despite the data's being presented differently. The gross savings for the period are shown in line 1 for each sector. These figures should be compared with private capital expenditures (line 5) to determine whether the sector is a savings-surplus or savings-deficit one. For example, the household sector is found to be the principal savings-surplus sector, while the business sector and the federal government sector are the major savings-deficit ones. Lines 6 through 9 give a breakdown of the various components of the change in real assets (line 5). This information is valuable in analyzing the impact of plant and equipment expenditures compared with those for construction and for consumer durables. The change in financial assets for a sector for the period is shown in line 11, and the change in financial liabilities is shown in line 12. The difference between the two changes is shown on line 10; and this amount is equal to gross savings (line 1) less private capital expenditures (line 5) for the sector.

As was true with Table 2-1, total uses of funds for a sector should equal total sources. For the economy as a whole, represented by the all-sectors column, gross savings should equal private capital expenditures, and changes in total financial assets should equal changes in total financial liabilities. We see, however, that these equalities are not the case, for there are slight discrepancies. For the individual sector, these discrepancies are shown on line 44; for all sectors, they are shown in the next to the last

---

[10]Technical information is available in "A Quarterly Presentation of Flow of Funds and Savings."

column. Although the flow of funds is an interlocking, balanced system in principle, discrepancies do occur because of unavoidable inconsistencies in timing, valuation, classification, coverage, and statistical errors in data collection.[11] As they tend to be small in relation to the totals involved, discrepancies, for the most part, can be ignored.

Lines 13 through 43 give the changes in specific financial assets and financial liabilities that constitute the total changes reflected in lines 11 and 12. This portion of the matrix is of particular interest to the capital-market analyst. It tells him which sectors finance with what financial instruments, and what sectors hold these instruments. For example, mortgages represent the largest single increase in financial liabilities for the household sector for the period, followed by consumer credit. Mortgage credit was extended primarily by the nonbank-finance sector, which includes savings and loan associations and insurance companies, by commercial banks, and by the U.S. government. Consumer credit was extended primarily by the commercial-bank sector, followed by the nonbank-finance and the business sectors for the period under review. The principal means of financing for the business sector was bonds, followed by bank loans and mortgages. By tracing across line 28, we find that the household, state and local government, and nonbank-finance sectors were the principal purchasers of the bonds. The increase in mortgage financing came principally from the nonbank-finance and the commercial-bank sectors.

State and local governments, on the other hand, were a savings-deficit sector for the period. As a result, the increase in financial liabilities for this sector exceeded its increase in financial assets. The principal means of financing was the issuance of municipal bonds, sold mostly to the commercial-bank sector. The portion of the net increase in municipals sold to banks indicates to a considerable extent the tone of the market for municipal securities. When money is tight and reserves supplied by the monetary authorities are curtailed, commercial banks reduce their commitment to municipal securities in order to service loan demand. Without the underlying support of the commercial-bank sector, yields on municipals tend to rise both in absolute terms and relative to yields for treasury and corporate bonds. For example, this occurrence was evident in 1966, when the banks accounted for only 43 per cent of the net increase in municipal bonds, compared with about 65 per cent the previous five years. As expected, yields on municipal securities rose very sharply in late 1966. In a similar manner, we can analyze other financial transactions occurring in lines 28 through 43.

Thus, the matrix of flows of funds for the entire economy, prepared by the Federal Reserve, contains a wealth of information for the capital-market analyst. Although the matrix will not enable him to analyze the behavior of individual economic units or small groups of economic units,

---

[11] For a discussion of discrepancies, see "A Quarterly Presentation of Flow of Funds and Savings," pp. 857–59.

TABLE 2-2 Summary of Flow of Funds Accounts for Second Quarter, 1968

| | Private Domestic Nonfinancial Sectors | | | | | | | | U.S. Government | |
| Sector | Households | | Business | | State and Local Governments | | Total | | U.S. Government | |
Transaction Category	U	S	U	S	U	S	U	S	U	S
1 **Gross saving**	—	144.7	—	82.0	—	−5.5	—	221.2	—	−12.2
2 Capital consumption	—	74.9	—	62.8	—	—	—	137.7	—	—
3 Net saving (1 − 2)	—	69.8	—	19.1	—	−5.5	—	83.5	—	−12.2
4 **Gross investment (5 + 10)**	141.8	—	79.5	—	−5.5	—	215.8	—	−12.4	—
5 **Private capital expenditures, net**	106.2	—	100.8	—	—	—	207.0	—	—	—
6 Consumer durables	81.0	—	—	—	—	—	81.0	—	—	—
7 Residential construction	21.6	—	8.0	—	—	—	29.5	—	—	—
8 Plant and equipment	3.7	—	82.2	—	—	—	85.9	—	—	—
9 Inventory change	—	—	10.6	—	—	—	10.6	—	—	—
10 **Net financial invesment (11 − 12)**	35.5	—	−21.3	—	−5.5	—	8.8	—	−12.4	—
11 **Financial uses, net**	67.0	—	20.7	—	6.0	—	93.7	—	−10.2	—
12 **Financial sources**	—	31.5	—	42.0	—	11.5	—	84.9	—	2.2
13 Gold and official U.S. foreign exchange	—	—	—	—	—	—	—	—	3.2	—
14 Treasury currency	—	—	—	—	—	—	—	—	—	0.2
15 Demand deposits and currency	—	—	—	—	—	—	—	—	—	—
16 Private domestic	21.4	—	−4.0	—	−1.4	—	15.9	—	—	—
17 U.S. government	—	—	—	—	—	—	—	—	−16.8	—
18 Foreign	—	—	—	—	—	—	—	—	—	—
19 Time and savings accounts	18.9	—	—	—	—	—	16.9	—	—	—
20 At commercial banks	6.3	—	−3.1	—	1.1	—	4.2	—	*	—
21 At savings institutions	12.7	—	—	—	—	—	12.7	—	—	—
22 Life insurance reserves	4.2	—	—	—	—	—	4.2	—	—	0.1
23 Pension fund reserves	16.1	—	—	—	—	4.4	16.1	4.4	—	1.9
24 Consolidated bank items[1]	—	—	—	—	—	—	—	—	—	—
25 Credit market instruments	10.3	26.5	6.2	37.6	5.9	7.0	22.4	71.0	8.2	1.7
26 U.S. government securities	10.5	—	0.7	—	0.5	—	11.6	—	—	1.7
27 State and local obligations	−1.6	—	0.7	—	−0.5	6.8	−1.4	6.8	—	—
28 Corporate and foreign bonds	7.3	—	—	13.7	5.3	—	12.5	13.7	—	—
29 Corporate stocks	−5.0	—	—	−0.6	—	—	−5.0	−0.6	—	—
30 1- to 4-family mortgages	−0.9	14.7	—	−0.7	0.7	—	−0.2	14.0	3.4	—
31 Other mortgages	—	0.8	—	9.5	—	—	—	10.3	1.0	—
32 Consumer credit	—	8.0	1.2	—	—	—	1.2	8.0	—	—
33 Bank loans n.e.c.	—	1.3	—	13.3	—	—	—	14.7	—	—
34 Other loans	—	1.6	3.6	2.4	—	0.2	3.6	4.2	3.8	—
35 Open market paper	—	—	3.6	1.1	—	—	3.6	1.1	—	—
36 Federal loans	—	0.1	—	1.4	—	0.2	—	1.7	3.8	—
37 Security credit	2.2	4.6	—	—	—	—	2.2	4.6	—	—
38 To brokers and dealers	2.2	—	—	—	—	—	2.2	—	—	—
39 To others	—	4.6	—	—	—	—	—	4.6	—	—
40 Taxes payable	—	—	—	−4.5	0.4	—	0.4	−4.5	−5.8	—
41 Trade credit	—	0.1	19.0	14.5	—	0.1	19.0	14.7	0.7	−0.5
42 Equity in noncorporate business	−7.8	—	—	−7.8	—	—	−7.8	−7.8	—	—
43 Miscellaneous financial transactions	1.6	0.3	2.7	2.2	—	—	4.3	2.5	0.4	−1.2
44 Sector discrepancies (1 − 4)	3.0	—	2.4	—	*	—	5.4	—	0.3	—

[1] Claims between commercial banks and monetary authorities: member bank reserves, vault cash, Federal Reserve loans to banks, Federal Reserve float, and stock at Federal Reserve Banks.

Source: *Federal Reserve Bulletin*, 54 (November, 1968), A-68.

Seasonally Adjusted Annual Rates, billions of dollars

| | | Financial Sectors | | | | | | | National | |
| Total | | Monetary Authorities | | Commercial Banks | | Nonbank Finance | | Rest of the World | | All Sectors | | Discrepancy | Saving and Investment | |
U	S	U	S	U	S	U	S	U	S	U	S	U		
—	2.0	—	0.1	—	2.7	—	-0.7	—	0.8	—	211.9	—	211.1	1
—	1.3	—	—	—	0.7	—	0.6	—	—	—	139.0	—	139.0	2
—	0.8	—	0.1	—	2.0	—	-1.3	—	0.8	—	72.9	—	72.1	3
1.8	—	0.1	—	2.6	—	-0.8	—	2.0	—	207.2	—	4.7	206.1	4
1.1	—	—	—	0.5	—	0.6	—	—	—	208.1	—	3.8	208.1	5
—	—	—	—	—	—	—	—	—	—	81.0	—	—	81.0	6
—	—	—	—	—	—	—	—	—	—	29.5	—	—	29.5	7
1.1	—	—	—	0.5	—	0.6	—	—	—	87.0	—	—	87.0	8
—	—	—	—	—	—	—	—	—	—	10.6	—	—	10.6	9
0.7	—	0.1	—	2.1	—	-1.4	—	2.0	—	-0.9	—	0.9	-2.0	10
55.3	—	*	—	17.4	—	37.9	—	7.2	—	146.1	—	—	5.2	11
—	54.6	—	-0.1	—	15.3	—	39.3	—	5.2	—	147.0	—	7.2	12
-2.6	—	-2.6	—	—	—	—	—	0.1	0.6	0.6	0.6	—	—	13
-0.4	—	-0.4	—	—	—	—	—	—	—	-0.4	0.2	0.6	—	14
—	5.2	—	3.5	—	1.7	—	—	—	—	3.6	5.2	—	—	15
2.5	22.5	—	2.0	—	20.5	2.5	—	—	—	18.5	22.5	4.0	—	16
—	-19.2	—	1.8	—	-21.0	—	—	—	—	-16.8	-19.2	-2.4	—	17
—	1.9	—	-0.2	—	2.1	—	—	1.9	—	—	1.9	—	—	18
1.0	17.4	—	—	—	—	1.0	—	—	—	—	17.4	—	—	19
0.2	4.0	—	—	—	4.0	0.2	—	-0.4	—	—	4.0	—	—	20
0.8	13.5	—	—	—	—	0.8	13.5	—	—	—	13.5	—	—	21
—	4.2	—	—	—	—	—	4.2	—	—	—	4.2	—	—	22
—	9.8	—	—	—	—	—	9.8	—	—	—	16.1	—	—	23
-5.3	-5.3	-2.7	-2.6	-2.6	-2.7	—	—	—	—	-5.3	-5.3	—	—	24
55.5	8.4	5.7	—	21.6	0.7	28.3	7.7	-2.3	2.5	83.8	83.7	—	—	25
-4.7	—	5.5	—	-8.2	—	-2.0	—	-5.2	—	—	1.7	—	—	26
8.2	—	—	—	6.3	—	1.9	—	—	—	—	6.8	—	—	27
2.2	0.8	—	—	—	0.7	2.2	0.1	*	0.3	—	14.7	—	—	28
7.4	4.9	—	—	—	*	7.4	4.9	2.1	0.2	—	4.5	—	—	29
11.2	0.3	—	—	2.9	—	8.3	0.3	—	—	—	14.3	—	—	30
9.3	—	—	—	3.3	—	5.9	—	—	—	—	10.3	—	—	31
6.7	—	—	—	3.8	—	2.9	—	—	—	—	8.0	—	—	32
13.8	-1.1	*	—	13.8	—	—	-1.1	—	0.1	—	13.8	—	—	33
1.4	3.5	0.2	—	-0.4	—	1.6	3.5	0.8	1.9	9.6	9.5	-0.1	—	34
*	4.1	0.2	—	-0.4	—	0.2	4.1	0.8	-0.8	—	4.4	—	—	35
—	-0.6	—	—	—	—	—	—	—	-0.6	—	3.8	—	—	36
2.9	0.5	—	—	—	-3.4	6.3	0.5	0.4	0.4	—	5.5	—	—	37
-2.1	0.5	—	—	—	-1.9	-0.2	0.5	0.4	—	—	0.5	—	—	38
5.0	—	—	—	—	-1.5	6.5	—	—	0.4	—	5.0	—	—	39
—	-0.8	—	*	—	-0.7	—	-0.1	—	—	-5.4	-5.3	0.1	—	40
0.3	—	—	—	—	—	0.3	—	—	—	20.0	14.2	-5.9	—	41
—	—	—	—	—	—	—	—	—	—	—	-7.8	—	—	42
1.4	15.2	—	-1.0	1.8	12.3	-0.4	3.8	7.5	1.7	13.5	18.1	4.6	—	43
0.2	—	*	—	0.1	—	0.1	—	-1.2	—	4.7	—	4.7	5.0	44

it does enable him to evaluate economic units which are reasonably homogeneous in their behavior as well as to trace the interaction of the financial system and the real system of the economy in a systematic and consistent manner. It tells him how various sectors financed the excess of their investment in real assets over savings and how these sectors changed their holdings of financial assets. The flow-of-funds framework provides a structured, interlocking means by which to analyze what has happened in the capital markets. The interrelation of sources and uses among sectors enables the analyst to trace the movement of funds through various sectors of the economy for the period of time under review.

Given the breakdown of financial assets and liabilities provided by the Federal Reserve, a fairly detailed analysis of specific types of financial instruments and markets is possible. For particular instruments, we are able to evaluate which sectors are important in the market and the magnitude of their purchases. When this analysis is extended over time, one is able to evaluate the degree of pressure in the various markets. Pressure arises whenever a traditional source of financing curtails its investment in the financial instrument. The curtailment of investment should be related to the savings and investment in real assets for the sector involved. Thus, a study of the behavior of individual sectors with respect to investment in financial assets and issuance of financial liabilities over time is useful in determining the impact of that sector in the capital markets.

Other Funds-Flow Information

In addition to the Federal Reserve, various private organizations provide useful data on the source and use of funds. Among these organizations are Bankers Trust Company and the Life Insurance Association of America, which publish information on the "final" sources and uses of funds, according to the institutions providing the funds, and the instrument in which the funds are used. This information differs from that provided by the Federal Reserve in that a flow-of-funds matrix for the entire economy is not given. Table 2-3 shows an example of the information provided by the Life Insurance Association of America for a single year. Note that the ultimate sources and uses of funds by sectors are not shown, only the final sources and uses. Although the former is sometimes implied, it is very difficult to evaluate savings-surplus and savings-deficit sectors on the basis of the information provided. The users shown may or may not be the ultimate investors in real assets. By the same token, the suppliers of funds may or may not be ultimate savers. Where financial institutions are the suppliers, for the most part they are not the ultimate savers. Although the rows and columns in Table 2-3 are interlocking and consistent, information is provided only on certain capital markets. Thus, only a portion of the flow-of-funds matrix of the entire economy is revealed.

Despite the fact that real and financial transactions in the economy are not linked together, source and use statements are useful to the capital-

TABLE 2-3 Sources and Uses of Funds in United States Money and Capital Markets in 1966, billions of dollars

Sources of Funds	Corporation Bonds	Corporation Stocks	State and Local	Federal Government	Federal Agency	1–4 Family	Other	Business Credit	Consumer Credit	All Other	Total Sources of Funds
	Securities					Mortgages		Loans and Credit			
Savings institutions	4.3	4.0	-0.5	-1.1	0.3	5.2	6.4	0.1	—	1.7	20.5
Life insurance companies	2.2	0.3	-0.4	-0.3	*	0.5	4.1	0.1	—	1.4	7.9
Savings and loan associations	—	—	—	0.4	0.1	2.7	1.2	—	—	—	4.3
Mutual savings banks	0.3	*	-0.1	-0.7	0.2	1.6	1.1	—	—	0.2	2.7
Noninsured pension funds	1.9	3.7	—	-0.5	*	0.5	—	—	—	—	5.5
Banking system	-0.2	—	2.3	0.1	0.8	2.4	2.2	9.3	3.1	1.6	22.7
Commercial banks	-0.2	—	2.3	-3.4	0.7	2.4	2.2	9.3	3.1	1.6	18.2
Federal Reserve banks	—	—	—	3.5	*	—	—	—	—	—	3.5
Government institutions	5.6	—	0.3	7.9	1.6	2.8	0.9	—	—	—	19.1
State and local funds	5.6	—	-0.4	1.0	0.4	0.4	—	—	—	—	6.9
U.S. investment accounts	—	—	—	6.8	1.3	—	—	—	—	—	3.1
Federal loan agencies	—	—	0.7	0.2	*	2.4	0.9	—	—	—	4.2
All other investors	1.3	-2.8	4.4	1.6	3.9	-0.5	1.2	3.2	3.8	—	16.0
Nonfinancial corporations	—	0.1	0.8	-1.0	-0.2	—	—	3.2	1.1	—	3.9
Fire and casualty companies	0.6	-0.3	0.7	0.2	*	—	*	—	—	—	1.6
Foreigners	1.0	—	—	-2.0	—	—	—	—	—	—	-1.3
Individuals and others	-0.3	-2.6	2.9	4.4	4.1	-0.5	1.1	—	2.7	—	11.8
Total uses of funds	11.1	1.2	6.6	8.5	6.6	10.0	10.7	12.6	6.9	3.3	77.4

*$50 million or less.

The uses of funds measure the net changes in outstanding loans and securities; the sources of funds measure the net changes in ownership. Because of rounding, components may not add to totals shown. Federal agency includes participation certificates.

Source: Kenneth M. Wright and Robert H. Parks, *1967 Economic and Investment Report* (New York: Life Insurance Association of America, 1967), p. 3.

market analyst in that they provide detailed information not available in the Federal Reserve flow-of-funds presentation. In addition, the presentation is clearer and easier to follow than the cumbersome matrix of the flow of funds. In particular, *The Investment Outlook* of the Bankers Trust Company provides considerable in-depth information about the major sources and uses of funds for the various capital and credit markets. With this information, the analyst is able to study the direct interaction between major suppliers and users of capital and credit.[12] The breakdown of the ownership of financial instruments and of the sources and uses of funds for financial institutions is far more detailed than that available in the flow-of-funds data. As a result, a penetrating analysis of the final sources and uses of funds as they relate to the various financial markets is possible. So far, we have considered only *ex post* data, whether it be flow of funds or source and use statements. Although these data are valuable in appraising past trends and in forming expectations of the future, we often need forecasts of the future involving *ex ante* estimates. To this aspect we now turn.

Forecasts

In addition to flows that actually have occurred, estimates of future funds flows are important in capital-market analysis. These estimates indicate likely strains in the system and the resulting pressure on interest rates. In this way, the analyst is able to get a better feel for desired demand and supply and for the change in interest rates necessary to bring about a balance between the two. He is interested both in the expected absolute change in interest rates for a particular market and in the change relative to changes in interest rates in other markets. Bankers Trust Company, Salomon Brothers & Hutzler, and Scudder, Stevens and Clark all make forecasts of future funds flows. Although Salomon Brothers & Hutzler makes more frequent forecasts in its *Comments on Credit*, the most extensive of these forecasts is *The Investment Outlook*, of Bankers Trust, which is published annually. In the preparation of these forecasts, independent estimates are made of the expected need for funds, classified according to the type of financial instrument, and of the expected funds available for investment by various financial institutions and by individuals.

Once independent estimates of supply and demand have been made, one benefit of the forecast comes in analyzing how supply and demand will come into balance. We know, of course, that on an *ex post* basis supply must equal demand.[13] The first step is simply to match the independently prepared estimates to determine the size and direction of any imbalance.

---

[12] See Sally S. Ronk, "Application of Flow of Funds Data to Capital Market Analysis: Comment," in *The Flow of Funds Approach to Social Accounting* (New York: National Bureau of Economic Research, 1962), p. 286.

[13] See James S. Duesenberry, "A Process Approach to Flow-of-Funds Analysis," in *The Flow-of-Funds Approach to Social Accounting* (New York: National Bureau of Economic Research, 1962), p. 174.

This imbalance indicates pressures that are likely to develop. Knowing these pressures, the analyst is able to predict the change in market interest rates necessary to bring about a balance in supply and demand. For example, suppose the need for mortgage funds is estimated to be $25 billion in the forthcoming year, but the supply of funds into this market is estimated at only $19 billion. As a result of this imbalance, there would likely be significant upward pressure on interest rates in order to bring about a balance between supply and demand for mortgages.

By analyzing imbalances across capital markets, the analyst can determine whether interest rates in one segment of the capital markets are likely to rise or fall relative to interest rates in other segments. In this way, he is able to forecast relative changes in interest rates. However, one must be careful not to lose sight of the interrelated nature of financial markets. Supply and demand forces in one market are not independent of those in other markets. Therefore, interest-rate changes in the various markets cannot be estimated independently. We shall examine this problem in detail in the subsequent chapter.

In the published forecasts, a balance is always shown between estimated sources of funds and estimated uses. In other words, adjustments are made until a balance is achieved. Consequently, certain valuable information is not available to the reader—namely, the independent estimates of supply and demand by the forecasters and the resulting *ex ante* gap. However, a residual category is shown, and this category gives us some information about any imbalance between supply and demand. To illustrate, an example of a source- and use-of-funds statement, prepared by Bankers Trust Company, is shown in Table 2-4. Historical sources and uses and also a forecast for the future are shown. In the table, the residual for individuals and others is reflected in the next to last line. In a certain sense, this residual can be regarded as a balancing factor in the forecast and can be used in judging strains in particular markets.[14] The larger the residual, the more "gap" there is for individuals and others to fill; and the higher interest rates would be expected to go in order to bring about a balance between supply and demand. Rising interest rates cause individuals and other residual investors to direct their savings to the purchase of financial instruments. In our example, the large residual in 1966 suggests that interest rates rose during that year. This was indeed the case; interest rates rose to unprecedented heights. Similar experiences were recorded in 1953, 1955–57, and 1959, when the portion of total funds supplied by residual investors was likewise relatively high. Because of the correlation between the residual and the level of interest rates, analysts are able to use, with a reasonable degree of success, the estimate of the residual as a basis for forecasting interest rates.

A forecast of sources and uses of funds differs from a forecast of the flow of funds for the entire economy. Whereas the former takes account of the

---

[14]See William C. Freund and Edward D. Zinbarg, "Application of Flow of Funds to Interest-Rate Forecasting," *Journal of Finance*, XVIII (May, 1963), 236–48.

TABLE 2-4 Summary of Sources and Uses of Funds, billions of dollars

	1961	1962	1963	1964	1965	1966	1967	1968 (estimated)	1969 (projected)
Uses (funds raised)									
Investment funds (Table 2)	30.6	34.0	40.7	43.1	45.9	42.6	54.1	55.6	57.3
Short-term funds (Table 3)	11.5	18.5	21.9	24.1	33.4	25.9	27.3	36.8	29.1
U.S. government and agency securities, publicly held (Table 4)	6.1	6.6	2.3	3.9	—	3.3	7.2	11.8	3.4
Total uses	48.2	59.0	64.8	71.1	79.4	71.9	88.7	104.2	89.8
Sources (funds supplied)									
Savings institutions									
Life insurance companies (Table 15)	5.6	6.4	6.6	7.4	8.3	8.1	8.4	8.3	8.9
Private noninsured pension funds (Table 16)	3.7	3.9	4.1	4.4	5.2	5.5	6.0	6.8	7.7
State and local government retirement funds (Table 17)	2.3	2.5	2.4	2.8	3.0	3.6	3.9	4.4	5.3
Fire and casualty insurance companies (Table 18)	1.3	1.2	1.3	1.1	0.9	1.6	2.2	2.7	3.0
Contractual-type savings institutions	12.9	14.1	14.4	15.7	17.4	18.8	20.5	22.2	24.9
Savings and loan associations (Table 19)	9.4	10.3	13.3	11.0	9.5	4.3	9.3	9.7	9.7
Mutual savings banks (Table 20)	2.1	3.1	3.5	4.2	3.9	2.5	5.1	4.3	4.3
Credit unions (Table 21)	0.4	0.6	0.7	0.9	1.1	1.0	0.8	1.4	1.5
Deposit-type savings institutions	11.9	14.0	17.5	16.1	14.5	7.8	15.1	15.4	15.5

Investment companies (Table 22)	1.4	1.2	0.8	1.1	1.6	2.0	1.1	2.5	1.8
Total savings institutions	26.2	29.3	32.6	32.8	33.5	28.6	36.7	40.1	42.2
Commercial banks (Table 25)	15.8	19.5	19.4	22.4	29.1	17.4	36.2	38.7	21.0
Business corporations									
Nonfinancial (Table 27)	3.1	5.2	6.1	6.0	5.8	6.6	6.4	9.3	7.6
Financial (Table 28)	0.4	3.1	4.6	4.2	5.8	3.5	0.9	4.0	3.3
Total business corporations	3.5	8.3	10.7	10.2	11.6	10.1	7.3	13.3	10.9
Other investor groups									
Federal agencies (Table 29)	0.8	0.8	−0.8	0.4	0.2	3.5	4.2	3.8	5.0
State and local governments (Table 29)	1.0	1.3	1.8	0.9	3.2	3.4	1.7	3.8	2.1
Brokers and dealers (Table 29)	1.0	−0.1	1.4	−0.4	0.4	−0.2	2.6	1.8	0.5
Other consumer lenders (Table 29)	0.4	0.6	0.6	0.7	0.7	0.7	0.7	1.1	0.7
Foreign investors (Table 30)	0.6	2.0	0.8	0.8	−0.2	−1.8	2.1	1.2	2.7
Total other investor groups	3.8	4.6	3.8	2.4	4.4	5.6	11.3	11.7	11.0
Residual: Individuals and others (Table 31)*	−1.1	−2.6	−1.7	3.3	0.8	10.2	−2.9	0.4	4.7
Total sources	48.2	59.0	64.8	71.1	79.4	71.9	88.7	104.2	89.8

*Includes revaluation of book assets of some holders.

Note: Figures have been rounded and thus do not necessarily add to totals shown.

Source: The Investment Outlook for 1969 (New York: Bankers Trust Company, 1969).

final sources and uses of funds for various financial instruments, a flow-of-funds forecast takes account of the source and use of funds for each sector of the economy. Because a simultaneous balance must be reached for each sector and across all sectors, a flow-of-funds forecast forces a much tighter analysis than does a forecast of sources and uses. The idea of having to force projections into the flow-of-funds framework may cause the analyst to be less conservative in his final estimates. To achieve a balance which satisfies the interlocking structure of the flow of funds, he sometimes must make fairly extreme estimates.[15] These estimates, however, may well be warranted by the conditions projected. A less rigorous framework, such as the source and use statements, encourages the common tendency to project only moderate changes and not to predict extreme changes and turning points. The flow-of-funds matrix forces the use of estimates that are consistent and in keeping with the initial assumptions. Therefore, they may tend to be more realistic.

The flow-of-funds framework and the source- and use-of-funds statement, which we have examined, provide a basis for analyzing financial markets. By comparing estimates of supply and demand, the analyst obtains insight into the likely strains in the system. Given these likely strains, he then is able to interpret their effect upon interest rates. Within either of these frameworks, the analysis of interest rates is likely to be far more rigorous, consistent, and comprehensive than it is if estimates are made on a market-by-market basis.

Summary

The flow of funds is a system of social accounting that permits the financial-market analyst to evaluate the flow of savings through various sectors of the economy. A sector consists of a grouping of economic units that are relatively homogeneous in their behavior. By combining source- and use-of-funds statements for all sectors, we may obtain a matrix for the entire economy. This matrix shows the interlocking nature of financial assets and liabilities among various sectors. It enables us to analyze savings-deficit sectors and the means by which they finance the excess of their investment in real assets over savings, together with the behavior of savings-surplus sectors and the way they invest in financial assets. Subject to certain limitations, the flow-of-funds data give the financial-market analyst rich insights. By tracing through the sources of funds for investment in a particular financial instrument, one gains much information on strains in the financial system and on interest rates.

In addition to the Federal Reserve flow-of-funds data, various source and use statements are published by several private organizations. However, these data do not show the interaction between the real and the

---

[15]See Stephen Taylor, "Uses of Flow-of-Funds Accounts in the Federal Reserve System," *Journal of Finance*, XVIII (May, 1963), 249–58.

financial segments of the economy. They are concerned only with the final supply and demand for funds. Nevertheless, source and use statements provide detailed information on financial markets not available in the flow-of-funds data. Consequently, this information is very valuable to the financial-market analyst.

The analyst gains insight not only from a study of flows that have occurred in the past but also from forecasts of the future. Here, independent forecasts should be made of the demand for and the supply of funds. If there is an imbalance, the analyst studies the change in interest rates necessary to bring about a balance. In the published forecasts, there usually is a residual category for individuals and other investors. The amount of the residual varies directly with the level of interest rates in financial markets. Consequently, the residual is useful in estimating future interest rates.

Selected References

The Flow-of-Funds Approach to Social Accounting. New York: National Bureau of Economic Research, 1962.

Freund, William C., and Edward D. Zinbarg, "Application of Flow of Funds to Interest-Rate Forecasting," *Journal of Finance,* XVIII (May, 1963), 231–48.

Goldsmith, Raymond W., *The Flow of Capital Funds in the Postwar Economy,* Chapter 2. New York: National Bureau of Economic Research, 1965.

The Investment Outlook for 1969. New York: Bankers Trust Company, 1969.

Moore, Basil J., *An Introduction to the Theory of Finance,* Appendix to Chapter 1. New York: The Free Press, 1968.

"A Quarterly Presentation of Flow of Funds and Savings," *Federal Reserve Bulletin,* 45 (August, 1959), 828–59.

Ritter, Lawrence S., *The Flow of Funds Accounts: A Framework for Financial Analysis.* New York: Institute of Finance, New York University, 1968.

Taylor, Stephen, "Uses of Flow-of-Funds Accounts in the Federal Reserve System," *Journal of Finance,* XVIII (May, 1963), 249–58.

```
33333333333333333333333333333333333333333333333333333333333333333333333333333333333333333333333
33333333333333333333333333333333333333333333333333333333333333333333333333333333333333333333333
3333333333333333333333333333333333333   333   333   3333333333333333333333333333333333333
33333333333333333333333333333333333333   333   333   3333333333333333333333333333333333333
33333333333333333333333333333333333333   333   333   3333333333333333333333333333333333333
33333333333333333333333333333333333333   333   333   3333333333333333333333333333333333333
33333333333333333333333333333333333333   333   333   3333333333333333333333333333333333333
33333333333333333333333333333333333333   333   333   3333333333333333333333333333333333333
33333333333333333333333333333333333333   333   333   3333333333333333333333333333333333333
33333333333333333333333333333333333333   333   333   3333333333333333333333333333333333333
33333333333333333333333333333333333333   333   333   3333333333333333333333333333333333333
33333333333333333333333333333333333333333333333333333333333333333333333333333333333333333333333
33333333333333333333333333333333333333333333333333333333333333333333333333333333333333333333333
```

The Role of Interest Rates

As we brought out in Chapter 1, the function of financial markets is to facilitate the flow of savings from savings-surplus economic units to savings-deficit ones. The allocation of these savings occurs primarily on the basis of price, expressed by interest rates. Economic units in need of funds must outbid others for the use of these funds. Although the allocation process is affected somewhat by capital rationing and government restrictions, interest rates are the primary mechanism whereby supply and demand are brought into balance for a particular financial instrument across financial markets. Those economic units willing to pay the highest interest rate for the use of funds, holding constant risk, are the ones entitled to their use. If rationality prevails, the economic units bidding the highest prices are the ones with the most promising investment opportunities. As a result, savings are allocated to the most efficient uses, and capital formation and want satisfaction in the economy tend toward optimality. In this chapter, we analyze how the price mechanism works to bring the supply of a financial instrument into balance with its demand. In subsequent chapters, the focus is on explaining relative yields, or yield differentials among various financial instruments.

Definition of Yield

Before we proceed, a brief discussion of the measurement of yields is in order. The yield on a financial instrument is the discount rate that equates the present value of expected cash inflows to the investor with the current market price of the security. If these inflows are assumed to occur at the end of the year, the yield can be determined by solving the following equation for r:

$$P_0 = \frac{C_1}{(1 + r)} + \frac{C_2}{(1 + r)^2} + \dots + \frac{C_n}{(1 + r)^n} \tag{3-1}$$

where P_0 is the current market price of the instrument, C_t is the expected cash inflow to the investor in period t, n is the final period in which a cash inflow is expected, and r is the yield to maturity for which we solve. C_t may be interest payments, repayment of principal, or dividend payments, depending upon the security being analyzed.

To illustrate the use of the equation, suppose that the current market price of a $1,000 face-value bond with 20 years to maturity were $894 and that this bond had a 6 per cent coupon, i.e., that it paid $60 in interest to the investor at the end of each of the next 20 years. The yield to maturity for this bond can be determined by solving the following equation for r:

$$894 = \frac{60}{(1 + r)} + \frac{60}{(1 + r)^2} + \dots + \frac{60}{(1 + r)^{20}} + \frac{1,000}{(1 + r)^{20}} \tag{3-2}$$

When the equation is solved for the discount rate that equates the current market price with the stream of interest payments plus the final redemption value of $1,000, it is found to be 7 per cent. Thus, the bond would yield 7 per cent to maturity.

If interest were paid more than once a year, equation (3-1) is modified to

$$P_0 = \frac{C_1}{\left(1 + \dfrac{r}{m}\right)} + \frac{C_2}{\left(1 + \dfrac{r}{m}\right)^2} + \frac{C_3}{\left(1 + \dfrac{r}{m}\right)^3} + \dots + \frac{C_n}{\left(1 + \dfrac{r}{m}\right)^{mn}} \tag{3-3}$$

where m is the number of times in the year interest is compounded. If interest were paid semiannually on a $1,000 face-value bond with 20 years to final maturity, a coupon rate of 5 per cent, and a current market price of \$1,032, the yield to maturity would be found by solving the following equation for r:

$$1,032 = \frac{25}{\left(1 + \dfrac{r}{2}\right)} + \frac{25}{\left(1 + \dfrac{r}{2}\right)^2} + \frac{25}{\left(1 + \dfrac{r}{2}\right)^3} + \dots +$$

$$\frac{25}{\left(1 + \dfrac{r}{2}\right)^{40}} + \frac{1,000}{\left(1 + \dfrac{r}{2}\right)^{40}} \qquad (3\text{-}4)$$

In this equation, r is 4.75 per cent. Fortunately, one need not solve for yield to maturity mathematically. Elaborate bond-value tables permit one to look up the yield, given the market price of the bond, the coupon rate, and the date of final maturity.

The yield to maturity, as calculated above, may differ from the holding-period yield on that security if the security is sold prior to maturity. The holding-period yield is the rate of discount that equates the present value of cash inflows (interest payments or dividends) plus the present value of terminal value at the end of the holding period with the price paid for the security. For example, suppose a share of stock were bought for \$50 on a net basis and sold three years later for \$70 net. Moreover, assume that the stock paid a \$1 cash dividend at the end of each year. The holding-period yield, or annual return, would then be found by solving the following equation for r:

$$50 = \frac{1}{(1 + r)} + \frac{1}{(1 + r)^2} + \frac{1}{(1 + r)^3} + \frac{70}{(1 + r)^3} \qquad (3\text{-}5)$$

where r is found to be 13.67 per cent. In the ensuing discussion, both yield to maturity and holding-period yield will be considered.

The Price Mechanism in Financial Markets

Interest rates in financial markets are determined by a complex inter-action of supply and demand forces. If financial assets already exist in an economy, supply and demand functions must be expressed in both stock and flow dimensions. Stocks relate to financial assets presently outstanding. Flows, on the other hand, relate to newly created financial assets as deter-mined by aggregate savings and investment over a period of time. Supply and demand schedules for newly created financial assets as well as those for existing financial assets are important in the determination of interest rates.

At a given instant, interest rates are determined only by the supply and demand schedules for existing financial assets. As time passes, however, new financial assets come into being and affect interest rates.[1] The importance of newly created financial assets compared with existing financial assets in determining interest rates depends upon the relative size of each and the degree of substitution between them. For most types of financial assets, the existing stock is large in relation to newly created financial assets.

Where both the existing stock is large and secondary markets are strong, it is contended that supply and demand functions for existing financial assets are the dominant factor in determining interest rates.[2] L.A. Metzler, for example, maintains that security markets are dominated by existing securities rather than by new securities. According to Metzler, savings and investment in the economy, and the new securities that result, do not have a direct effect upon market rates of interest.[3] This position is an extension of that of Keynes, who held that interest rates were determined solely by the supply and demand for existing securities. In his system, supply and demand for newly created securities did not influence market rates of interest directly.[4]

The view that interest rates are determined independently of newly created securities contrasts with the views of George Horwich and of Basil J. Moore and with the position taken here—that supply and demand forces for newly created financial assets have a direct impact on market rates of interest.[5] Interest rates are determined by supply and demand for newly created financial assets as well as for existing financial assets. Because the two sets of supply and demand equations interact, it is not possible to separate them; therefore, savings and investment in an economy have a direct influence upon market rates of interest. To be sure, either existing securities or newly created ones may have more influence than the other. The appropriate comparison, however, is not the existing stock of securities with the amount of newly created securities over a period of time; such a comparison invariably shows the dominance of existing securities. The more relevant comparison is the volume of transactions in existing securities with the amount of newly created securities for a particular period of time.

Equilibrating Process

The equilibrating process in financial markets depends upon the behavior of investors in financial assets, the behavior of issuers of financial

[1] See George Horwich, *Money, Capital, and Prices* (Homewood, Ill.: Richard D. Irwin, Inc., 1964), p. 402.

[2] Basil J. Moore, *An Introduction to the Theory of Finance* (New York: The Free Press, 1968), pp. 121–24, analyzes the relative importance of each according to the speed of portfolio adjustment by existing financial-asset holders to disequilibrium conditions.

[3] "Wealth, Saving, and the Rate of Interest," *Journal of Political Economy*, LIX (April, 1951), 115.

[4] John Maynard Keynes, *The General Theory of Employment Interest and Money* (New York: Harcourt, Brace & World, Inc., 1936), Chapters 13, 15, 17, and 18.

[5] Horwich, *Money, Capital, and Prices*, Chapter X; and Moore, *An Introduction to the Theory of Finance*, Chapter 4.

liabilities, and the efficiency of the financial markets in which they operate. Financial markets are continually subject to disequilibrium conditions, which may be caused by (1) changes in the portfolio preferences of investors in financial assets, (2) changes in the preferences of economic units for issuing financial liabilities, and (3) changes in private wealth which result from capital formation and government savings or dissavings. The movement toward equilibrium in each financial market is accomplished through changes in interest rates.[6] With multiple financial instruments, equilibrium must be achieved *across* financial markets; otherwise, an interest-rate change to bring supply and demand into balance in one market would create an imbalance in another market. For example, suppose that interest rates rose in the municipal-bond market to eliminate a previous excess supply. Municipal bonds then would be more attractive than corporate and treasury bonds. If investors in these bonds were to sell them to purchase municipals, excess supply in the first two markets and excess demand in the latter would change interest rates in all three markets. The equilibrating process, then, is across financial markets.

The time required for adjustment to disequilibrium conditions differs among different financial markets according to the causes of disequilibrium. If the adjustment period were instantaneous, economic units would constantly hold assets and issue liabilities that maximized their utility. These assets and liabilities would be adjusted instantaneously to changing market conditions. The action of all economic units behaving in this manner would assure that financial markets were constantly in equilibrium. When a disequilibrium condition arose, economic units would adjust to it immediately, thereby bringing financial markets back into equilibrium. When there is a delay in reaction time, however, it complicates the equilibrating process. Take the situation where the lag in adjustment to disequilibrium conditions is infinite. Under these circumstances, existing financial assets would be neither bought nor sold, and there would be no adjustments in portfolios to changed conditions.[7] Utility preferences for holding financial assets would have to be satisfied entirely by newly created financial instruments. The length of time for adjustment to disequilibrium conditions obviously lies somewhere between these two extremes.

This adjustment is affected by information lags in financial markets and by the efficiency of secondary markets. To react to disequilibrium conditions, economic units first must recognize them. The longer the information lag, the slower the speed of adjustment. For example, in-

---

[6] See James Tobin, "A Process Approach to Flow-of-Funds Analysis: Comment," in *The Flow-of-Funds Approach to Social Accounting* (New York: National Bureau of Economic Research, 1962), p. 191.

[7] See Moore, *An Introduction to the Theory of Finance*, pp. 119–20.

formation lags in the secondary market for mortgages are much longer than those in the market for treasury bonds. We should therefore expect the adjustment process for mortgages to be much longer than that for treasury bonds. Also, the efficiency of the secondary market is important. An efficient secondary market speeds the adjustment process considerably. If the potential seller of a financial asset must seek out a buyer on his own, he tends to hold the asset and not to adjust his financial-asset portfolio to changing conditions. The same applies to an economic unit issuing financial liabilities. The greater the information lag and the less marketable the claims it issues, the slower the adjustment to changing conditions.

Closely allied to the factors which impede adjustment are the transaction costs involved in a purchase or sale. The greater the spread between bid and ask prices or the greater the brokerage commission or both, the slower the adjustment process. Red tape also slows adjustment. The necessary amount of paper work involved in mortgage lending makes the adjustment process rather slow in this market. Moreover, tradition, inertia on the part of individual economic units, and institutional and legal restrictions also tend to slow the speed of adjustment. These factors all affect the time lag in which individual economic units adjust their portfolios of financial assets and financial liabilities to disequilibrium conditions. Clearly the adjustment process varies among economic units and among financial markets. As can well be imagined, the process is very complex.[8] For simplicity, comparative statics will be used in our illustration of the role of interest rates. In equilibrium, of course, the structure of interest rates is such that desired holdings of financial assets conform exactly to the financial claims which economic units desire to issue. It is this conformity and how it comes about that we investigate.

Behavior of Individual Economic Units

Interest rates in a financial market cannot be analyzed in isolation. They are dependent not only upon interest rates in other financial markets but also upon the real sector of the economy and upon consumption. All these factors interact to determine an equilibrium structure of interest rates. In this section, we study the behavior of individual economic units in choosing assets and issuing financial liabilities. An understanding of this behavior allows us later to examine how economic units interact to determine interest rates in the economy.

---

[8] For further discussion of lags in the adjustment process, see James S. Duesenberry, "A Process Approach to Flow-of-Funds Analysis," in *The Flow-of-Funds Approach to Social Accounting* (New York: National Bureau of Economic Research, 1962), pp. 178–82.

As recalled from Chapter 2, the balance sheet for an economic unit at any moment is

Assets	*Liabilities and Net Worth*
Money	Financial liabilities
	#1
Other financial assets	#2
#1	.
#2	.
.	.
.	#n
.	
#n	
Real assets	
#1	
#2	
.	
.	Net worth
.	
#n	

It is assumed that the economic unit adjusts its balance sheet toward a desired, or preferred, mix of assets and liabilities in keeping with changes in interest rates, investment opportunities, wealth, and other factors. It may increase its total asset holdings only if its net worth increases, it issues additional financial liabilities, or both. In turn, a change in net worth can be the result of two occurrences: (1) current expenditures less than or more than current income and (2) capital gains or losses on financial assets and liabilities and on real assets over the period.

Consumption clearly represents an alternative to holding assets or issuing financial liabilities and accordingly influences the desired totals in the balance sheet for the economic unit. A household, for example, has several choices to make in the allocation of its wealth and income. To purchase a house, it may have to save, by consuming less than its income, until it has accumulated sufficient funds for a down payment. The alternative to purchasing a house in this case would be increased consumption. If the household were already consuming less than its current income, the alternative might be increasing its financial assets. A household must decide not only on the proportion of income to save but also on where these savings are to be employed—that is, what type of asset is to be increased (money, other financial assets, or real assets) or what type of financial liability is to be paid off. A business corporation, on the other hand, may purchase a piece of capital equipment by retaining its earnings, by reducing its financial assets, or by increasing its financial liabilities.[9] These examples are sufficient to illustrate the complexities that face the individual economic unit in determining the total amount and composition of financial assets it holds and the amount and composition of financial liabilities it issues. Too often, the holding of financial assets is analyzed independent of these alternatives. Often assumed is that the individual economic unit has a given endowment for investment in financial assets and that the number and types of financial instruments in the economy are fixed. Although this assumption is understandable for practical reasons, it overlooks the behavioral interaction of holding financial assets with holding money and real assets, issuing financial liabilities, and consuming. All these factors affect the total amount and composition of financial assets held.

How does the individual economic unit adjust its holdings of assets, its financial liabilities, and its consumption to achieve a preferred position? It does so on the basis of maximizing total utility. At a moment in time, the economic unit increases its financial liabilities to finance its holding of money, other financial assets, and real assets as long as it can increase its total utility by doing so. Over time the economic unit can increase or decrease its marginal propensity to consume. Changes in net worth affect and are affected by consumption, the holdings of various assets, and the financial liabilities issued. Thus, all of these factors are interdependent with respect to the utility preferences of an economic unit and its behavior.

Utility for Financial Assets

Assuming that economic units attempt to maximize their total utility, we must consider now the utility derived from holding various assets and from issuing financial liabilities. This consideration is fundamental to understanding how economic units in an economy interact to determine interest rates. For financial assets other than money, we assume that the preferences of economic units are based upon a two-parameter utility function; these parameters are (1) the expected return from the instrument and (2) the risk involved in holding it.[10] If the future were known, no risk would be involved in holding a financial asset. The income stream would be certain. Because utility is associated positively with return, all economic units would try to maximize their total return from the holding

---

[9]For a discussion of the rationale for optimal corporate behavior, see James C. Van Horne, *Financial Management and Policy* (Englewood Cliffs, N.J.: Prentice-Hall, Inc., 1968), Chapters 1 through 9. An analysis of household behavior is found in Moore, *An Introduction to the Theory of Finance*, Chapter 3.

[10]For a justification of this approach, see James Tobin, "Liquidity Preference as Behavior Towards Risk," *Review of Economic Studies*, XXV (February, 1958), 65–86.

of financial assets by investing in that financial asset which promised the greatest return. With certainty about the future and perfect capital markets, however, arbitrage would assure that every financial asset yielded no more than the risk-free rate, i.e., the time value of money.

When the future is not known, the utility function of the economic unit becomes more complex. Decision situations of this sort can be broken down into two types: risk and uncertainty. The distinction between the two is that risk involves situations in which the probabilities of a particular event occurring are known; whereas, with uncertainty, they are not known.[11] In the remainder of this chapter, we assume that economic units can be analyzed as though they formulated subjective probability distributions of possible returns from the holding of financial assets.

The expected value of the probability distribution is calculated by

$$\bar{R} = \sum_{x=1}^{n} R_x P_x \qquad (3\text{-}6)$$

where $\bar{R}$ is the expected value, R_x is the return for the xth possibility, P_x is the probability of occurrence of that return, and n is the total number of possibilities. It is assumed that investors associate risk with the dispersion of the probability distribution. The greater the dispersion, the more risky the financial asset, and vice versa. The conventional measure of dispersion of a probability distribution is the standard deviation, which is calculated by

$$\sigma = \sqrt{\sum_{x=1}^{n} (R_x - \bar{R})^2 P_x} \qquad (3\text{-}7)$$

Equation (3-7) gives only the standard deviation for a single financial asset. However, an economic unit usually has more than one investment opportunity available. Rather than evaluate the expected value of return and the standard deviation for a single financial asset, one must evaluate them for a portfolio of financial assets. Implied is that economic units maximize the utility arising from holding a portfolio of financial assets. The expected value of return for a portfolio is simply the sum of the expected values of returns for the financial assets making up the portfolio. The standard deviation, however, is not the sum of the individual standard deviations, but

$$\sigma = \sqrt{\sum_{j=1}^{m} \sum_{k=1}^{m} A_j A_k r_{jk} \sigma_j \sigma_k} \qquad (3\text{-}8)$$

[11]See Frank H. Knight, *Risk, Uncertainty and Profit* (Boston: Houghton Mifflin Company, 1921), and R. Duncan Luce and Howard Raiffa, *Games and Decisions* (New York: John Wiley & Sons, Inc., 1957), p. 13.

where m is the total number of financial assets under consideration, A_j is the proportion of total funds invested in financial asset j, A_k is the proportion invested in financial asset k, r_{jk} is the expected correlation between returns for financial assets j and k, σ_j is the standard deviation about the expected value of return for financial asset j, and σ_k is the standard deviation for financial asset k. These standard deviations are calculated with equation (3-7). The correlation between returns may be positive, negative, or zero, depending upon the nature of the association. A correlation coefficient of 1.00 indicates that the returns from two financial assets vary positively, or directly, in exactly the same proportions; a correlation coefficient of -1.00 indicates that they vary inversely in exactly the same proportions; and a zero coefficient indicates an absence of correlation.[12]

By diversifying its holdings to include financial assets with less than perfect positive correlation among themselves, the risk averse economic unit is able to reduce the dispersion of the probability distribution of possible returns for its portfolio in relation to the expected value of return for that portfolio. In so doing, it reduces the risk of holding financial assets. However, this diversification must be among the right financial assets. It is not enough for an economic unit simply tb spread its endowment among a number of financial assets; diversification must be among financial assets not possessing high degrees of positive correlation among themselves.[13] It is evident from equation (3-8) that the dispersion of the probability distribution for a portfolio could be reduced to zero if financial assets with negative correlation could be found. The objective of diversification, however, is not to reduce dispersion per se but to obtain the best combination of expected value of return and standard deviation.

The individual economic unit is assumed to have a preference function with respect to the expected value of return and risk from holding a portfolio of financial assets. In other words, it is assumed to make optimal portfolio decisions on the basis of these two parameters. If an economic unit is averse to risk and associates risk with divergence from expected return, its utility schedule may be similar to that shown in

[12] Rather than estimate the correlation between each financial instrument under consideration, it is easier to estimate the correlation between an instrument and some market factor, such as the GNP or some index. Using William F. Sharpe's "diagonal model," we can make estimates of the total variance of a portfolio, given these correlation estimates. This procedure reduces considerably the necessary computations when a portfolio is large. "A Simplified Model for Portfolio Analysis," *Management Science*, 9 (January, 1963), 277–93.

[13] For a more detailed analysis of diversification, see John Lintner, "Security Prices, Risk, and Maximal Gains from Diversification," *Journal of Finance*, XX (December, 1965), 587–615. See also William F. Sharpe, "Capital Asset Prices: A Theory of Market Equilibrium Under Conditions of Risk," *Journal of Finance*, XIX (September, 1964), 425–42; Eugene F. Fama, "Risk, Return and Equilibrium: Some Clarifying Comments," *Journal of Finance*, XXIII (March, 1968), 29–40, who reconciles the positions of Lintner and Sharpe; and Michael C. Jensen, "Risk, the Pricing of Capital Assets, and the Evaluation of Investment Portfolios," *Journal of Business*, XXXXII (April, 1969), 167–247. In general, mean-variance portfolios are based on the assumptions of returns which are normally distributed and of investors' utility functions which are quadratic.

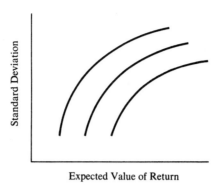

Fig. 3-1.

Fig. 3-1. There, expected value of return is plotted on the horizontal axis, while standard deviation is along the vertical. The curves are known as indifference curves; the economic unit is indifferent between any combination of expected value and standard deviation on a particular curve. Its utility is constant along the curve. As we move to the right in Fig. 3-1, each successive curve represents a higher level of expected utility. The utility schedule shown in the example is a monotonic increasing-concave one to the origin, indicating diminishing marginal rates of substitution between expected value of return and standard deviation. The greater the slope of the indifference curves, the more averse the economic unit is to risk. Because the risk averter prefers less variance to more, with the expected value of return being constant, $\partial U/\partial V < 0$, where V is the standard deviation of the probability distribution of possible returns.

A risk seeker, on the other hand, may have a utility schedule similar to that shown in Fig. 3-2. These indifference curves imply that an investor's preference for additional dispersion is an increasing function of the dis-

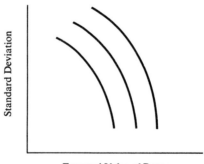

Expected Value of Return

Fig. 3-2.

persion already present.[14] Here $\partial U/\partial V > 0$. We assume that all economic units prefer more expected value of return to less—assuming constant risk—so $\partial U/\partial E > 0$, where E is the expected value of return.

The risk averter and the risk seeker each desires that portfolio of financial assets that places him on the highest indifference curve, choosing it from the opportunity set of available portfolios. An example of an opportunity set, based upon the subjective probability beliefs of an individual economic unit, is shown in Fig. 3-3. This opportunity set reflects all possible portfolios of financial assets as envisioned by the economic unit. The dark line at the bottom of the set is the line of efficient combinations, or the efficient frontier; its slope depends upon the degree of correlation among combinations of financial assets along the line. This line depicts the tradeoff between risk and expected value of return. According to the Markowitz mean-variance maxim, an economic unit should seek a portfolio of securities that lies on the efficient frontier.[15] A portfolio is not efficient if there

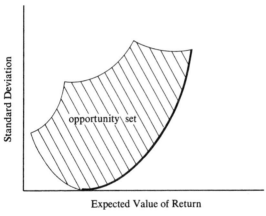

Expected Value of Return

Fig. 3-3.

is another portfolio with a higher expected value of return and a lower standard deviation, a higher expected value and the same standard deviation, or the same expected value but a lower standard deviation. If an economic unit's portfolio does not lie on the efficient frontier, it can increase the expected value of return without increasing the risk, decrease the risk without decreasing the expected value of return, or obtain some combination of increasing expected value of return and decreasing risk by switching to a portfolio along the efficient frontier. For all economic units, the portfolio providing the maximum utility is determined by the point of inter-

---

[14] For an analysis of the utility function of risk averters and risk seekers, see James Tobin, "Liquidity Preference as Behavior Towards Risk," pp. 74–77.

[15] Harry M. Markowitz, *Portfolio Selection: Efficient Diversification of Investments* (New York: John Wiley & Sons, Inc., 1959), Chapters VII and VIII.

section of the opportunity set with the highest indifference curve. For the risk averter, this point must lie on the efficient combination line and be a point of tangency, as illustrated in Fig. 3-4.[16] The portfolio represented by this point is the optimal one for an economic unit with those expectations and utility preferences.

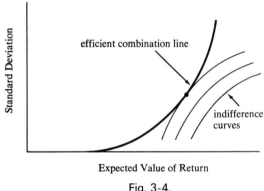

Fig. 3-4.

It is assumed that all economic units select portfolios of financial assets in such a way as to maximize their utility.[17] Because the opportunity sets of attainable portfolios are formulated on the basis of subjective probability beliefs, these opportunity sets are likely to differ among economic units. Their expectations are not homogeneous. In addition, the utility preferences with respect to expected value of return and risk for different economic units differ. For these reasons, the optimal portfolio of financial assets will vary considerably for different economic units in an economy. As we will discuss in the latter part of this chapter and in the appendix, heterogeneous expectations, together with differences in utility preferences among economic units, have a major bearing upon the structure of interest rates.

One difficulty with a two-parameter approach to portfolio selection is that it ignores the shape of the probability distribution. Most economic

---

[16] For the risk seeker, the point of intersection of the opportunity set with the highest indifference curve need not lie on the efficient combination line.

[17] One approach for specifying utility preferences as to expected value of return and risk is the von Neumann-Morgenstern measure of cardinal utility. Here, the utility preferences of an individual economic unit are specified numerically for risk situations, usually by having it consider various groups of lotteries. With the specification of an individual's utility function, possible outcomes in risk situations can be assigned utility values, called *utiles*. By multiplying the utile value of an outcome by the probability of occurrence for that outcome and totaling the products, we obtain the expected utility value of a financial asset or of a portfolio of financial assets. In this way, the portfolio with the highest expected utility value from the opportunity set is selected. John von Neumann and Oscar Morgenstern, *Theory of Games and Economic Behavior* (2nd ed.) (Princeton, N.J.: Princeton University Press, 1947). The method is illustrated in Van Horne, *Financial Management and Policy*, pp. 82–86.

units associate risk with the possibility of loss; downside fluctuations in return, not dispersion per se, are important. As a result, investors may well be influenced by the skewness of the probability distribution of possible returns. A distribution skewed to the left would involve more chance for low or negative returns than a distribution skewed to the right, all other things the same. Harry M. Markowitz, recognizing the limitations in the use of variance, considered semivariance a measure of risk.[18] This measure is the variance of the probability distribution to the left of the expected value of return and may be expressed as

$$SV(R) = \sum_{x=1}^{m} (R_x - \bar{R})^2 P_x \tag{3-9}$$

where R_x is the xth possible rate of return, P_x is the probability of that rate of return, $\bar{R}$ is the expected value of return, and where the possible rates of return are ordered from low to high so that m represents the last of the possible returns less than the expected value of return $\bar{R}$. For a measure of relative skewness, Markowitz proposed the use of $V(R)/2SV(R)$, which is the variance of the probability distribution over twice its semivariance. For symmetrical distributions, $V(R)/2SV(R)$ equals one; it is greater than one for distributions skewed to the right and less than one for distributions skewed to the left.

Obviously, a measure of downside potential would be useful. Unfortunately, mathematical calculation of a skewness measure is possible only for a very simple problem; it is unfeasible for a portfolio with a large number of possible combinations of return. Because of the difficulty of dealing mathematically with moments of a probability distribution higher than the second, our analysis is confined to the first two moments—the expected value and the standard deviation.[19] We assume that individual economic units may be analyzed as though their utilities for holding financial assets were governed by the mean and standard deviation of the probability distributions of possible returns.[20]

---

[18] *Portfolio Selection*, Chapter IX.

[19] An alternative to the use of probability distributions is the state-preference approach to security selection. In this approach, the outcomes for various states of nature are specified for each security. Utility preferences are expressed in terms of these states, such as depression or boom, as well as in terms of the timing of return. See J. Hirshleifer, "Investment Decision Under Uncertainty: Application of the State-Preference Approach," *Quarterly Journal of Economics*, LXXX (May, 1966), 252–77; J. Hirshleifer, "Investment Decisions Under Uncertainty: Choice-Theoretic Approaches," *Quarterly Journal of Economics*, LXXIX (November, 1965), 509–36; and Stewart C. Myers, "A Time-State-Preference Model of Security Valuation," *Journal of Financial and Quantitative Analysis*, III (March, 1968), 1–33.

[20] Assumed in this approach is the existence of a finite variance. Eugene F. Fama, "The Behavior of Stock-Market Prices," *Journal of Business*, XXXVII (January, 1965), 34–105; and earlier, Benoit Mandelbrot showed that stock market prices conformed to a stable paretian distribution—a "fat-tailed" distribution—for which the variance (and standard deviation) does not exist. Fama concluded, however, that the insights on diversification gained from the mean-standard–deviation model are valid when the distribution is a member of the stable family. Fama, "Risk, Return and Equilibrium," p. 30.

Utility for Financial Liabilities

We assume also that the issuance of financial liabilities can be analyzed on the basis of a two-parameter utility function. Because an economic unit must pay the return on a financial liability, it would have a negative utility for doing so, all other things the same. Consequently, $\partial U/\partial e < 0$, where e is the expected value of return on the financial liability. If an economic unit is a risk averter, it would prefer less variance to more variance, holding constant the expected value of return, so $\partial U/\partial v < 0$, where v is the standard deviation for the financial liability. For the risk seeker, $\partial U/\partial v > 0$.

For a financial liability, variance pertains to the dispersion of the probability distribution of possible future market prices. For fixed-income financial liabilities, the issuer knows with certainty its contractual obligation to meet interest and principal payments. After issuance, however, the instrument fluctuates in market price because of changes in the overall level of interest rates and because of changes in the perceived risk of the borrower by investors. To the extent that a borrower is unconcerned with the future market price of its financial liability, it would have a one-parameter utility function. In other words, its preferences would be governed only by the yield to be paid at the time of issuance. In this case, e, the expected value of return, would correspond to the initial yield.

Although diversification is possible by issuing different financial liabilities, the potential is not nearly so great as for financial assets because the financial risk of the issuer is the same, regardless of the instrument issued. However, the economic unit can diversify its "portfolio" of financial liabilities by issuing claims with different lengths of time to maturity. In addition, it can issue different types of claims with respect to security. In this way, an economic unit is able to reduce somewhat the dispersion of possible returns for a combination of financial liabilities relative to the expected value of those returns. However, financial liabilities are less divisible than financial assets. Flotation costs, inconvenience, and institutional factors make issuing financial liabilities somewhat "lumpy." This lack of divisibility impedes diversification. Overall, then, the potential for diversification of financial liabilities is more limited than with financial assets.

Utility for Other Assets

In the previous discussion, we considered the effect of holding financial assets and issuing financial liabilities on the utility of an economic unit. We now must consider the utility arising from the holding of other assets. Because our primary interest is in financial instruments, however, our examination necessarily will be brief. Afterward, the maximization of utility for an economic unit in its holdings of assets, in its issuance of financial liabilities, and in its consumption will be considered. Having established these building blocks, we will deal in the remainder of the chapter and in the appendix with how economic units interact to determine interest rates in an economy.

Because money is a medium of exchange and other financial assets are not, it was not included in our previous discussion. For purposes of analysis, we use the "narrow" definition of money—currency in circulation and demand deposits. This definition differs from a "broad" one, where money is taken to include currency, demand deposits, time deposits at commercial banks, and sometimes time deposits at other financial intermediaries.[21] If it were not for money, of course, trading would have to be done on the basis of exchanging one good for another. Such a barter system allows little or no store of purchasing power, no common unit of account in which different goods can be expressed, and little divisibility. Because of these obvious inefficiencies, money has come to serve as the accepted medium of exchange in acquiring goods and services. In addition, it serves as the unit of account, or common denominator, in the pricing of goods and services. For example, a good or service does not have to be priced in terms of so many units of other goods and services. It can be priced in terms of units of money. Although money additionally serves as a store of value, other assets, of course, also serve this function.

Keynes has identified three motives for holding money—the transactions motive, the precautionary motive, and the speculative motive.[22] The transactions motive is the desire to hold money to pay for goods and services. This need tends to rise with the level of income and expenditures of an economic unit. The precautionary motive for holding money involves maintaining a cushion, or buffer, to meet unexpected contingencies. The more predictable the money needs of an economic unit, the less precautionary balances are needed. If an economic unit is able to borrow on short notice to meet emergency money drains, the need for this balance also is reduced. The last motive, the speculative one, means holding money to take advantage of expected changes in security prices. When interest rates are expected to rise and security prices to fall, this motive would suggest that the economic unit should hold money until the rise in interest

---

[21] Friedman is the best known advocate of a broad definition. He defines money as being not only a medium of exchange but also a temporary store of purchasing power. He and others suggest that bank time deposits are a close substitute for currency and demand deposits and, therefore, should be included in the definition. See M. J. Friedman and A. J. Schwartz, *A Monetary History of the United States, 1867–1960* (New York: National Bureau of Economic Research, 1963), p. 650. Gurley-Shaw and Lee contend that savings deposits at nonbank financial institutions are close substitutes and should be included. John G. Gurley and Edward S. Shaw, *Money in a Theory of Finance* (Washington, D.C.: The Brookings Institution, 1960); and Tong Hun Lee, "Substitutability of Non-Bank Intermediary Liabilities for Money: The Empirical Evidence," *Journal of Finance*, XXI (September, 1966), 441–57. Although the controversy over the proper definition of money is interesting, space does not permit its consideration.

[22] *The General Theory of Employment Interest and Money*, pp. 170–74.

rates ceases, in order to avoid a loss in security value. When interest rates are expected to fall, money may be invested in securities; the economic unit will benefit by any subsequent fall in interest rates and rise in security prices.

The marginal utility for holding money can be related to these three motives, and it is assumed that economic units formulate utility preferences for money on these bases. The expected value of return for holding paper money is zero. However, no risk is involved, for the future price is known. To be sure, there may be an opportunity loss in the form of eroded purchasing power. However, there is no dispersion of the probability distribution of possible monetary returns. X dollars of paper money held today will be worth X dollars tomorrow. With demand deposits, a commercial bank may possibly fail, and the depositor may suffer a loss. However, with deposit insurance and a central bank, the probability for actual loss is rather small if not negligible. Consequently, we will regard money as having no uncertainty as to future price.

Unlike financial assets, real assets are held for the physical services they provide the owner. These assets may be productive, such as a machine tool, or may be designed to satisfy the wants of economic units, such as a house or a consumer durable. Real assets are tangible; they cannot be produced instantaneously but only over time. The marginal utility arising from owning a real asset must be related to the services it provides. In the case of a productive asset, it usually is related to the marginal profitability of another unit of input. In analyzing profitability, one must take account of the interdependence of inputs in the production function. It is the partial derivative of profitability with respect to the asset that is important. The marginal utility of consumer durables and dwellings is much more difficult to measure. Here, marginal utility must be related to the want satisfaction the asset provides the owner.

The holding of certain real assets can be explained in terms of the overall portfolio of the owner. Business firms, on one hand, hold capital assets for the return they are expected to provide. Many firms combine these assets with attention to the overall risk of the enterprise, undertaking diversification to reduce risk relative to expected return. The most striking example is the acquisition of other companies through mergers in order to stabilize fluctuations in operating income.[23]

Households, on the other hand, do not appear to acquire consumer durables on the basis of portfolio considerations. However, the acquisition of a home seems to have portfolio implications, for generally it is the largest asset holding of the household.[24] Although the model developed in this chapter implies an independence of the utility function for real assets from that for financial assets, the holding of certain real assets can be explained in terms of an expected return-risk tradeoff for the economic

[23] For an analysis of this risk-return tradeoff for business firms, see Van Horne, *Financial Management and Policy*, Chapters 4 and 5.

[24] See Moore, *An Introduction to the Theory of Finance*, p. 69.

unit as a whole. In these cases, the interdependence of real and financial assets must be recognized in the final determination of an optimal portfolio.

Equilibrium for an Economic Unit

The amount of money, financial assets, and real assets held, the amount of financial liabilities issued, and consumption are determined by an economic unit on the basis of maximizing its total utility, subject to net worth and income constraints. In equilibrium, the marginal utility derived from holding each asset is the same. *Marginal utility* is defined as the change in total utility that accompanies an increase of one dollar in a particular asset. Thus, the marginal utility derived from the last dollar increase in financial asset 1 must equal the marginal utility derived from the last dollar increase in money, in financial assets 2, 3, and n, and in real assets 1, 2, ..., n. In equilibrium, the following equation holds:

$$\frac{MU \text{ money}}{P \text{ money}} = \frac{MU \ FA1}{P \ FA1} = \frac{MU \ FA2}{P \ FA2} = \frac{MU \ FAn}{P \ FA} =$$

$$\frac{MU \ RA1}{P \ RA1} = \frac{MU \ RA2}{P \ RA2} = \frac{MU \ RAn}{P \ RAn} \tag{3-10}$$

Here MU stands for marginal utility, P for price per unit, FAn for financial asset n, and RAn for real asset n. In other words, maximum satisfaction occurs at the point at which the marginal utility of a dollar's worth of money equals the marginal utility of a dollar's worth of financial asset n and the marginal utility of a dollar's worth of the other assets held. If this equation is not satisfied, an economic unit can increase its total utility by shifting from an asset with a lower ratio of marginal utility to price to one with a higher ratio. By such shifting, equilibrium will eventually be achieved where the ratios of marginal utility to price are all equal to some constant λ. If the price of money is 1, $\lambda = MU$ money$/1$, or the marginal utility of money.

For simplicity in analysis, we hold constant the effect of consumption by considering the balance sheet of an economic unit at only a moment in time. Over time, of course, an economic unit can have current expenditures. Then, in equilibrium, the marginal utility derived from a dollar's worth of current expenditures must equal that derived from a dollar's worth of each asset held. In other words, consumption competes with the holding of assets in the maximization of total utility. This implies that the marginal utility of savings (current income less current expenditures) must be evaluated in relation to the satisfaction derived from the assets into which savings are put. To facilitate later analysis, however, we hold constant the effect of savings and consumption and assume that an economic unit will not sell assets, use money, or issue financial liabilities for consumption.

Financial liabilities represent a negative marginal utility to the issuer. An economic unit does not issue a financial liability for its own sake but to acquire assets. As long as the positive marginal utility from an additional dollar's worth of assets exceeds in absolute magnitude the negative marginal utility from the issuance of an additional dollar of financial liabilities, the economic unit will issue financial liabilities. In equilibrium, the negative marginal utility per dollar's worth of each financial liability should be the same. Moreover, the ratio of marginal utility to price for each financial liability should equal the ratio of marginal utility to price for each asset (if we ignore the sign of the ratio). For the risk averter, we would expect the negative ratio of marginal utility to price to increase at an increasing rate as a financial liability is increased beyond some point. This occurrence is a result not only of the utility preferences of the economic unit but also of possible increases in the interest rate as more financial liabilities are issued. Because of the decreasing positive ratio of marginal utility to price for acquiring additional assets and the increasing negative ratio of marginal utility to price for issuing financial liabilities, an equilibrium will be achieved for the individual economic unit.

In the model developed so far, we assumed that the utility function for financial liabilities was independent of that for financial assets. However, some theorists argue that the same utility function should be applied to both functions. According to them, issuing a financial liability is the same as selling a financial asset short; the negative marginal utility associated with issuing a liability is of the same magnitude as the positive marginal utility associated with investing in a financial asset, all other things the same. However, many economic units would appear to regard the negative marginal utility associated with issuing a financial liability of a given amount as greater in magnitude than the positive marginal utility of investing in a financial asset of the same amount, all other things the same. Over and above the difference in sign, they simply view borrowing and lending in a different light. Moreover, the utility function for issuing financial liabilities for certain economic units may involve only one parameter, the yield paid (as brought out in our previous discussion), whereas that for investing in financial assets may involve two parameters. For these reasons, it is important to allow for differences in utility functions for investing in financial assets and issuing financial liabilities.

At a moment in time, the holding of financial assets and the issuance of financial liabilities are constrained by the net worth of the individual economic unit.

$$
\begin{aligned}
M &+ FA1P_{FA1} + FA2P_{FA2} \\
&+ \ldots + FAnP_{FAn} + RA1P_{RA1} + RA2P_{RA2} \\
&+ \ldots + RAnP_{RAn} - FL1P_{FL1} - FL2P_{FL2} \\
&- \ldots - FLnP_{FLn} = \text{NW}
\end{aligned} \tag{3-11}
$$

where $FA1$ is the quantity of financial asset n, P_{FAn} is the price per unit of that asset, FLn is the quantity of liability n, and P_{FLn} is the price per unit of that financial liability. The individual economic unit will try to maximize its total utility by changing its asset holdings and liabilities issued, subject to its net worth constraint. Its objective function is

$$\max X = U(M, X, R, Y) \qquad (3\text{-}12)$$

subject to

$$M + \sum_i P_i x_i + \sum_k P_k r_k - \sum_j P_j y_j = \text{NW} \qquad (3\text{-}13)$$

where X = a column vector of x_i, where x_i is the quantity of the ith financial asset
P_i = price per unit of the ith financial asset
R = a column vector of r_k, where r_k is the quantity of the kth real asset
P_k = price per unit of the kth real asset
Y = a column vector of y_j, where y_j is the quantity of the jth financial liability
P_j = price per unit of the jth financial liability

Recall that the utility to an economic unit of holding financial assets and issuing financial liabilities was assumed to be based upon the expected value and standard deviation of the probability distributions of possible returns. Each economic unit forms expectations about possible returns from all feasible portfolios of financial assets and all feasible combinations of financial liabilities. We recognize, however, that an economic unit is limited in the number of financial assets it can consider at one time. It simply is unable to form expectations about the universe of financial assets available to it for investment; consequently, the number of feasible portfolios is restricted. Once the optimal portfolio of financial assets and the optimal combination of financial liabilities are determined by an economic unit, it then increases or decreases them to maximize its total utility in keeping with equations (3-12) and (3-13).

In summary, the individual economic unit maximizes its utility according to equation (3-12) by varying M, X, R, and Y, subject to the net worth constraint. In equilibrium, the marginal utility per dollar of money equals the marginal utility per dollar of the optimal financial-asset portfolio, which, in turn, equals the marginal utility per dollar of real assets held. In addition, the negative marginal utility per dollar of the optimal combination of financial liabilities must equal the ratio for the assets (if we ignore the sign). If it were less, an economic unit could increase its total utility by increasing its financial liabilities and increasing its holdings of assets.

Market Equilibrium

The action of all economic units in an economy maximizing their utility according to equation (3-12) determines market prices for real and financial assets in that economy. Whereas prices in equation (3-13) are assumed to be given for the individual economic unit, they are not given for economic units collectively. These economic units act to maximize their individual utilities, and in doing so, they determine market prices and interest rates in the economy. For the economy as a whole, financial assets equal financial liabilities. Accordingly, market prices must adjust so that in equilibrium there is no excess demand or excess supply.

The equilibrium structure of financial-asset prices and interest rates is the result of a complex blending of the expectations, net worths, incomes, and utility functions of all economic units in an economy. This structure is affected by the utility preferences of economic units regarding money, real assets, financial assets, and financial liabilities. For example, an increase in the marginal utility of all economic units toward holding real assets would lead, ceteris paribus, to a greater aggregate demand for real assets, higher prices for these assets, a lower aggregate demand for financial assets, and a greater aggregate supply of financial liabilities. For equilibrium to be achieved, prices of financial instruments would have to decline and interest rates rise.

Equilibrium in financial markets requires that the total quantity of a financial instrument demanded equal the total quantity an economic unit desires to issue. The relative influence of an economic unit on market price depends on its net worth, its utility preferences, its expectations, and its existing holding of assets and liabilities. On the supply side of the market, the quantity of a particular financial liability that an economic unit desires to issue also depends on these factors. In a modern economy, most economic units exert at least some influence on interest rates. Differing expectations, net worths, and utility functions of economic units, however, make determination of equilibrium prices of financial instruments in an economy an extremely complex process involving the interaction of all economic units in the economy. Perhaps the key element in this process is expectations. On the basis of expectations as to return, variance, and covariance, different financial instruments are perceived differently by different economic units. Economic units in need of funds must compete for them on the basis of the expected return paid. (Actually, the need for funds and the expected return paid are determined simultaneously.) Through the interaction of the various economic units, interest rates are determined and savings are allocated in the economy.

Because of the mathematical complexity of the process, it is examined in detail in the appendix to this chapter.

Summary

Savings in an economy are allocated primarily through interest rates. The *yield* on a financial instrument is the discount rate that equates the present value of expected future cash inflows, including the redemption price, with the current market price. The yield to maturity on an instrument differs from its *holding-period yield* in that the latter encompasses both the cash inflows and the capital gain or loss for the holding period. Interest rates in financial markets are determined by the interaction of both the supply and the demand for existing financial assets and the supply and demand for newly created financial assets. Thus, savings and investment in the economy have a direct influence upon market rates of interest.

The equilibrating process in financial markets depends upon the behavior of investors in and issuers of financial instruments and upon the efficiency of these markets. The process may be subject to lags that impede the adjustment to disequilibrium conditions. The individual economic unit continually adjusts its asset holdings and liabilities toward a preferred mix of assets, liabilities, and consumption. At the preferred mix, the wealth and income of the unit are allocated optimally. The economic unit adjusts its mix to maximize its total utility. In equilibrium, the marginal utilities of each dollar of money, each dollar of each financial asset, and each dollar of each real asset are the same. These ratios are equal also to the negative marginal utility of each dollar of each financial liability (if we ignore the sign).

The utility preferences for holding financial assets and issuing financial liabilities are assumed to be based upon the expected value and the dispersion of the probability distribution of possible returns. In either case, it is the portfolio of assets or liabilities that is important, for an economic unit can reduce dispersion of its portfolio through diversification. The behavior of risk averters and risk seekers with respect to an optimal portfolio was examined. Individual economic units maximize their total utility arising from holding money, financial assets, and real assets, from issuing financial liabilities, and from consuming, subject to wealth and income constraints. The behavior of all economic units in a closed economy maximizing their total utility in this manner determines interest rates on financial instruments in that economy. In equilibrium, the total amount of financial assets demanded must equal the total amount supplied; there can be no excess demand or excess supply in financial markets. Interest rates adjust to clear these markets and are the result of a complex interaction of all economic units in the economy.

Appendix: The Equilibrium Prices of Financial Assets*

The purpose of this appendix is to develop a model of financial-asset prices in a closed economy. We begin by assuming that at a moment in time an individual economic unit may hold money, financial assets, and real assets. In addition, it may issue a variety of financial liabilities to finance its holding of assets. Consider a simplified situation with only one financial asset—a fixed-income security—in which an individual economic unit may invest and with only one type of financial liability which it may issue—also a fixed-income security. The asset and the liability are assumed to have a zero coupon with interest expressed as a discount. Moreover, we assume no transaction costs, no short sales, and no taxation. The economic unit will attempt to maximize its total utility arising from holding money, the financial asset, and real assets, and from issuing the financial liability. The amounts of the various assets are constrained by the net worth of the economic unit at time t plus the amount of the financial liability it issues.[1] The relationship for the individual economic unit may be expressed as

$$\max \mathcal{Z} = U(M, x, R, y) + \lambda(N - M - P_x x - R + P_y y) \qquad (1)$$

where M = money, expressed in units of one dollar, and assumed to be nonnegative[2]

x = quantity of the financial asset held at time t

P_x = price of the financial asset at time t

R = market value of real assets held at time t, expressed in units of one dollar, and assumed to be nonnegative

y = quantity of the issued financial liability at time t

P_y = price of the financial liability at time t

N = net worth of economic unit at time t, expressed in units of one dollar

λ = a Lagrangian multiplier

It is evident from equation (1) that the individual economic unit will increase its financial liability to finance its holding of money, the financial asset, and real assets as long as it can increase its total utility by doing so. Assuming no short sales, so that $x \geq 0$ and $y \geq 0$, the equilibrium conditions for the financial asset and liability are

---

*I am grateful to Professor Robert Wilson for helpful comments in the development of this appendix.

[1] The net worth of an individual economic unit is assumed to be constant. We assume that it will not sell assets, use money, or borrow to consume.

[2] We assume that the economic unit analyzed is not able to issue money.

$$\frac{\partial U}{\partial x} - \lambda P_x \le 0, \qquad x \ge 0, \qquad x\left[\frac{\partial U}{\partial x} - \lambda P_x\right] = 0 \qquad (2)$$

$$\frac{\partial U}{\partial y} + \lambda P_y \le 0, \qquad y \ge 0, \qquad y\left[\frac{\partial U}{\partial y} + \lambda P_y\right] = 0 \qquad (3)$$

We assume a one-period horizon and that the future price of the financial asset and the future price of the financial liability at time $t + 1$ are subjective random variables.[3] We also assume that the individual economic unit knows the mean and variance of the probability distributions. Thus, the value of the financial asset to rule at time $t + 1$ is a random variable with a mean of

$$E = \bar{\rho}_x x \qquad (4)$$

and a variance of

$$V = \sigma_x^2 x^2 \qquad (5)$$

where $\bar{\rho}_x$ is the mean of the probability distribution of possible prices one period hence, σ_x^2 is the variance, and x is the quantity of the asset held.

Similarly, the value of the financial liability to rule at time $t + 1$ is also a random variable with a mean of

$$e = \bar{\rho}_y y \qquad (6)$$

and a variance of

$$v = \sigma_y^2 y^2 \qquad (7)$$

where $\bar{\rho}_y$ is the mean of the probability distribution, σ_y^2 is the variance, and y is the quantity of the liability issued.

We assume that individual economic units may be analyzed as though their utilities with respect to holding and issuing a financial asset and a liability were governed by the mean and variance of the respective probability distributions. We assume also that the price of money and the prices of real assets at time $t + 1$ are known with certainty and that these prices are the same as those that prevailed at time t. Thus, we consider only a subset of prices of financial assets and liabilities within which equilibrium can occur. Moreover, we assume that the prices of the financial asset and the financial liability are stochastically independent.

---

[3]The immediate subsequent analysis draws upon G. O. Bierwag and M. A. Grove, "On Capital Assets Prices: Comment," *Journal of Finance*, XX (March, 1965), 89–93; and J. R. Hicks, "Liquidity," *The Economic Journal*, LXXII (December, 1963), 795, 798–802.

Under conditions (4) through (7), equations (2) and (3) become

$$\frac{\partial U}{\partial E}\frac{\partial E}{\partial x} + \frac{\partial U}{\partial V}\frac{\partial V}{\partial x} - \lambda P_x \leq 0, \qquad x \geq 0,$$

$$x\left[\frac{\partial U}{\partial E}\frac{\partial E}{\partial x} + \frac{\partial U}{\partial V}\frac{\partial V}{\partial x} - \lambda P_x\right] = 0 \tag{8}$$

or $\quad \dfrac{\partial U}{\partial E}\bar{\rho}_x + \dfrac{\partial U}{\partial V}2x\sigma_x^2 - \lambda P_x \leq 0, \qquad x \geq 0,$

$$x\left[\frac{\partial U}{\partial E}\bar{\rho}_x + \frac{\partial U}{\partial V}2x\sigma_x^2 - \lambda P_x\right] = 0$$

and $\quad \dfrac{\partial U}{\partial e}\dfrac{\partial e}{\partial y} + \dfrac{\partial U}{\partial v}\dfrac{\partial v}{\partial y} + \lambda P_y \leq 0, \qquad y \geq 0,$

$$y\left[\frac{\partial U}{\partial e}\frac{\partial e}{\partial y} + \frac{\partial U}{\partial v}\frac{\partial v}{\partial y} + \lambda P_y\right] = 0 \tag{9}$$

or $\quad \dfrac{\partial U}{\partial e}\bar{\rho}_y + \dfrac{\partial U}{\partial v}2y\sigma_y^2 + \lambda P_y \leq 0, \qquad y \geq 0,$

$$y\left[\frac{\partial U}{\partial e}\bar{\rho}_y + \frac{\partial U}{\partial V}2y\sigma_y^2 + \lambda P_y\right] = 0$$

The equilibrium quantity of the financial asset held is

$$x = \max\left\{\left(\frac{-\dfrac{\partial U}{\partial E}\bar{\rho}_x + \lambda P_x}{2(\partial U/\partial v)}\right)\bigg/\sigma_x^2, 0\right\}$$

$$= \max\left\{\left(k\frac{\partial U}{\partial E}\bar{\rho}_x - k\lambda P_x\right)\bigg/\sigma_x^2, 0\right\} \tag{10}$$

where $k = -[1/2(\partial U/\partial V)]$ or a measure of risk aversion.

For the risk averter who associates risk with variance, $\partial U/\partial V$ will be negative and k positive; for the risk seeker, $\partial U/\partial V$ will be positive and k negative. We assume, of course, that $\partial U/\partial E > 0$.

For the issuance of a financial liability, the equilibrium quantity is

$$y = \max\left\{\left(\frac{-\dfrac{\partial U}{\partial e}\bar{\rho}_y - \lambda P_y}{2(\partial U/\partial v)}\right)\bigg/\sigma_y^2, 0\right\}$$

$$= \max\left\{\left(l\frac{\partial U}{\partial e}\bar{\rho}_y + l\lambda P_y\right)\bigg/\sigma_y^2, 0\right\} \tag{11}$$

where $l = -[1/2(\partial U/\partial v)]$, or a measure of risk aversion for the issuance of the financial liability. For the issuer, we assume $\partial U/\partial e < 0$.

Market Equilibrium: Two Economic Units

In a closed economy of two economic units, if unit b is to issue a financial liability, unit a must invest in it. In market equilibrium, $x_a = y_b$, the amount of the financial asset demanded by a must equal the amount that b desires to issue. Thus,

$$\max\left\{\left(k\,\frac{\partial U}{\partial E}\,\bar{\rho}_{xa} - k\lambda_a P\right)\middle/\sigma_{xa}^2,\, 0\right\}$$

$$= \max\left\{\left(l\,\frac{\partial U}{\partial e}\,\bar{\rho}_{yb} + l\lambda_b P\right)\middle/\sigma_{yb}^2,\, 0\right\} \quad (12)$$

If both x_a and y_b are greater than zero, the equilibrium price at time t of the financial asset is

$$P = \frac{k\,\dfrac{\partial U}{\partial E}\,\bar{\rho}_{xa}/\sigma_{xa}^2 - l\,\dfrac{\partial U}{\partial e}\,\bar{\rho}_{yb}/\sigma_{yb}^2}{k\lambda_a/\sigma_{xa}^2 + l\lambda_b/\sigma_{yb}^2} \quad (13)$$

Equation (13) suggests that the equilibrium price of the financial asset is a balancing of the expectations, net worths, and utility functions of the economic units involved. If both a and b are risk averters, an assumption we continue throughout this section, the price of the financial asset will vary directly, ceteris paribus, with the means of the probability distributions of prices that a and b expect at time t to prevail at time $t + 1$.

The direction of the variation with the variances of the probability distributions will depend upon the relative marginal utilities of units a and b. When $(\partial U/\partial E)\bar{\rho}_{xa}/\lambda_a = (\partial U/\partial e)\bar{\rho}_{yb}/\lambda_b$, price does not vary with either the variance of a's probability distribution, σ_{xa}^2, or that of b's, σ_{yb}^2. When $(\partial U/\partial E)\bar{\rho}_{xa}/\lambda_a < (\partial U/\partial e)\bar{\rho}_{yb}/\lambda_b$, price varies directly with σ_{xa}^2 and inversely with σ_{yb}^2. Finally, when $(\partial U/\partial E)\bar{\rho}_{xa}/\lambda_a > (\partial U/\partial e)\bar{\rho}_{yb}/\lambda_b$, price varies inversely with σ_{xa}^2 and directly with σ_{yb}^2.

If expectations are homogeneous, so that the probability distributions of a and b are the same, equation (13) becomes

$$P = \frac{\bar{\rho}\left(k\,\dfrac{\partial U}{\partial E} - l\,\dfrac{\partial U}{\partial e}\right)}{k\lambda_a + l\lambda_b} \quad (14)$$

For the actual price at time t to equal the mean of the probability distribution of prices expected by a and b at time t to prevail at time $t + 1$,

$[k(\partial U/\partial E) - l(\partial U/\partial e)]$ must equal $(k\lambda_a + l\lambda_b)$. If $\partial U/\partial E$ and $-\partial U/\partial e$ are less than λ_a and λ_b, respectively, P, the actual price at time t, will be less than $\bar{p}$, the mean of the probability distribution.

Market Equilibrium: Multiple Financial Assets

Clearly, it is inappropriate to consider an economy of only one financial asset and two economic units. An individual economic unit may both invest in and issue a variety of financial assets and liabilities. Thus, equation (1) must be expanded as follows:[4]

$$\max Z = U(M, X, R, Y) + \lambda(N - M - \sum_i P_i x_i - R + \sum_j P_j y_j) \quad (15)$$

where X = a column vector of x_i, where x_i is the quantity of the ith financial asset

P_i = price of the ith financial asset at time t

Y = a column vector of y_j, where y_j is the quantity of the jth financial liability

P_j = price of the jth financial liability at time t

For the individual economic unit in equilibrium,

$$\frac{\partial U}{\partial x_i} - \lambda P_i \leq 0, \qquad x_i \geq 0,$$

$$x_i \left[\frac{\partial U}{\partial x_i} - \lambda P_i \right] = 0 \qquad (i = 11, ..., mn) \tag{16}$$

$$\frac{\partial U}{\partial y_j} + \lambda P_j \leq 0, \qquad y_j \geq 0,$$

$$y_j \left[\frac{\partial U}{\partial y_j} + \lambda P_j \right] = 0 \qquad (j = 1, ..., n) \tag{17}$$

where mn is security n issued by the mth economic unit in the economy. We assume that individual economic units do not issue financial liabilities to themselves. As before, the utilities of holding financial assets and issuing financial liabilities are assumed to be functions of the mean and variance of the probability distributions of prices expected by the economic unit at time t to prevail at time $t + 1$. The value of an individual's entire portfolio of financial assets expected at time t to rule at time $t + 1$ is a random variable with a mean of

---

[4] Again, we assume that R for each economic unit in the economy is nonnegative. However, M for certain units now may be negative. The monetary authorities and commercial banks are assumed to be able to issue money, while all other economic units cannot.

$$E = \sum_{i=11}^{mn} \bar{p}_i x_i \tag{18}$$

where $\bar{p}_i$ is the mean of the probability distribution of prices of the ith financial asset expected to prevail at time $t + 1$. The variance of the random variable is

$$V = \sum_{i=11}^{mn} \sum_{q=11}^{mn} x_i x_q \sigma_{iq} \tag{19}$$

where σ_{iq} is the covariance between the price of financial asset i expected at time t to prevail at time $t + 1$ and the price of financial asset q expected at time t to prevail at time $t + 1$.

In equilibrium, equation (17) becomes[5]

$$\left[\frac{\partial U}{\partial E}\bar{p}_i + \frac{\partial U}{\partial V}2\sum_{q=11}^{mn} x_q \sigma_{qi} - \lambda P_i\right] \leq 0, \qquad x_i \geq 0,$$

$$x_i\left[\frac{\partial U}{\partial E}\bar{p}_i + \frac{\partial U}{\partial V}2\sum_{q=11}^{mn} x_q \sigma_{qi} - \lambda P_i\right] = 0 \qquad (i = 11, \ldots, mn) \tag{20}$$

Assuming $\partial U/\partial V < 0$, this equation becomes

$$\left[\sum_{q=11}^{mn} x_q \sigma_{qi} - k\left(\frac{\partial U}{\partial E}\bar{p}_i - \lambda P_i\right)\right] \geq 0, \qquad x_i \geq 0,$$

$$x_i\left[\sum_{q=11}^{mn} x_q \sigma_{qi} - k\left(\frac{\partial U}{\partial E}\bar{p}_i - \lambda P_i\right)\right] = 0 \qquad (i = 11, \ldots, mn) \tag{21}$$

In matrix notation, condition (21) becomes[6]

$$X \geq 0 \leq CX - k\left(\frac{\partial U}{\partial E}\theta - \lambda\Phi\right) \tag{22}$$

where C is the matrix of variances and covariances, X is a column vector of the quantities of financial assets $(x_{11}, \ldots, x_{mn})$, where x_{mn} is security n issued by the mth economic unit, θ is a column vector of the means of the probability distributions of prices expected at time t to prevail at time $t + 1$ for these financial assets $(\bar{p}_{11}, \ldots, \bar{p}_{mn})$, and Φ is a column vector of their

[5]The development of the following equations is similar to that of Bierwag and Grove, "On Capital Assets Prices," p. 93.

[6]We shall follow the notational convention that triplets of the form $[a \geq 0, b \geq 0, ab = 0]$ are represented as $[a \geq 0 \leq b]$.

actual prices at time t $(P_{11}, ..., P_{mn})$. The equilibrium X vector for the individual economic unit may be expressed as

$$X = C^{-1}k\left(\frac{\partial U}{\partial E}\theta - \lambda\Phi\right) + C^{-1}\epsilon \tag{23}$$

where $X \geq 0 \leq \epsilon$, and where C^{-1} is an inverse matrix.

In addition to investing in financial assets, the individual economic unit may issue a number of different financial liabilities.[7] As with financial assets, the risk averter will issue less of a particular financial liability as its contribution to the total variance of his financial liabilities increases. Assuming $\partial U/\partial v < 0$, the equilibrium Y vector of financial liabilities for the economic unit is

$$Y = T^{-1}l\left(\frac{\partial U}{\partial e}\Psi + \lambda\Phi\right) + T^{-1}\delta \tag{24}$$

where $Y \geq 0 \leq \delta$, and where T^{-1} is an inverse matrix of variances and covariances, Y is a column vector of the quantities of financial liabilities $(y_{1m}, ..., y_{nm})$, where y_{nm} is the quantity of security n issued by economic unit m, Ψ is a column vector of the means of the probability distributions of prices expected at time t to prevail at time $t + 1$ for the financial liabilities, and Φ is a column vector of their actual prices at time t.

Equilibrium in the market requires that the total quantity of a financial asset demanded equal the quantity of the financial liability an economic unit desires to issue. If X and Y are greater than or equal to zero,

$$\sum_{f=1}^{m} X_f = W \tag{25}$$

where f is the economic unit investing in a financial asset and W is a column vector of financial liabilities for economic units 1 through m (ordered such that the Y column vector of financial liabilities for economic unit 1 is followed by the Y column for unit 2, and so on all the way through unit m). Substituting equations (23) and (24) into (25), we obtain[8]

$$\sum_{f=1}^{m} C_f^{-1}k_f\left(\frac{\partial U}{\partial E_f}\theta_f - \lambda_f\Phi\right) = T^{-1}l\left(\frac{\partial U}{\partial e}\Psi + \lambda\Phi\right) \tag{26}$$

---

[7] Again, we assume that individual economic units do not issue themselves financial liabilities.

[8] For the right-hand side of the equation, we assume the ordering mentioned earlier, namely, that the Y column vector, or $T^{-1}l[\partial U/\partial e)\Psi + \lambda\Phi]$, for unit 1 is followed by the Y column vector for unit 2, and so on through unit m.

The Φ vector of equilibrium prices of financial assets in the market is

$$\Phi = \frac{\displaystyle\sum_{f=1}^{m} C_f^{-1} k_f \frac{\partial U}{\partial E_f} \theta_f - T^{-1} l \frac{\partial U}{\partial e} \Psi}{\displaystyle\sum_{f=1}^{m} C_f^{-1} k_f \lambda_f + T^{-1} l \lambda} \tag{27}$$

According to this equation, the price of a financial asset in the market is an intricate blending of the expectations, net worths, and utility functions of all economic units in an economy. The relative influence of an investor on market price varies according to his net worth, his utility functions, his probability distributions of prices expected at time t to prevail at time $t + 1$, the covariances for the financial asset under consideration, and his probability distributions and covariances for all other financial assets and for all financial liabilities he may issue. Because expectations, net worths, and utility functions of the different economic units in the economy differ, determination of the equilibrium price of a financial asset is an extremely complex process.

Selected References

Bierwag, G. O., and M. A. Grove, "On Capital Asset Prices: Comment," *Journal of Finance*, XX (March, 1965), 89–93.

———, "Slutzky Equations for Assets," *Journal of Political Economy*, 76 (January–February, 1968), 114–27.

Duesenberry, James S., "A Process Approach to Flow-of-Funds Analysis," in *The Flow-of-Funds Approach to Social Accounting*. New York: National Bureau of Economic Research, 1962.

Fama, Eugene F., "Risk, Return, and Equilibrium: Some Clarifying Comments," *Journal of Finance*, XXIII (March, 1968).

Horwich, George, *Money, Capital, and Prices*. Homewood, Ill.: Richard D. Irwin, Inc., 1964. Chapter X.

Jensen, Michael C., "Risk, the Pricing of Capital Assets, and the Evaluation of Investment Portfolios," *Journal of Business*, XXXXII (April, 1969), 167–247.

Keynes, John Maynard, *The General Theory of Employment Interest and Money*. New York: Harcourt, Brace & World, Inc., 1936.

Lintner, John, "Security Prices, Risk, and Maximal Gains from Diversification," *Journal of Finance*, XX (December, 1965), 587–615.

Lutz, Friedrich A., *The Theory of Interest*. Dordrecht, Holland: D. Reidel Publishing Co., 1967.

Markowitz, Harry M., *Portfolio Selection*. New York: John Wiley & Sons, Inc., 1959.

Metzler, L. A., "Wealth, Saving and the Rate of Interest," *Journal of Political Economy*, LIX (April, 1951).

Moore, Basil J., *An Introduction to the Theory of Finance*. New York: The Free Press, 1968. Chapters 3 and 5.

Mossin, Jan, "Equilibrium in a Capital Asset Market," *Econometrica*, 34 (October, 1966), 768–83.

Patinkin, Don, *Money, Interest, and Prices*. New York: Harper & Row, Publishers, 1965.

Sharpe, William F., "Capital Asset Prices: A Theory of Market Equilibrium Under Conditions of Risk," *Journal of Finance*, XIX (September, 1964), 425–42.

————, "A Simplified Model for Portfolio Analysis," *Management Science*, 9 January, 1963), 273–93.

Tobin, James, "A Process Approach to Flow-of-Funds Analysis: Comment," in *The Flow-of-Funds Approach to Social Accounting*. New York: National Bureau of Economic Research, 1962.

————, "Liquidity Preference as Behavior Towards Risk," *Review of Economic Studies*, XXV (February, 1958), 65–86.

```
4444444444444444444444444444444444444444444444444444444444444444444444444444444444
4444444444444444444444444444444444444444444444444444444444444444444444444444444444
44444444444444444444444444444444   444   444444444444   4444444444444444444444444444
44444444444444444444444444444444   4444   444444444   4444444444444444444444444444444
44444444444444444444444444444444   44444   44444444   44444444444444444444444444444444
44444444444444444444444444444444   444444   4444444   44444444444444444444444444444444
44444444444444444444444444444444   4444444   44444   444444444444444444444444444444444
44444444444444444444444444444444   4444444   444   44444444444444444444444444444444444
44444444444444444444444444444444   44444444   4   44444444444444444444444444444444444
44444444444444444444444444444444   444444444   44444444444444444444444444444444444444
44444444444444444444444444444444   4444444444   444444444444444444444444444444444444
4444444444444444444444444444444444444444444444444444444444444444444444444444444444444
4444444444444444444444444444444444444444444444444444444444444444444444444444444444444
```

The Term Structure of Interest Rates

IN the previous chapter, our focus was on how equilibrium rates of interest
were determined for financial instruments in the economy. We analyzed
the desired quantities of financial assets held and liabilities issued in
relation to the total utility of an economic unit. In this chapter and the
next two, we are concerned with why rates of interest differ for different
financial instruments. We shall study the relationship among yields on
fixed-income securities by examining the term structure of interest rates
in this chapter, the risk structure and marketability in Chapter 5, and
callability and taxability in Chapter 6. These factors should allow us to
explain most of the observed differences in yield for nonequity securities.

The relationship between yield and maturity on securities differing
only in length of time to maturity is known as the *term structure of interest
rates*. Factors other than maturity must be held constant if the relationship
studied is to be meaningful. In practice, this usually means holding constant the degree of default risk. The term structure may be studied
graphically by plotting yield and maturity for equivalent-grade securities
at a moment in time. Maturity is plotted on the horizontal axis and yield
on the vertical axis, and their relationship is described by a yield curve
fitted to the observations. An example of a yield curve for default-free
Treasury securities is shown in Fig. 4-1. The yield curves in this figure

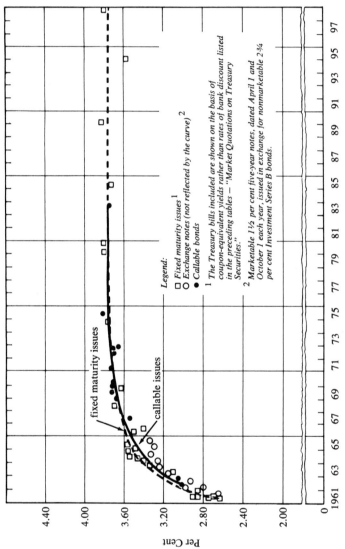

Explanation: The points represent yields to call when prices are above par, and to maturity date when prices are at par or below. The smooth curves for the two classes of points are fitted by eye. Market yields on regular weekly bills other than those offered the latest week and on maturing coupon issues for which an exchange offer has been made and on any issues which are due in less than three months are excluded.

Fig. 4-1. Yields of taxable Treasury securities, Feb. 28, 1961, based on closing bid quotations. Source: *Treasury Bulletin* (March, 1961).

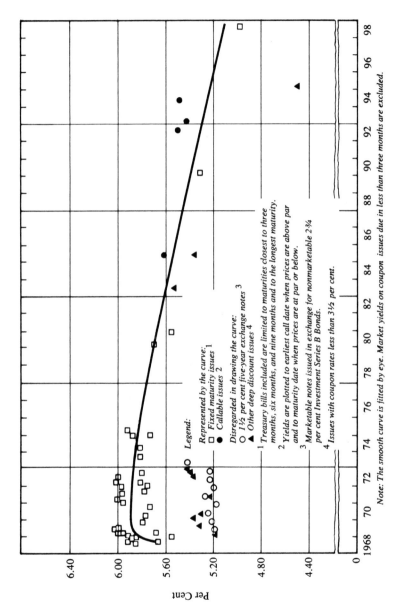

Fig. 4-2. Yields of Treasury securities, April 30, 1968, based on closing bid quotations. Source: *Treasury Bulletin* (May, 1968).

Note: *The smooth curve is fitted by eye. Market yields on coupon issues due in less than three months are excluded.*

Legend:

Represented by the curve:
□ *Fixed maturity issues* [1]
● *Callable issues* [2]

Disregarded in drawing the curve:
○ *1½ per cent five-year exchange notes* [3]
▲ *Other deep discount issues* [4]

[1] *Treasury bills included are limited to maturities closest to three months, six months, and nine months and to the longest maturity.*

[2] *Yields are plotted to earliest call date when prices are above par and to maturity date when prices are at par or below.*

[3] *Marketable notes issued in exchange for nonmarketable 2¾ per cent Investment Series B Bonds.*

[4] *Issues with coupon rates less than 3½ per cent.*

67

are upward-sloping ones. However, yield curves may have other shapes; a downward-sloping one is illustrated in Fig. 4-2.

In this chapter, we investigate why the term structure of interest rates has different shapes and different overall levels over time. It generally is agreed that expectations of the future course of interest rates are an important influence;[1] controversy arises, however, as to whether there are other important factors. We begin by considering the unbiased expectations theory, where the term structure is explained entirely by interest-rate expectations. Using this theory as a building block, we then consider rival theories for explaining the yield-maturity relationship on securities differing only in the length of time to maturity.

The Unbiased Expectations Theory

In its basic form, the unbiased expectations theory states that the long-term rate of interest is an unbiased average of the current short-term rate and future short-term rates expected to prevail during the long-term obligation. This theory was first expressed by Irving Fisher and was developed further by Friedrich Lutz.[2] When considering the theory, we find it helpful to transform actual interest rates into forward rates of interest. J. R. Hicks analyzes the term structure as a market for funds similar to the futures market in commodities.[3] For example, a borrower obtains funds from a current spot transaction. At the same time, he executes a forward contract in which he promises to pay back the money at some future date or at a series of future dates. Implied in the term structure at any moment is a set of forward rates:[4]

$$(1 + {}_tR_n)^n = (1 + {}_tR_1)(1 + {}_{t+1}r_{1t})(1 + {}_{t+2}r_{1t}) \cdots (1 + {}_{t+n-1}r_{1t}) \quad (4\text{-}1)$$

where ${}_tR_n$ represents the actual rate of interest at time t on an N-period loan, ${}_tR_1$ is the actual rate on a one-period loan at time t, and ${}_{t+1}r_{1t}, {}_{t+2}r_{1t}$, and ${}_{t+n-1}r_{1t}$ are forward rates for one-period loans beginning at times $t + 1, t + 2$, and $t + n - 1$, implied in the term structure at time t. Thus, a loan for four years is equivalent to a one-year loan plus a series of forward contracts, each renewing the loan for a successive year. The formula for

---

[1] See Burton G. Malkiel, *The Term Structure of Interest Rates* (Princeton, N.J.: Princeton University Press, 1966), Chapters 2 and 4; and L. G. Telser, "A Critique of Some Recent Empirical Research on the Explanation of the Term Structure of Interest Rates," *Journal of Political Economy*, 75 (Supplement: August, 1967), 546–61.

[2] Irving Fisher, "Appreciation and Interest," *Publications of the American Economic Association*, XI (August, 1896), 23–29, 91–92; and F. A. Lutz, "The Structure of Interest Rates," *The Quarterly Journal of Economics*, LV (November, 1940), 36–63.

[3] *Value and Capital* (2nd ed.) (London: Oxford University Press, 1946), pp. 141–45.

[4] This formula assumes implicitly that coupon payments are reinvested, the lender receiving the principal and reinvested interest at maturity. The formula contrasts with one in which all payments are discounted back to present value in accordance with the times when they are to be paid.

deriving the one-period forward rate beginning at time $t + n$, implied in the term structure at time t, is

$$1 + {}_{t+n}r_{1t} = \frac{(1 + {}_{t}R_{1t})(1 + {}_{t+1}r_{1t}) \cdots (1 + {}_{t+n-1}r_{1t})(1 + {}_{t+n}r_{1t})}{(1 + {}_{t}R_{1t})(1 + {}_{t+1}r_{1t}) \cdots (1 + {}_{t+n-1}r_{1t})}$$

$$= \frac{(1 + {}_{t}R_{n+1})^{n+1}}{(1 + {}_{t}R_{n})^{n}}$$

$${}_{t+n}r_{1t} = \frac{(1 + {}_{t}R_{n+1})^{n+1}}{(1 + {}_{t}R_{n})^{n}} - 1 \qquad (4\text{-}2)$$

This formula permits calculation of the implied one-period forward rate for any future period based upon actual rates of interest prevailing in the market at a specific time. The forward rate computed need not be a one-period rate but may span any useful length of time. The calculation of the J-period forward rate beginning at time $t + n$ implied in the term structure at time t is

$$_{t+n}r_{jt} = \sqrt[j]{\frac{(1 + {}_{t}R_{n+jt})^{n+j}}{(1 + {}_{t}R_{nt})^{n}}} - 1 \qquad (4\text{-}3)$$

The forward rate defined in this way is merely a mathematical calculation which has no behavioral meaning. The unbiased expectations theory, however, adds behavioral content to the concept of the forward rate by implying that expected future interest rates are equivalent to the computed forward rates. According to this theory, ${}_{t+n}\rho_{1t} = {}_{t+n}r_{1t}$, where ρ_1 is the future one-period rate expected at time t to prevail at time $t + n$. To illustrate, suppose that the actual rates of interest prevailing in the market were 5 per cent for a two-year bond and $5\frac{1}{2}$ per cent for a three-year bond. The implied forward rate on a one-year loan two years hence would be

$$_{t+2}r_{1t} = \frac{(1 + {}_{t}R_3)^3}{(1 + {}_{t}R_2)^2} - 1 = \frac{(1.055)^3}{(1.050)^2} - 1 = 6.50 \text{ per cent} \qquad (4\text{-}4)$$

Because forward rates are equivalent to expected future rates, the unbiased expectations theory implies that the expected one-year rate two years hence is 6.50 per cent.

If we ignore transaction costs and assume for the moment that the unbiased expectations theory is valid, securities of different maturity would be perfect expected substitutes for one another. The prospective investor at any time has three choices: He may invest in an obligation having a maturity corresponding exactly to his anticipated holding period; he may invest in short-term securities, reinvesting in short terms at each maturity over his holding period; or he may invest in a security having a maturity longer than his anticipated holding period. In the last case, he would sell the security at the end of the given period, realizing either a capital gain or a loss. According to the unbiased expectations theory, the investor's expected return for any holding period would be the same, regardless of the alternative or combination of alternatives he chose. This return would be a weighted average of the current short-term interest rate plus future short rates expected to prevail over the holding period; this average is the same for each alternative. To illustrate, suppose that the following yields prevailed in the market for default-free treasury securities:

Maturity	*Yield*
One year	4.00 per cent
Two year	5.00
Three year	6.00
Four year	6.50

The one-year forward rates, implied in this term structure, may be derived with equation (4-2) and are found to be

Forward Rate	
$_{t+1}r_{1t}$	6.01 per cent
$_{t+2}r_{1t}$	8.03
$_{t+3}r_{1t}$	8.02

If an investor has an anticipated holding period of three years, he may invest in the three-year security, from which he will obtain a 6.00 per cent yield to maturity. However, he may also invest in a one-year security and reinvest in one-year securities at maturity over his holding period. In this case, his expected return is

$$\sqrt[3]{(1.0400)(1.0601)(1.0803)} - 1 = 6.00 \text{ per cent} \qquad (4\text{-}5)$$

or the same as that for investment in the three-year security. Finally, the investor can invest in a four-year security and sell it at the end of three years. If the security had a zero coupon rate, its price would have to be $77.73 (per $100 face value) for it to yield 6.5 per cent to maturity. Moreover, its expected market price at the end of the third year would have to be $92.58 for it to yield 8.02 per cent to maturity. The expected return to the investor can be found by solving the following equation for r:

$$77.73 = \frac{92.58}{(1 + r)^3} \qquad (4\text{-}6)$$

Solving for r, one finds it also to be 6.00 per cent. Thus, the investor could expect to do no better by investing in securities with maturities other than three years. Regardless of the maturity in which an investment is made, the expected return at the time of initial investment is the same.

Behaviorally, support for the unbiased expectations theory comes from the presence of market participants who are willing and able to exploit profit opportunities. Should forward rates differ from expected future rates, a large enough speculative element is said to exist in the market to drive the two sets of rates together.[5] With different rates, various market participants, sensing opportunity for expected gain, would exploit the opportunity until it was eliminated. As a result, forward rates would be unbiased estimates of expected future rates—i.e., the two would be the same. This does not imply that individual investors calculate expected future short rates mathematically for all maturities and then invest accordingly. As Joseph Conard points out,

> The thought process implied is not one of investors estimating future bill rates and then calculating the yield to be expected on other securities. Rather, it is one of estimating whether it will be more profitable to invest funds over a given period by purchasing shorts and reinvesting as they mature, or by buying a security whose term matches the time funds are to be invested, or by buying a still longer-term issue and considering the capital gain or loss as well as the yield for the period involved.[6]

Market participants seek to maximize their return based upon their expectations. By buying and selling securities of different maturities, the individual can, in effect, engage in forward transactions. Such a transaction may consist only of shifting from a six-year bond to a seven-year one, a shift that is marginally the same as making a forward contract for a one-year loan six years in the future.

The action of these market participants seeking profit results at any point in the term structure's being determined solely by expectations about future interest rates. According to the unbiased expectations theory, a horizontal yield curve implies that market participants expect future short rates to be the same as the current short rate. A downward-sloping yield curve signifies that future short rates are expected to fall. Investors are willing to buy long-term securities yielding less than short-term ones because they can expect to do no better by the continual reinvestment in short-term securities. On the other hand, a positively sloped yield curve implies that future short rates are expected to rise. Investors are then unwilling to invest in long-term securities unless the yield is in excess of that on short-terms. They would be better off investing

---

[5] David Meiselman, *The Term Structure of Interest Rates* (Englewood Cliffs, N.J.: Prentice-Hall, Inc., 1962), p. 10.

[6] *An Introduction to the Theory of Interest* (Berkeley, Calif.: University of California Press, 1959), p. 357.

in short terms and reinvesting at maturity. With forward rates as unbiased estimates of expected future rates, different maturity securities must be perfect expected substitutes.

The previous discussion does not imply that long-term interest rates are caused by short rates. Instead, all rates depend upon the interaction of present and expected future supply and demand for funds over the span of the loan.[7] For purposes of analysis, expectations are reduced to the short rate. However, it is possible to build a system based upon long-rate expectations without disturbing the role of expectations. J. R. Hicks suggests that in practice, relevant expectations are concerned with the whole system of interest rates.[8] Although expectations can be reduced to a short rate, a long rate, or, for that matter, any rate, the important question is whether expectations are operative in determining the term structure. For simplicity, we shall use the one-year rate as the unit of measure; but this does not imply that market participants gear their individual expectations to this unit of measure.

Expectations and Inflation

Inflation influences expectations about future interest rates. Because interest is expressed in terms of money and because the monetary standard changes over time, the real rate of return on a security can differ considerably from its money, or nominal, return. If the purchasing power of the dollar increases or decreases, the real *ex post* interest rate, adjusted for the change in purchasing power, will be either higher or lower than the nominal *ex post* interest rate. For example, if the nominal rate on a ten-year bond were 7 per cent and prices increased at a compound annual rate of 4 per cent over this time span, the real rate of return on the investment would be 3 per cent. The real and nominal rates are the same only if prices are stable over the length of the loan contract.

The *ex ante* rate of interest depends not upon actual or past changes in purchasing power but upon anticipated ones.[9] At a moment in time, it is the change in prices which people anticipate that is important in determining the nominal rate of interest. If 3 per cent annual inflation over a loan contract were anticipated, and if the real rate of interest justified on the contract were 4 per cent, the nominal rate would be 7 per cent.[10] Because of uncertainty, the actual rate of inflation over the loan contract need not equal the previously anticipated rate. Borrowers and lenders do not have perfect foresight in predicting future variation in price level.

---

[7] Conard, *An Introduction to the Theory of Interest*, p. 301.

[8] *Value and Capital*, pp. 149–52.

[9] See Irving Fisher, *The Theory of Interest* (New York: The Macmillan Company, 1930), Chapter 2.

[10] See Milton Friedman, "Factors Affecting the Level of Interest Rates," in *Conference on Savings and Residential Financing* (Chicago: U.S. Savings and Loan League, 1968), p. 20.

The anticipated rate of price change may vary with the length of the loan contract. The longer the contract, the longer the period for which the price change must be predicted. For example, if the current rate of inflation were 5 per cent and this rate were expected to decline gradually to 2 per cent over five years and level off thereafter, the anticipated rate of price change for a one-year loan would be much higher than that for a ten-year one. As a result, the nominal rate of interest on the one-year loan would be higher than that on the ten-year loan, all other things being the same. In the subsequent discussion, we assume that the anticipated rate of price change for a future period is embodied in interest-rate expectations for that period. Thus, if inflation of 3 per cent were anticipated for a one-year period two years in the future and the real rate of interest expected for that period were $3\frac{1}{2}$ per cent, the expected nominal rate of interest for a one-year loan two years hence would be $6\frac{1}{2}$ per cent.

Uncertainty and Liquidity Preference

Although a number of factors must be considered when evaluating the role of expectations, uncertainty is perhaps the key issue. If complete certainty existed in the market, forward rates would be exact forecasts of future short-term interest rates. Arbitrage would make all maturities consistent with expectations, so that the investor would receive the same return regardless of the maturity in which he invested. However, uncertainty raises the question of risk.

Here, Hicks and others argue, the unbiased expectations theory must be modified. The longer the maturity of the security, the greater the risk of fluctuation in value of principal to the investor. Because of this greater risk, investors are said to prefer to lend short. Borrowers, however, are said to prefer to borrow long in order to reduce the risk of inability to meet principal payments. Because of this "constitutional weakness" on the long side, a risk, or liquidity, premium must be offered to induce investors to purchase long-term securities. This premium is over and above the average of the current short rate and expected future short rates. The premium structure itself is said to correspond to "normal backwardation" in the commodities futures market.[11]

The theory of normal backwardation supposes that the securities market is dominated by risk averters, who prefer to lend short unless offered a premium sufficient to offset the risk of lending long. Forward rates, therefore, would be biased estimates of future interest rates, exceeding them by the amount of the risk, or liquidity, premium. Thus,

$$_{t+n}r_{1t} = {}_{t+n}\rho_{1t} + {}_{t+n}L_{1t} \tag{4-7}$$

where $_{t+n}r_{1t}$, as before, is the forward one-period rate beginning at $t + n$ implied in the term structure at time t, $_{t+n}\rho_{1t}$ is the expected future rate

[11] *Value and Capital*, pp. 146–47.

for that period, and $_{t+n}L_{1t}$ is the Hicksian liquidity premium embodied in the forward rate. If risk increases with the remoteness of the future, liquidity premiums would be an increasing function of this distance.

$$0 < {}_{t+1}L_{1t} < {}_{t+2}L_{1t} < \ldots < {}_{t+n}L_{1t} \tag{4-8}$$

The presence of liquidity premiums implies a bias toward upward-sloping yield curves. Indeed, the yield curve could decrease monotonically only when expected future short rates were lower than the current short rate by amounts exceeding their respective liquidity premiums. To illustrate, suppose that market participants expected future short-term interest rates to be the same as the current short rate. On the basis of these expectations alone, the yield curve would be horizontal. However, with liquidity premiums embodied in forward rates, it would be upward-sloping, as illustrated in Fig. 4-3. If a positive bias does exist in forward rates, securities of different maturities would not be perfect expected sub-

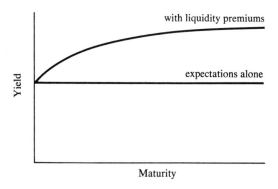

Fig. 4-3.

stitutes for one another. Investment in a long-term security would provide a higher expected return than would investment in a short-term security and reinvestment in short-terms at each maturity. As we shall see, much of the empirical work on the term structure has been directed toward determining whether there is a systematic bias embodied in forward rates of interest.

Proponents of the unbiased expectations theory contend that speculators need not be offered a liquidity premium because they are risk seekers and will search for advantages in the term structure where forward rates exceed corresponding expected future rates. Speculators, together with investors who are indifferent as to maturity, are said to squeeze out any premium that might exist in the forward rate. All maturities then would have expected equal liquidity, according to the unbiased expectations theory.

Level of Interest Rates

If forward rates do contain liquidity premiums, these premiums are not necessarily constant over time. Investors' views of the risk of holding a particular maturity can change over time. In particular, risk may vary according to the relative level of interest rates. In this regard, we are concerned with *interest-rate risk*, defined as the risk of loss of principal resulting from future changes in the general level of interest rates.

A widely held rationale for investor behavior suggests that risk in the market for loans varies with the overall level of interest rates.[12] If, on one hand, interest rates in general were believed to be high by "recent historical standards" and were not expected to go much higher, interest-rate risk would seem to be relatively moderate. Risk averters would not be overly fearful about loss of principal. Additionally, those long-term investors primarily interested in certainty of income probably would be actively seeking investments, thereby exerting pressure analogous to a negative liquidity premium.

If overall interest rates were believed to be low and susceptible to a rise, we would expect the balance to shift in the direction of a greater positive liquidity premium. Risk averters would demand a higher liquidity premium in forward rates, anticipating a probable rise in interest rates and a corresponding drop in security prices. It would follow also that those long-term investors interested in income certainty would be less active in seeking investments at these lower prevailing rates of interest. However, the role of long-term investors seeking income is constrained by the amount of funds that they have available for investment over an interest-rate cycle.

Borrowers, on the other hand, would have an incentive to issue securities if interest rates were low and expected to rise because of the lower interest cost. By the same token, they would want to refrain from borrowing when interest rates were believed to be high and were expected to fall. This behavior prediction must be modified, of course, to take into account the capital needs of borrowers and their interest elasticity. If the need for funds were great when interest rates were high and borrowers were relatively insensitive to interest costs, they would tend to borrow anyway. Corporations, for example, are said to invest in projects when they believe the climate is favorable and are not said to be overly sensitive to the level of interest rates.

It is important to recognize that "recent historical standards" are subject to change. This is the perspective, expressed as an accustomed or normal interest-rate range, with which market participants view probable movements in interest rates. What is considered the normal or typical interest-rate range may differ significantly over time. Consider, for example, the

---

[12] See John Maynard Keynes, *The General Theory of Employment Interest and Money* (New York: Harcourt, Brace & World, Inc., 1936), pp. 201–2.

1966–68 period relative to 1962–64. The accustomed range in 1966–68 was substantially higher than that in 1962–64. In the analysis of interest-rate risk, it is the probability distribution of possible future interest rates that is important. The perspective of an accustomed interest-rate range is valid only if future variations in interest rates are expected to conform to this historical pattern. This is not to say that rates of interest which eventually prevail need conform to the pattern, only that expectations at a moment in time conform to it.

For any given change in prevailing yields, the prices of fixed-income securities mathematically either rise or fall at a decreasing rate as maturity increases. To illustrate, Fig. 4-4 shows the market prices for issues with maturities ranging from one to fifty years, all issues having a $5\frac{1}{2}$ per cent coupon. If the prevailing yield in the market remained at $5\frac{1}{2}$ per cent for

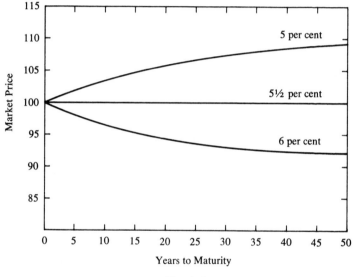

Fig. 4-4.

all maturities, the price of all issues would be $100, as denoted by the horizontal line. The lower curve represents the market price at which securities of different maturities would have to sell to yield 6 per cent to maturity. The upper curve represents the price at which they would have to sell to yield 5 per cent. As can be seen, both curves change at a decreasing rate with respect to maturity, although the upper one reflects greater absolute changes in price. These relationships can be confirmed mathematically through the use of the yield formulas given in equations (3-1) and (3-3) in Chapter 3.[13]

[13] For a detailed examination of the mathematics of interest, see Burton G. Malkiel, "Expectations, Bond Prices, and the Term Structure of Interest Rates," *Quarterly Journal of Economics*, LXXVI (May, 1962), 197–218.

In the market, however, yields do not fluctuate by the same amount for all maturities but by different amounts depending upon the maturity. Short-term rates fluctuate over a far wider range than do long-term rates. This is illustrated for Treasury securities in Fig. 4-5, which shows the bill rate and the rate on long-term bonds over the 1946–68 period. The greater fluctuation of short-term yields over long-term ones offsets somewhat the effect illustrated in Fig. 4-4. Because of the combined influence of these factors, the risk associated with the level of interest rates would not be expected to increase proportionally with maturity, but at a decreasing rate. This occurrence would tend to produce yield curves which flatten as maturity increases.

The foregoing discussion suggests that the level of interest rates may have an influence apart from that of expectations in determining the term structure of interest rates. Interest-rate risk is postulated as varying inversely with the level of interest rates, relative to an accustomed interest-rate range. Forward rates would then be altered, depending upon whether interest rates were high or low relative to what was considered normal. To illustrate, suppose that the forward rate for a one-year loan ten years in the future implied in the term structure at time t were

$$_{t+10}r_{1t} = 6.50 \text{ per cent} \qquad (4\text{-}9)$$

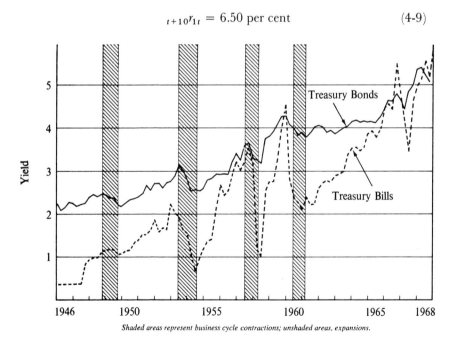

Shaded areas represent business cycle contractions; unshaded areas, expansions.

Fig. 4-5. Yields on three-month Treasury bills and long-term Treasury bonds, 1946–1968. Source: *Moody's Municipal & Government Manual.*

Also, suppose that somehow we knew that the one-year rate expected at time t to prevail ten years hence was 5.50 per cent. Therefore, the risk premium embodied in the forward rate would be 1.00 per cent:

$$_{t+10}L_{1t} = {}_{t+10}r_{1t} - {}_{t+10}\rho_{1t} = 6.50 - 5.50 = 1.00 \text{ per cent} \quad (4\text{-}10)$$

Assume that at time t, interest rates were at the midpoint of an accustomed interest-rate range; market participants gave the same probability to a rise in interest rates as they did to a fall. Thus, $_{t+1}L_{1t} = 1.00$ per cent represents the "average" liquidity premium embodied in the forward rate for a one-year loan ten years in the future.

Now suppose that interest rates were to fall and that at time $t + 1$ the future interest rate expected to prevail on a one-year loan ten years in the future were

$$_{t+11}\rho_{1t+1} = 4.25 \text{ per cent} \quad (4\text{-}11)$$

Moreover, suppose this rate were on the lower side of the accustomed interest-rate range and that market participants expected interest rates to rise in the future. As a result, they would demand a risk premium higher than 1 per cent because of the greater probability of interest rates rising and security prices falling. If the new risk premium were 1.50 per cent, the forward rate would be

$$_{t+11}r_{1t+1} = {}_{t+11}\rho_{1t+1} + {}_{t+11}L_{1t+1} = 4.25 + 1.50 = 5.75 \text{ per cent} \quad (4\text{-}12)$$

Although the expected future rate on a one-year loan ten years in the future declines by 1.25 per cent from time t to time $t + 1$, the forward rate declines by only 0.75 per cent because of the increase in risk premium. Assumed then is that the risk premium embodied in the forward rate varies inversely with the level of interest rates. This behavior would tend to accentuate the positive slope of the yield curve in cyclical troughs and to accentuate the downward-sloping portion of the yield curve at cyclical peaks.

The idea of an inverse relationship between risk premiums and the level of interest rates contrasts with the view of Reuben A. Kessel, who claims the relationship is direct.[14] His position stems from the belief that securities serve as money substitutes. Kessel reasons that because a rise in interest rates increases the cost of holding money, this rise increases also the cost of holding money substitutes. Because short-term securities are better money substitutes than longer-term securities, an increase in interest rates implies that the opportunity cost of holding short-term securities rises relative to the opportunity cost for holding longer-term, less liquid, secu-

---

[14] *The Cyclical Behavior of the Term Structure of Interest Rates* (New York: National Bureau of Economic Research, 1965), pp. 25–26.

rities. With the greater relative opportunity cost for holding short-term securities, Kessel holds that yields on longer-term securities increase relative to those on short-term securities. As a result, liquidity premiums embodied in forward rates must rise. Contrarily, when interest rates fall, opportunity costs decline, and as a result liquidity premiums embodied in forward rates fall. Thus, Kessel maintains that liquidity premiums vary directly with the level of interest rates. This argument ignores altogether the notion of risk associated with the loss of principal that was analyzed earlier, a notion that many feel governs investor behavior. More will be said about the effect of the level of interest rates on the term structure when we take up empirical testing later in this chapter.

Market Segmentation

Some see the impact of "hedging" or institutional pressures in the market for loans as the principal explanation of the term structure of interest rates, thereby justifying modification or even rejection of the expectations theory.[15] Hedging consists of offsetting a liability with an asset of equal maturity, and vice versa. In order to hedge against uncertain fluctuations in prices and yields, financial institutions are said to manage their investments so that the maturity composition of the portfolio matches to some extent the maturity composition of liabilities or prospective commitments. For example, commercial banks typically prefer short- to medium-term maturities because of the nature of their deposit liability and a traditional emphasis upon liquidity. Insurance companies and other lenders with long-term liabilities prefer longer maturities. On the other hand, borrowers are described as relating the maturity of their debt to their need for funds. Thus, a corporation constructing a plant often takes steps to assure that the maturity of the debt it undertakes in financing the plant corresponds to the expected cash flow to be generated from the plant.

The market is characterized as having participants who have preferred maturity ranges in which they operate. Maturities on either side of this range involve risk. Suppose that a long-term investor wishes to remain invested for 15 years. If he invests in a 25-year bond, he is assured of a steady flow of income over his holding period but is uncertain of the value of his investment at the end of the period. Thus, he incurs risk of loss of principal. If he invests in short-term securities, he is assured of receiving his capital in a short period of time but uncertain of the return he will be able to obtain upon reinvestment. This risk is known as *income risk*. Because the Hicksian liquidity premium model only takes into account the risk associated with a loss of principal, it thereby implies a positive premium that rises with maturity. Income risk, on the other hand, implies

---

[15] J. M. Culbertson, "The Term Structure of Interest Rates," *Quarterly Journal of Economics*, LXXI (November, 1957), 489–504; and Charls E. Walker, "Federal Reserve Policy and the Structure of Interest Rates on Government Securities," *Quarterly Journal of Economics*, LXVIII (February, 1954), 22–23.

a negative risk premium. In the total market for loans, the direction and magnitude of the net risk are what matters. The market segmentation theory suggests that both the principal risk and the income risk are important to market participants and that this double risk causes them to hedge. Thus, market participants are characterized as having definite maturity preferences and as not being likely to move from their preferred maturity ranges.

The presence of borrowers and lenders with rather strict maturity preferences is said to lead to segmented markets, with interest rates determined by supply and demand forces in each market. Moreover, the interaction of supply and demand in one sector of maturities may be somewhat different from that occurring in other sectors. Because maturity preferences are strong, participants in one market would not be inclined to leave that market to take advantage of a favorable yield in another market. Effective shiftability among maturities, essential for the expectations theory, would not exist in a hedger-dominated market. As a result, forward rates would not necessarily equal expected future short rates. What bias there is in forward rates as estimates of expected future interest rates would not likely be systematic.

In practice, institutional portfolios are seldom completely fixed with respect to the maturity composition of the institution's liabilities. Usually there is a certain amount of leeway for adaption to market conditions. David Meiselman, in defense of the unbiased expectations theory, points out that although investors may specialize, there are many overlapping areas of interest in the term structure which give the market a continuity.[16] Even if institutions had rigid maturity needs, enough market participants with maturity indifference might prevent market segmentation. However, the argument that institutional lenders and borrowers have maturity preferences cannot be dismissed. In a practical sense, the theory of market segmentation does not mean that each borrower and lender has but one preferred maturity position and will never shift from that position. Rather, it means that institutions may have to be paid a differential premium to induce them to move from their preferred position.[17] Moreover, this premium can be in either direction; it is not confined necessarily to the long side, as implied by Hicksian liquidity premiums.

Transaction Costs

In addition to the factors already considered, transaction costs also may have an influence upon the shape of the yield curve.[18] On the basis of number of transactions alone, the long-term investor would find holding long-terms more attractive than holding short-terms and reinvesting in

---

[16] *The Term Structure of Interest Rates*, p. 53.

[17] See Malkiel, *The Term Structure of Interest Rates*, Chapter 6, for an analysis of the behavioral patterns of institutional investors.

[18] This section draws on Malkiel, *The Term Structure of Interest Rates*, Chapter 5.

short-terms at maturity. If he had a ten-year holding period, investment in a ten-year bond would involve only one transaction. If he were to invest in one-year securities, there would be ten transactions. In contrast, if the investor had a holding period of only one year, the purchase of a one-year security would involve only one transaction, whereas the purchase of a ten-year security would involve two—the purchase and the sale. All other things being the same, each investor would have an incentive to invest in a security with a maturity corresponding to his holding period. If the distribution of holding periods for all investors were shorter in maturity than that of securities outstanding, and if transaction costs per transaction for all maturities were equal, a bias toward a positively sloped yield curve would exist. All other things being the same, longer-term securities would have to yield more than securities which corresponded in maturity to investors' holding periods to offset the higher total transaction costs for investment in them. The opposite is implied if the distribution of holding periods is longer in maturity than the distribution of securities outstanding. The net impact of transaction costs on the term structure depends upon the distribution of holding periods for all investors relative to the maturity distribution of securities outstanding.

Another factor that must be considered, however, is that transaction costs in the secondary market for fixed-income securities tend to increase with the length of time to maturity. Table 4-1 shows the bid-ask prices for Treasury bonds of different maturity on a particular day. It is seen that the turn-around costs of buying and selling a security, as depicted by the spread, increase with maturity. One reason for this occurrence is the greater risk of long-term securities to dealers who make the market. The increase in transaction costs with maturity offsets in whole or in part the previously described disadvantage to the long-term investor of investing in short-term securities and reinvesting in short-terms upon maturity. Contrarily, the short-term investor must pay substantially higher transaction costs to purchase a long-term security and to sell it at the end of his holding period than he does to purchase a security which corresponds to his holding period.

Malkiel contends that the extremely low transaction costs for very short-term securities make it possible for a long-term investor to buy short-terms, as total transaction costs would be very similar to the cost of a single long-term purchase.[19] If this were true, there would be a bias toward an upward-sloping yield curve, all other things being the same. Long-term investors would be roughly indifferent to transaction costs, while short-term investors would prefer short-term securities. Accordingly, there would be buying pressure in favor of short-term securities relative to long-term ones, resulting in a decline of interest rates on short-terms relative to long-terms and a tendency toward a positively sloped yield curve.

[19] Malkiel, *The Term Structure of Interest Rates*, Chapter 5.

TABLE 4-1   Bid and Ask Prices
Treasury Bonds—January 31, 1969

Treasury Bonds			Bid	Asked
4s,	1969	Feb.	99.28	99.29
$2\frac{1}{2}$s,	1964–69	June	98.20	98.24
4s,	1969	Oct.	98.19	98.23
$2\frac{1}{2}$s,	1964–69	Dec.	97.13	97.17
$2\frac{1}{2}$s,	1965–70	Mar.	96.19	96.23
4s,	1970	Feb.	97.27	97.31
4s,	1970	Aug.	96.30	97.2
$2\frac{1}{2}$s,	1966–71	Mar.	94.11	94.19
4s,	1971	Aug.	95.11	95.19
$3\frac{7}{8}$s,	1971	Nov.	94.16	94.24
4s,	1972	Feb.	94.12	94.20
$2\frac{1}{2}$s,	1967–72	June	90.26	91.2
4s,	1972	Aug.	93.24	94.0
$2\frac{1}{2}$s,	1967–72	Sept.	90.10	90.18
$2\frac{1}{2}$s,	1967–72	Dec.	89.26	90.2
4s,	1973	Aug.	92.14	92.22
$4\frac{1}{8}$s,	1973	Nov.	92.14	92.22
$4\frac{1}{8}$s,	1974	Feb.	92.6	92.14
$4\frac{1}{4}$s,	1974	May	92.15	92.23
$3\frac{7}{8}$s,	1974	Nov.	90.6	90.14
4s,	1980	Feb.	82.28	83.12
$3\frac{1}{2}$s,	1980	Nov.	78.22	79.6
$3\frac{1}{4}$s,	1978–83	June	73.30	74.14
$3\frac{1}{4}$s,	1985	May	72.14	72.30
$4\frac{1}{4}$s,	1975–85	May	80.30	81.14
$3\frac{1}{2}$s,	1990	Feb.	71.2	71.18
$4\frac{1}{4}$s,	1987–92	Aug.	75.30	76.14
4s,	1988–93	Feb.	74.6	74.22
$4\frac{1}{8}$s,	1989–94	May	74.2	74.18
3s,	1995	Feb.	71.4	71.20
$3\frac{1}{2}$s,	1998	Nov.	71.2	71.18

Note: Two digits after decimal point refer to thirty-seconds. For example, 90.26 refers to $90 and 26/32.

Source: *The Wall Street Journal*, February 3, 1969.

From the standpoint of the borrower, transaction costs (comprised of underwriting and selling costs, legal fees, and inconvenience) make the relative cost per unit of time higher for short-term securities than for long-term securities.[20] Available evidence on corporate and municipal offerings suggests that the percentage cost of flotation varies inversely with the absolute amount of the issue being offered. As a result of these factors, debt financing tends to be "lumpy." Thus, issuers are not inclined to sell bonds with maturities shorter than the time for which they will need the funds.

[20]See Lutz, "The Structure of Interest Rates," pp. 41–46.

To the extent that the maturity distribution of debt outstanding is longer than the distribution of desired holding periods by investors, there is a bias toward a positively sloped yield curve. However, if the distribution of debt outstanding is shorter than the distribution of desired holding periods, the effect of transaction costs on the term structure will be neutral, according to Malkiel's analysis. The longer the holding periods of investors, then the less the effect of transaction costs on the term structure, all other things the same.

Cylical Behavior of the Term Structure

In the preceding sections, several factors were considered that may influence the term structure of interest rates: expectations, liquidity preference, the level of interest rates (or interest-rate risk), institutional pressures, and finally transaction costs. The support of these various theories must be based upon empirical testing, a subject we shall consider shortly. However, a certain amount of insight can be gained by examining the shape of the yield curve over various interest-rate cycles.[21]

Since World War II, the term structure for Treasury securities has shown the greatest positive slope at cyclical troughs and usually has evidenced a hump and downward slope during the peaks. In Figs. 4-1 and 4-2, early in the chapter, yield curves appearing at a cyclical trough and at a peak were illustrated. If the term structure were determined solely by interest-rate expectations, we might expect the negative yield differential between long- and short-term securities at cyclical peaks to approximate the positive differential at cyclical troughs. Since World War II, however, the positive yield differential between long- and short-term Treasury securities has been quite pronounced at cyclical troughs, the negative differential at cyclical peaks being relatively small in comparison. This relationship may be seen in Fig. 4-5, where yields on three-month Treasury bills were compared with long-term Treasury bond yields. While the use of bills, as opposed to a slightly longer obligation, distorts the relationship somewhat, we still are able to see the contrast between differentials.

This evidence is consistent with an expectations theory modified for liquidity preference. Hicksian liquidity premiums would tend to cushion any downward slope in the yield curve at cyclical peaks and to accentuate the upward slope at the troughs. Thus, the bias would be toward a positively sloped yield curve, holding expectations constant. To illustrate this notion, consider the yield curves in Fig. 4-6. In the upper panel of the figure, a yield curve based upon expectations alone is assumed to be downward sloping.[22] However, when liquidity premiums are added, the

---

[21] For a more detailed analysis of interest-rate cycles, see Kessel, *The Cyclical Behavior of the Term Structure of Interest Rates*, Chapters 3 and 4; and Phillip Cagan, *Changes in the Cyclical Behavior of Interest Rates* (New York: National Bureau of Economic Research, 1966).

[22] See Kessel, *The Cyclical Behavior of the Term Structure of Interest Rates*, pp. 84–92.

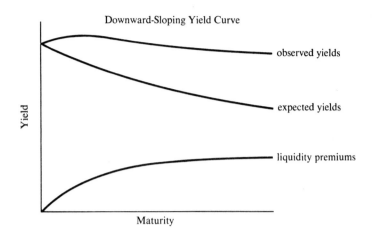

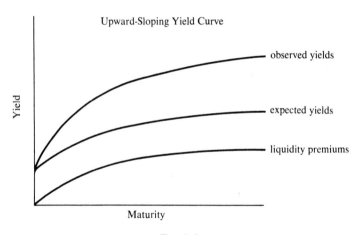

Fig. 4-6.

yield curve becomes humped in the early maturities and downward sloping thereafter. Thus, liquidity premiums cushion the downward slope. The lower panel of the figure depicts a positively sloped yield curve based upon expectations alone. Here, liquidity premiums result in the slope becoming more accentuated. A theory of expectations, modified for liquidity premiums, then is consistent with the observed predominance of yield differentials in favor of long-term over short-term yields. As discussed previously, if interest-rate risk increases with the length of time to maturity, there will be a positive bias at cyclical troughs when interest rates are expected to rise and a negative bias at the peaks when they are expected to fall. The evidence, therefore, is not inconsistent with the presence of interest-rate risk in the market for Treasury securities.

We see in Fig. 4-5 that the cyclical behavior of interest rates has corresponded closely to cyclical fluctuations in business: The troughs appear during recessions and the peaks during periods of prosperity. Over a longer horizon, from 1900 to 1960, Philip Cagan found that long-term interest rates tended to lag significantly behind the business cycle prior to World War I.[23] However, this lag became quite small by the fifties. For short-term interest rates, Cagan found a mixture of leads and lags. During cyclical troughs, the short rates examined (Treasury bills, call money, commercial paper, bankers' acceptances, and bank loans) tended to lag the business cycle. In contrast, Treasury bills and call loans tended to lead the business cycle at cyclical peaks. Whereas in the past short-term rates led long-term rates by a significant margin, the turning points have clustered close together in recent years, according to Cagan. In summary, there currently is a strong degree of correspondence between interest-rate cycles and business cycles despite certain small leads and lags.

Empirical Studies

Most of the empirical studies dealing with the term structure of interest rates have been concerned either directly or indirectly with whether forward rates are accurate forecasts of future rates of interest. If it can be shown that forward rates correspond exactly to expected future rates, the unbiased expectations theory is supported. However, if the forward rates are found to be systematically biased in a particular direction, the evidence casts light on other theories of the term structure. The difficulty in testing is that expectations by market participants are not directly observable. Consequently, only indirect estimates can be made.

Probably the first empirical contribution of significance on the effect of interest-rate expectations was that of Frederick R. Macaulay.[24] Before the establishment of the Federal Reserve system, both call-money and 90-day loan rates displayed definite seasonal fluctuations. By comparing the movements for the two series of rates, Macaulay found that the time-money seasonal showed clear signs of attempted forecasting of the call-money seasonal. It tended to move ahead of the call-money seasonal, thus anticipating known seasonal movements in the latter. Macaulay concluded that this constituted evidence of relatively successful forecasting. However, when the seasonal factor was removed from both series, the evidence showed no attempted forecasting.

More recent attempts to analyze coincidence in the movement of rates for various maturity securities have used cross-spectral analysis, in which pairs of interest-rate time series are analyzed to estimate the covariance between the two series. Thomas J. Sargent studied these relationships

---

[23] *Changes in the Cyclical Behavior of Interest Rates.*

[24] *The Movement of Interest Rates, Bond Yields, and Stock Prices in the United States Since 1856* (New York: National Bureau of Economic Research, 1938).

for 1951–1960 Treasury securities.[25] He found in general that longer-term rates led three-month Treasury bill rates and that, in several cases, the lead tended to increase with increases in maturity. This evidence is consistent with an expectations hypothesis, which implies that long rates should lead short rates.[26]

One way that various investigators have tested the unbiased expectations theory is through the use of a perfect-foresight model. Such a model assumes that not only are expectations held by market participants but also, on the average, they are realized. As expectations cannot be determined directly, the *actual* short rate for a given period of time is substituted for the rate predicted at some earlier time to prevail during the given period. If the long rate at the earlier point in time agrees closely with the average of actual short rates, substituted for expected short rates, the unbiased expectations theory is supported. Although this model provides meaningful information, it is not a truly valid test of the unbiased expectations theory. Actual short rates (*ex post*) cannot be substituted for expected short rates (*ex ante*) and then be used to determine long rates.

Another variation of a perfect-foresight model is to compare forward rates, as implied in the term structure at one point in time, with the actual short rates that they attempt to forecast. Regardless of which variation is used, it is not possible to refute the unbiased expectations theory simply by showing that implied forward rates at one point in time were poor forecasts of actual short rates. In essence, a perfect-foresight model tests whether predictions in the market, as evidenced by various forward rates, are accurate. Culbertson employed a variation of the perfect-foresight model in his analysis of holding-period yields in order to determine whether holding-period yields for securities of different maturity were equal for all holding periods. For his analysis, he used Treasury bills and long-term Treasury bonds for one-week and three-month holding periods during 1953. He concluded that the wide differences in holding-period yields that he found rendered the unbiased expectations theory inadequate as a means of explaining the term structure of interest rates.[27] Like Culbertson, W. Braddock Hickman also used a perfect-foresight model. He compared actual rates with previously predicted rates, implied in the term structure, and concluded that forward rates did not forecast actual rates successfully.[28]

---

[25] "Interest Rates in the Nineteen Fifties," *Review of Economics and Statistics*, L (May, 1968), 164–72.

[26] In contrast, C. W. J. Granger and H. J. B. Rees, "Spectral Analysis of the Term Structure of Interest Rates," *Review of Economic Studies*, XXXV (January, 1968), 67–76, found for British government securities that the one-year rate tended to lead longer-term rates for long-run frequencies. This lead pattern was not evident for shorter frequencies. The data employed were computed by J. A. G. Grant using varying maturities for the 1924–1962 period. As these data are subject to question (see notes 34 and 35 of this chapter), so may be the results of the cross-spectral analysis.

[27] "The Term Structure of Interest Rates," pp. 499–502, 507–9.

[28] "The Term Structure of Interest Rates: An Explanatory Analysis," Mimeographed Manuscript (New York: National Bureau of Economic Research, 1942).

While it is reasonable to have errors in prediction, we would not expect these errors to take on any pattern or bias. Over a sufficient period of time, errors should be distributed randomly about the actual rate, with forward-rate forecasts being above actual rates about as often as below them. However, if a bias in one direction were evident, it would suggest that factors other than pure expectations were at work in the determination of the term structure. In computing the average forecasting error, one should try to eliminate any secular trend. Otherwise, the bias in forecasting error may be attributable to this trend.

Error-Learning Models

Until the work of David Meiselman, comprehensive empirical testing of interest-rate expectations was lacking.[29] Previous work had been hampered by an absence of direct evidence concerning expectations. Meiselman, however, maintained that since expectations were reflected already in the term structure, they could be analyzed. He asserted that interest-rate expectations are revised whenever previously held expectations prove to be in error. An error-learning model was introduced, which implied that expectations are a function of past and present learning experience. As new information is received, expectations are adjusted in keeping with the learning process. In his model, changes in one-year forward rates are related to errors in forecasting the actual one-year rate of interest:

$$_{t+n}r_{1t} - {}_{t+n}r_{1t-1} = a + b(Et_1) + u \qquad (4\text{-}13)$$

where u is the error term, and Et_1 is the one-year forecasting error, defined as

$$Et_1 = {}_tR_{1t} - {}_tr_{1t-1} \qquad (4\text{-}14)$$

Thus, the forecasting error is the actual one-year rate in period t minus the forward-rate forecast of a one-year loan beginning at time t embodied in the term structure one year earlier.

Market participants are assumed to adjust their expectations in keeping with unanticipated changes in the actual one-year rate of interest. Using the Durand basic corporate bond yield data, Meiselman computed the degree of correlation between forecasting errors and changes in various forward rates for the period 1900–1954.[30] He assumed a linear function and found that correlation coefficients ranged from 0.95 for changes in forward rates one year from t to 0.59 for changes eight years from t. In

---

[29] *The Term Structure of Interest Rates.*

[30] In the Durand annual basic yield data, estimates are made of the yield on the highest grade corporate bonds. David Durand, *Basic Yields on Corporate Bonds, 1900–1942* (New York: National Bureau of Economic Research, 1942); and David Durand and Willis J. Winn, *Basic Yields of Bonds, 1926–1947: Their Measurement and Pattern* (New York: National Bureau of Economic Research, 1947).

addition to high positive association, Meiselman found that the regression coefficients reflecting the responsiveness of dependent-variable changes to forecasting errors decreased with the remoteness in the future of the dependent variable.

Moreover, the constant terms were not found to differ significantly from zero. Meiselman argued that constant-term values were measures of liquidity premiums; and since these values did not differ significantly from zero, liquidity premiums were not present in the term structure. From this evidence, it was inferred that a significant portion of the variation in expectations could be explained by the one-year forecasting error. Meiselman contended that the evidence was consistent with the unbiased expectations theory, in which forward rates are equivalent to expected future short rates.[31]

It is important to recognize that the error-learning model by itself does not corroborate the equality of forward rates and expected future short rates. Although Meiselman maintained that forward rates were unbiased estimates of expected future short rates, he was unable to substantiate this equality adequately in attempting to refute the Hicksian liquidity-premium theory. This logical weakness was brought out by John H. Wood in his review of Meiselman's book. Wood demonstrated that constant terms not significantly different from zero are consistent theoretically with forward rates as biased estimates of expected future rates.[32] Moreover, the 1900–1954 Durand yield-curve data do not entirely substantiate the equality of forward rates with expected future short rates. If we use a perfect-foresight model and subtract the actual rate obtained from the forward-rate forecast, we find that the average forecasting error over the 1900–1954 period was positive and increased from 0.14 for $_{t+1}r_{1t}$ to 0.83 for $_{t+9}r_{1t}$.[33] Thus, the evidence suggests that forward

---

[31] Meiselman, *The Term Structure of Interest Rates*, pp. 21–22, 45–47, 60.

[32] John H. Wood, "Expectations, Errors, and the Term Structure of Interest Rates," *The Journal of Political Economy*, LXXI (April, 1963), 165–66. If liquidity premiums are embodied in the forward rate, Meiselman's error-learning model, equation (4–13), becomes

$$(_{t+n}\rho_{1t} + _{t+n}L_{1t}) - (_{t+n}\rho_{1t-1} + _{t+n}L_{1t-1}) = a + b[_tR_{1t} - (_t\rho_{1t-1} + _tL_{1t-1})]$$

Rearranging them gives

$$(_{t+n}\rho_{1t} - _{t+n}\rho_{1t-1}) + (_{t+n}L_{1t} - _{t+n}L_{1t-1}) = a + b[_tR_{1t} - (_t\rho_{1t-1} + _tL_{1t-1})]$$

where, as before, ρ is the expected future rate, and L is the liquidity premium. We can see readily that when the expectations are realized and the constant term is zero, the first term above equals $b[_tR_{1t} - _t\rho_{1t-1}]$, and we are left with

$$(_{t+n}L_{1t} - _{t+n}L_{1t-1}) = b(_tL_{1t-1})$$

Thus, a constant term of zero can be consistent with the presence of liquidity premiums embodied in forward rates.

[33] See James Van Horne, "The Expectations Hypothesis, the Yield Curve, and Monetary Policy: Comment," *Quarterly Journal of Economics*, LXXIX (November, 1965), 666–68.

rates were biased and high estimates of actual rates, consistent with the Hicksian liquidity-premium theory. This finding, however, must be qualified for a moderate downward trend in interest rates over the period. If this trend were unanticipated, expected short rates would exceed the actual rates that they attempted to forecast. The error-learning model has been applied to other sets of data. Using data on British government securities, J. A. G. Grant concluded that the error-learning model could not be used to predict successfully changes in expectations.[34] However, his data consisted of observations connected by straight lines, resulting in a jagged rather than a fitted yield curve. In light of these data, the lack of results is not surprising. A. Buse also used data on British government securities but worked with yield curves that were fitted. He found that the error-learning model was of value in explaining changes in expectations. Moreover, he discovered that the constant terms differed significantly from zero, supporting the notion of liquidity preference.[35]

Using U.S. Treasury yield-curve data for the 1954–1963 period, I tested certain variations of the error-learning model.[36] A high degree of positive correlation was discovered between changes in forward rates and errors in forecasting the one-year actual rate. For all of the forward rates tested, the Treasury data resulted in a higher degree of correlation than that which Meiselman had found using the Durand basic corporate yield data. The results supported the notion that interest-rate expectations are important in explaining the term structure of interest rates and that they are revised systematically when actual rates of interest differ from those that had been anticipated.

Furthermore, all of the constant-term values were significantly different from zero, a finding that supports the hypothesis that forward rates of interest contain both expectations and a liquidity premium. Moreover, the pattern of intercepts on the horizontal axis for the various regression studies was consistent with liquidity premiums increasing at a diminishing rate with the remoteness of the future period.[37]

---

[34] "Meiselman on the Structure of Interest Rates: A British Test," *Economica*, XXXI (February, 1964), 36–38.

[35] "Interest Rates, the Meiselman Model and Random Numbers," *Journal of Political Economy*, LXXV (February, 1967), 49–62.

[36] James Van Horne, "Interest-Rate Risk and the Term Structure of Interest Rates," *Journal of Political Economy*, LXXIII (August, 1965), 344–51; and "Liquidity Preference, Interest-Rate Risk, and the Term Structure of Interest Rates" (unpublished Ph.D. dissertation, Northwestern University, 1964).

[37] If liquidity premiums are embodied in forward rates and no other factors exist that would cause the regression line not to pass through the origin, we have from footnote 32 in this chapter:

$$({}_{t+n}\rho_{1t} - {}_{t+n}\rho_{1t-1}) + ({}_{t+n}L_{1t} - {}_{t+n}L_{1t-1}) = b[{}_{t}R_{1t} - ({}_{t}\rho_{1t-1} + {}_{t}L_{1t-1})]$$

We assume that $({}_{t+n}\rho_{1t} - {}_{t+n}\rho_{1t-1})$ is revised relative to ${}_{t}R_{1t} - {}_{t}\rho_{1t-1}$. If ${}_{t+n}L_{1t}$ equaled

Although the one-year error-learning model shows a high degree of correlation, it is possible also to devise multiple-year error-learning models.[38] Consider the responsiveness of changes in forward rates to errors in forecasting the five-year rate. The error, $Et5$, would be

$$Et5 = {}_tR_{5t} - {}_tr_{5t-1} \qquad (4\text{-}15)$$

Similarly, the error variable for any error-learning model is simply

$$EtN = {}_tR_{nt} - {}_tr_{nt-1} \qquad (4\text{-}16)$$

The question raised is whether the one-year forecasting error takes account of the entire error-learning process, thereby being most representative of changes in expectations. Expectations beyond one year may not always vary proportionately to errors in forecasting the one-year actual rate. To the extent that interest-rate expectations for various future periods are less than perfectly elastic, use of the one-year error would not be representative of the entire change in expectations because it would not take account of the complete error-learning process.

When multiple-year error-learning models were employed with the Treasury yield-curve data and the Durand basic corporate yield data, some interesting relationships were evident. As the remoteness of the dependent variable increased with successive regression studies, higher correlation coefficients were obtained when using multiple-year errors that roughly corresponded to, or were somewhat greater in length than, the remoteness of the dependent variable.[39] The results supported the

---

${}_{t+n}L_{1t-1}$, then the constant term would be $b({}_tL_{1t-1})$. The intercept on the horizontal axis would be $-{}_tL_{1t-1}$ and would be the same for all regression studies.

Now, if ${}_{t+n}L_{1t-1}$ exceeds ${}_{t+n}L_{1t}$, the regression line and the constant term would be lower than if the two liquidity premiums were equal. If liquidity premiums increase with the remoteness of the future period, ${}_{t+n}L_{1t-1}$ would exceed ${}_{t+n}L_{1t}$. Thus, the intercept on the X, or horizontal, axis would be

$$X \text{ intercept} = -{}_tL_{1t} - [({}_{t+n}L_{1t} - {}_{t+n}L_{1t-1})/b]$$

If the negative X intercepts increased in magnitude with successive regression studies, this occurrence would be consistent with liquidity premiums increasing at a diminishing rate with the remoteness of the future period. The X intercepts in the results for the Treasury securities followed this pattern through $n = 8$ for the dependent variable, after which point ($n = 9$ through 11) they leveled off and fluctuated. Thus, the evidence on Treasury securities for the 1958–1963 period was consistent with liquidity premiums, increasing at a diminishing rate.

[38] See James Van Horne, "Interest-Rate Expectations, the Shape of the Yield Curve, and Monetary Policy," *The Review of Economics and Statistics*, XLVIII (May, 1966), 211–15.

[39] For certain multiple-year error-learning model regression studies, common elements appear on both sides of the regression equation. However, when the remoteness of the last forward-rate period in the independent variable is less than that of the dependent variable forward-rate period, common elements do not appear. Inasmuch as correlation

notion that expectations beyond the immediate future may change somewhat independently of near-term expectations, not always varying proportionately with the one-year error. Thus, interest-rate expectations for various future periods appear to be less than perfectly elastic.[40]

Additional Tests for Liquidity Premiums

Kessel, in his investigation of the term structure, also tested for the presence of liquidity premiums in forward rates of interest. Using error-learning models similar to those discussed, he analyzed the residuals in the regression results when the models were applied to the Durand yield-curve data and to certain Treasury-bill data. In both cases, he found systematic positive bias in forward rates as estimates of expected future interest rates—i.e., they were high estimates.[41] In addition to this evidence and his theoretical argument for liquidity preference, Kessel pointed out that on the average, long-term yields on government securities exceeded short-term yields over the period 1921–1961. This finding also might be considered to be consistent with liquidity preference, if one isolated the effect of trend.

Joseph W. Conard and Jonathan Freudenthal conducted tests similar to those of Kessel and some additional ones.[42] While their results supported the idea that liquidity premiums are embodied in forward rates, they found that these premiums diminish rapidly beyond intermediate-term maturities. Moreover, they observed that if the depression of the thirties and World War II and the post-war period of the forties were treated as abnormal, average yields on short-term securities over the period 1900–1961 exceeded those on long-term securities. Clearly, yield curves observed through the 1920s were not consistent with liquidity preference in the market for loans. Only since 1930 has there been a predominance of positively sloped yield curves.

Tests Concerning the Level of Rates

If liquidity premiums are embodied in forward rates and affect the term structure, it is important to know whether they vary with the level of interest rates over time. Recall from our earlier discussion that one widely held rationale for investor behavior suggests that risk premiums vary inversely with the level of interest rates relative to an accustomed

---

coefficients for regression studies not affected by the presence of common terms showed this clear pattern of variation, the conclusions reached were meaningful.

[40] Van Horne, "Interest-Rate Expectations, the Shape of the Yield Curve, and Monetary Policy," p. 214. These findings have important implications for monetary policy and "Operation Twist," which are taken up in the article.

[41] *The Cyclical Behavior of the Term Structure of Interest Rates*, pp. 12–25; Chapter 3.

[42] Conard, *The Behavior of Interest Rates* (New York: National Bureau of Economic Research, 1966), Chapter 7.

(normal) interest-rate range. If interest rates were low and were expected to rise, investors would be expected to demand a relatively high risk premium; the opposite would hold if interest rates were high and were expected to fall.

Malkiel tested the hypothesis that the spread between long-term and short-term interest rates varied inversely with the deviation of the long rate from the midpoint of a "normal" range.[43] After transforming the variables to eliminate certain statistical problems, he tested this hypothesis on the Durand basic corporate yield data for the period 1900–1942. The results were found to support the hypothesis of an inverse relationship, thereby supporting indirectly the idea of an inverse relation between liquidity premiums and the level of interest rates relative to a normal level. He also tested for the combined periods 1900–1942 and 1951–1965, and again the results were found to be consistent with an inverse relationship between the yield spread and the level of interest rates.

Conard and Freudenthal also tested the effect of the level of interest rates on the behavior of 28-day Treasury bills, three-month bills, one-year government securities, and five-year government securities.[44] They regressed "last year's forward rate minus today's actual rate" against both the change in interest rates and the level of interest rates for various periods during 1958–1963. They found that when changes in interest rates were held constant, the influence of level of interest rates on the dependent variable was positive for 28-day and three-month Treasury bills, but negative for one-year and five-year government securities. Their findings confirmed Kessel's results of a positive relationship between the level of interest rates and liquidity premiums for Treasury bills.[45] However, the generalization of a direct relationship cannot be extended to the entire term structure because the results for one- and five-year government securities were consistent with liquidity premiums varying inversely with the level of interest rates. The Treasury bill evidence of Kessel and of Conard and Freudenthal merely supports the notion that the positive slope of the shortest-maturity portion of the yield curve tends to rise and fall directly in keeping with the level of interest rates.

Finally, certain empirical studies I undertook supported in some measure the notion that interest-rate risk varies inversely with the level of interest rates. In these studies, changes in forward rates were made a function of the one-year forecasting error and of the deviation of the level of forward rates from an accustomed level.[46] The results of regression studies using Treasury yield-curve data over the period 1958–1963 indicated alteration of forward rates depending upon whether interest rates were

---

[43] *The Term Structure of Interest Rates*, Chapter 3.

[44] Conard, *The Behavior of Interest Rates*, pp. 83–85, 100–105.

[45] *The Cyclical Behavior of the Term Structure of Interest Rates*, pp. 22–26.

[46] Van Horne, "Interest-Rate Risk and the Term Structure of Interest Rates"; Richard Roll, "Comment," *Journal of Political Economy*, LXXIV (December, 1966), 629–32; and Van Horne, "Reply," *Journal of Political Economy* (December, 1966), 633–35.

believed to be high or low with respect to an accustomed interest-rate range. These results, like the other two, were consistent with the idea of an inverse relationship between liquidity premiums and the relative level of interest rates. The empirical studies discussed suggest that interest-rate risk, or risk associated with the loss of principal, is a factor in determining the term structure of interest rates. Not only do liquidity premiums appear to be embodied in the term structure, but they appear to vary relative to the level of interest rates.

Tests Concerning Maturity Composition of the Debt

The last category of empirical studies we shall consider involves using the maturity composition of securities outstanding as an explanatory variable. These studies cast light on the theory of market segmentation discussed earlier. If the term structure is compartmentalized into separate markets, a change in relative supply in one of these markets should change the shape of the yield curve. For example, an increase in the relative supply of long-term securities should result in an increase in long rates relative to short rates, all other things being the same. In this type of study, the explanatory variable usually employed is either the relative proportion of securities outstanding in various maturity categories or the average length of the debt. With maturity categories, the proportions of debt maturing within one year, one to five years, five to ten years, etc., are used. The categories themselves are arbitrary, however, and their use often results in serious discontinuities. For example, if the categories employed were within five years, five to ten years, and over ten years, and a large block of outstanding debt had ten years, five months to maturity, it would pass into another category in six months. However, there would not be nearly as much shortening of the debt as implied by the passing of the block from one category to the other. On the other hand, an average length-of-time-to-maturity measure represents a weighted average, with the amounts outstanding for each security as weights multiplied by their length of time to maturity. This measure suffers from the assumption of a linear relationship between liquidity and maturity. For example, the sacrifice in liquidity that accompanies a change in maturity from one to two years is assumed to be the same as that which accompanies a change from 11 to 12 years.

Another problem in testing for market segmentation is that the effect of maturity composition on the term structure is not likely to be restricted to one market. Because the various markets for securities are inter-dependent, the more appropriate variable would be the maturity composition of all marketable debt instruments. However, information of this sort is not available; the only complete data are for U.S. Treasury securities. Apart from the problems of measurement, a serious question raised is whether a maturity-composition variable should be used in addition to an expectations variable. A change in the maturity composition of securities outstanding would seem to be a factor shaping interest-rate expectations; and to include it as an additional explanatory variable may be redundant.

Still another problem in testing for market segmentation is that the maturity composition of the debt outstanding is treated as the independent variable and interest rates are treated as the dependent variable. In reality, these two variables are jointly determined, with interest rates affecting the supply of securities offered as well as supply affecting interest rates. Both variables, then, would be endogenous. In the single-equation models employed, however, the maturity-composition variable is treated as an exogenous rather than an endogenous variable. As a result of these problems and others, the results of most empirical studies using supply variables have been conflicting and generally inconclusive.[47]

One of the most interesting studies of this sort, however, was by Franco Modigliani and Richard Sutch, who employed a variant of an expectations model.[48] They labeled their theory "preferred habitat"; supposedly it blended the theories of expectations, liquidity preference, and market segmentation. The authors suggested that expectations of future interest rates are formed on the basis of past interest rates. However, there are two distinct influences in this history: the recent trend in interest rates and the "normal" level of interest rates based upon long-run experience. These influences were used first by Frank deLeeuw[49] to explain the term structure, and his work inspired the Modigliani-Sutch study. The first influence suggests that over the short run market participants expect current trends in interest rates to continue. The second influence is that interest rates are expected to regress toward a normal level.

Modigliani and Sutch combine both of these expectational influences into a single expectations variable, using an Almon lag structure, which resembles an inverted U. The yield differential between long and short rates is made a function of a moving average of past short rates, weighted according to the lag structure. Their model is

$$R_{Lt} - R_{st} = a + b_0 R_{st} + \sum_{i=1}^{16} B_i R_{st-i} + u \qquad (4\text{-}17)$$

[47] See, for example, Arthur M. Okun, "Monetary Policy, Debt Management, and Interest Rates: A Quantitative Appraisal," in *Stabilization Policies*, Commission on Money and Credit (Englewood Cliffs, N.J.: Prentice-Hall, Inc., 1963), pp. 331–80; Robert H. Scott, "Liquidity and the Term Structure of Interest Rates," *Quarterly Journal of Economics*, LXXIX (February, 1965), 135–45; and Neil Wallace, "The Term Structure of Interest Rates and the Maturity Composition of the Federal Debt," *Journal of Finance*, XXII (May, 1967), 301–12.

[48] "Innovations in Interest Rate Policy," *American Economic Review*, LVI (May, 1966), 178–97; and Modigliani and Sutch, "Debt Management and the Term Structure of Interest Rates: An Empirical Analysis of Recent Experience," *Journal of Political Economy*, LXXXV (Supplement: August, 1967), 569–89.

[49] "A Model of Financial Behavior," in *Brookings Quarterly Econometric Model of the United States Economy* (Chicago: Rand McNally & Company, 1965), pp. 465–530.

where R_{Lt} is the long rate at time t, R_{st} is the short rate, the third term on the right represents the lag structure, and u is the error term. Through various tests, the most suitable lag was found to be 16 quarters. It should be noted that there is no explicit use of future rates; Modigliani and Sutch relate current spot rates to current and past spot rates. The data used to test the model was based on three-month Treasury bills and the average yield on long-term government securities, both on a quarterly basis over the 1952–1961 period. Overall, the model was successful in explaining the *ex post* differential between the long and short rates; the regression coefficients had the right sign and size. Because the lag structure had the predicted shape, the authors concluded that interest-rate expectations are based upon both of the influences discussed above.

In their first paper (*American Economic Review*, 1966), Modigliani and Sutch added various supply variables to their model and found that these variables exerted no significant influence upon the spread between the long and the short rate. Also, the authors tested for the effectiveness of "Operation Twist." This operation involved efforts by the Federal Reserve and Treasury in the early sixties to affect the shape of the yield curve. The idea was to keep short-term interest rates fairly high for balance-of-payments purposes while keeping intermediate and long rates at moderate levels to stimulate domestic growth. In essence, "Operation Twist" affected the maturity composition of the marketable government debt held by the public. Modigliani and Sutch used parameter estimates for the period 1952–1961 to extrapolate for the period 1962–1965. Because these predictions were accurate, they concluded that "Operation Twist" had little effect upon the term structure.[50]

Elsewhere (*Journal of Political Economy*, 1967), they tested in more depth the influence of maturity composition of the debt upon the spread between the long and short rates. Their approach consisted of adding various maturity-composition variables to their expectations model and seeing if the effect of these additions was significant. Using their original data for the 1952–1965 period, they failed to uncover any significant relationships between the yield spread and the various measures of maturity composition. However, when the authors used average yield-to-maturity data prepared by Morgan Guaranty Trust Company, they discovered significant and positive relationships between the yield spread of intermediate and very short rates and variations in the supply of debt in the intermediate range. However, these relationships were not evident for yield spreads involving longer-term securities. Even from the evidence for intermediate-term securities, the term structure could not be considered very responsive to changes in the maturity composition of the debt.[51] The problems cited earlier make it extremely difficult to test

---

[50]In Van Horne, "Interest-Rate Expectations, the Shape of the Yield Curve and Monetary Policy," I concluded that "Operation Twist" may have had at least some influence, albeit slight, in altering the shape of the yield curve.

[51]Modigliani and Sutch, "Debt Management and the Term Structure," 588–89.

for the influence of maturity composition.[52] In the case of Modigliani
and Sutch, its influence may already be reflected in their expectations
variable. Thus, the basic contribution of Modigliani and Sutch is the
insight they provide into interest-rate expectations rather than into the
effect of maturity composition on the term structure.

Another means for investigating the effect of maturity composition
on the term structure, as well as on interest-rate expectations, is the use of
term structure models to predict future rates. If investors base expectations of future rates on a weighted average of current and past rates in
the manner suggested by Modigliani and Sutch, one might expect
such a weighted average to have predictive value. Using this argument,
Alan Kraus compared the ability of four basic models to forecast rates
for Treasury bonds of different maturity for varying lengths of time into
the future.[53] One model employed a simple "inertia" hypothesis; it
used the current spot rate as a prediction of the future rate. A second
model was based on fitting a relation between the *ex post* "forecast error"
(forward rate less subsequently observed actual rate) and the current
spot rate. The third model, based on the Modigliani and Sutch research,
used a fitted relation between the subsequently observed actual rate and a
series of current and past spot rates. The fourth model incorporated the
maturity composition of the debt as well as relative holdings of Treasury
securities by various investor groups as variables for explaining the
ex post forecast error.[54]

The statistical estimation of parameters for the models was made
using monthly data for the period 1960–1964. For each model, the parameter values obtained were used in conjunction with monthly data for the
1965–1967 period to generate a series of predicted rates. The predictions
were then compared with the actual 1965–1967 rates. The results Kraus
obtained indicated that the model which incorporated the maturity
composition and holdings of Treasury securities had more predictive
value than the other three models. Although the model based on the
Modigliani and Sutch research produced high multiple correlation
coefficients during its fitting to the 1960–1964 data, it gave the least accurate predictions of rates during the 1965–1967 period. Kraus interpreted
these results as evidence for the effect of maturity composition on the term
structure.

---

[52] For criticism of the Modigliani-Sutch approach, see Neil Wallace, "Comment," and
Reuben A. Kessel, "Comment," *Journal of Political Economy*, 75 (Supplement: August,
1967), 590–95.

[53] "The Forecasting Accuracy of Models of the Term Structure of Interest Rates"
(Ph.D. dissertation, Cornell University, 1969).

[54] In attempting to avoid the difficulties in using either broad maturity categories or
average length of time to maturity as measures of maturity composition, Kraus employed
a large number of very narrow maturity categories, with coefficients estimated by using a
variation of the Almon distributed-lag procedure.

Empirical Studies: Summary

In summary, the evidence cited, plus additional empirical studies, attests to the importance of interest-rate expectations in the term structure of interest rates. The market appears to forecast the future course of interest rates, and these forecasts are important in determining the yield on securities. In addition, empirical studies dealing with post-World War II data suggest that forward rates are biased and high estimates of expected future rates. Market participants during this period appear to have gauged their activities on expected future interest rates plus a Hicksian liquidity premium. This premium allows compensation for the sacrifice of liquidity that accompanies investment in any but the shortest of maturities. Thus, the market as a whole appears to associate risk with uncertainty of principal; and this risk dominates any risk associated with uncertainty of income on the part of individual market participants.

In addition, certain empirical studies suggest that liquidity premiums vary inversely with the relative level of interest rates. The widely held notion that interest rates fluctuate around a normal, or accustomed, level is associated with Keynes; and it implies that the risk of loss of principal varies inversely with the level of rates relative to a "normal" level based upon past experience. The market-segmentation theory has been tested mostly in relation to changes in the maturity composition of outstanding debt. If a shift in the maturity composition of the debt alters the term structure, it would be concluded that market segmentation has some influence upon the term structure. A number of problems have made the evidence in this regard inconclusive.

It must be pointed out that the generalizations brought out in this summary are not universally accepted. The question of what theory best explains the term structure of interest rates remains a subject of heated controversy.

Summary

The term structure of interest rates portrays the yield-maturity relationship on securities differing only in length of time to maturity. A number of theories attempt to explain the term structure. The unbiased expectations theory states that expectations of the future course of interest rates are the sole determinant. When the yield curve is upward sloping, this theory implies that market participants expect interest rates to rise in the future; a downward-sloping curve implies that interest rates are expected to fall; while a horizontal yield curve suggests that interest rates are not expected to change. The theory implies also that securities of different maturity are perfect expected substitutes in the sense that the expected return is the same. Most analyses have used the unbiased expectations theory as a point of departure.

A combined theory of expectations and liquidity preference suggests that market participants generally prefer to lend short unless offered a premium sufficient to offset the risk of lending long. Thus, the term structure would be affected not only by expectations but also by Hicksian liquidity premiums. If risk increases with the remoteness of the future, these premiums would be an increasing function of remoteness. The presence of liquidity premiums in the term structure implies a bias toward upward-sloping yield curves. These premiums may vary with the level of interest rates; when interest rates are low and are expected to rise, there is a greater risk associated with investment in securities, particularly long-term securities, than there is when these rates are high and are expected to fall. This pattern suggests that liquidity, or risk, premiums vary inversely with the level of interest rates relative to an accustomed level.

A market segmentation theory implies that maturity preferences of lenders and borrowers are so strong that they usually will not leave their preferred maturity range to take advantage of yield differentials. As a result, there are a number of different markets, and interest rates are said to be determined by the interaction of supply and demand in each. Because these markets are separate, interest rates for various maturities would be largely independent of each other. In addition to the theories considered, transaction costs also may influence the yield curve. We examined the role of these costs and their effect on the term structure. We analyzed also cyclical changes in the term structure over time.

The empirical studies examined give considerable insight into the factors that best explain the term structure. Most of the studies show the important role of expectations of the future course of interest rates. In recent years, there has been evidence of a bias toward positively sloped yield curves, all other things being the same. This evidence is consistent with an expectations theory modified for liquidity preference. In addition, certain empirical studies have given modest indication of liquidity premiums varying inversely with the level of interest rates, in keeping with the changing risk of capital loss. Finally, tests of the market segmentation theory largely have been inconclusive. The term structure appears to be best explained by a combined theory of expectations and risk aversion.

Selected References

Buse, A., "Interest Rates, the Meiselman Model and Random Numbers," *Journal of Political Economy*, LXXV (February, 1967), 49–62.

Cagan, Philip, *Changes in the Cyclical Behavior of Interest Rates*. New York: National Bureau of Economic Research, 1966.

Conard, Joseph W., *Introduction to the Theory of Interest.* Berkeley, Calif.: University of California Press, 1959.

———, *The Behavior of Interest Rates.* New York: National Bureau of Economic Research, 1966.

Culbertson, John M., "The Term Structure of Interest Rates," *Quarterly Journal of Economics,* LXXI (November, 1957), 485–517.

Hicks, J. R., *Value and Capital* (2nd ed.) London: Oxford University Press, 1946.

Kessel, Reuben H., *The Cyclical Behavior of the Term Structure of Interest Rates.* New York: National Bureau of Economic Research, 1965.

Kraus, Alan D., "The Forecasting Accuracy of Models of the Term Structure of Interest Rates." Ph.D. dissertation, Cornell University, 1969.

Lutz, Friedrich A., "The Structure of Interest Rates," *Quarterly Journal of Economics,* LV (November, 1940), 36–63.

Malkiel, Burton G., "Expectations, Bond Prices, and the Term Structure of Interest Rates," *Quarterly Journal of Economics,* LXXVI (May, 1962), 197–218.

———, *The Term Structure of Interest Rates.* Princeton, N.J.: Princeton University Press, 1966.

Meiselman, David, *The Term Structure of Interest Rates.* Englewood Cliffs, N.J.: Prentice-Hall, Inc., 1962.

Modigliani, Franco, and Richard Sutch, "Innovations in Interest Rate Policy," *American Economic Review,* LVI (May, 1966), 178–97.

———, "Debt Management and the Term Structure of Interest Rates: An Empirical Analysis of Recent Experience," *Journal of Political Economy,* 75 (Supplement: August, 1967), 569–89.

Telser, L. G., "A Critique of Some Recent Empirical Research on the Explanation of the Term Structure of Interest Rates," *Journal of Political Economy,* 75 (Supplement: August, 1967), 546–61.

Van Horne, James, "Interest-Rate Expectations, the Shape of the Yield Curve, and Monetary Policy," *Review of Economics and Statistics,* XLVIII (May, 1966), 211–15.

———, "Interest-Rate Risk and the Term Structure of Interest Rates," *Journal of Political Economy,* LXXIII (August, 1965), 344–51.

———, "The Expectations Hypothesis, the Yield Curve, and Monetary Policy: Comment," *Quarterly Journal of Economics,* LXXIX (November, 1965), 664–68.

Van Horne, James C., and David A. Bowers, "The Liquidity Impact of Debt Management," *The Southern Economic Journal,* XXXIV (April, 1968), 526–37.

Wood, John H., "Expectations, Error, and the Term Structure of Interest Rates," *Journal of Political Economy,* LXXI (April, 1963), 160–71.

The Risk Structure of Interest Rates
and Marketability

IN the preceding chapter, we examined one reason for relative differences in market rates of interest—the term to maturity. In this chapter, two additional reasons are examined—differences in financial, or default, risk and differences in marketability. Our focus is on fixed-income securities. While the factors discussed also affect common stocks, the circumstances are sufficiently different to warrant special consideration of equity securities in Chapter 7.

Risk Structure

The risk structure of interest rates depicts the relationship between the yield on securities and their risk of default, holding all other factors constant. In particular, maturity is held constant by studying different financial instruments of the same maturity. The relationship between yield and default risk may be similar to that shown in Fig. 5-1. In the figure, yield is plotted along the horizontal axis and risk along the vertical. The intercept on the horizontal axis represents the yield on a default-free security; for all practical purposes, it represents the yield on Treasury securities. The figure shows that investors demand a higher yield, the greater the risk of default. This relationship is assumed to be concave to

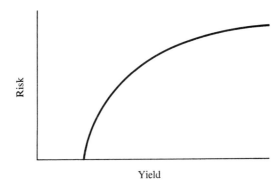

Fig. 5-1.   Yield-risk relationship.

the origin, indicating that yield must increase at an increasing rate with risk.

Promised and Expected Rates

In this chapter, a *risk premium* is defined as the differential in yield between a security being studied and a default-free one, with all factors other than default risk constant. It is represented by the distance on the horizontal axis in Fig. 5-1 between the intercept and the yield on the security being studied.

The *promised rate* on a security is the *ex ante* yield at a moment in time. If a corporation issues a bond with a $7\frac{1}{2}$ per cent coupon rate at a price of $1,000 to the public, the rate promised by the issuer is $7\frac{1}{2}$ per cent. However, if the bond rises in price so that one month later it yields $7\frac{1}{4}$ per cent to maturity, the promised rate at that time would be $7\frac{1}{4}$ per cent. It is important to recognize that the promised rate is not necessarily the rate actually realized if the bond is held to maturity.

The *realized rate* is the rate of discount that equates all payments actually received by investors with the market price of the security at the time the security was purchased. Any difference between the promised rate at the time the security was bought and the realized rate is known as the *loss rate* attributable to default.[1] It is clear that, if the issuer does not default in the payment of principal and interest, the promised and the realized rates are the same.

At a moment in time, the risk structure of interest rates is determined by differences between promised rates and *expected* rates—the latter being the rate investors at the margin actually expect to receive. If there is a

---

[1] This assumes that we have held constant all other factors, in particular callability. See W. Braddock Hickman, *Corporate Bond Quality and Investor Experience* (New York: National Bureau of Economic Research, 1958), introductory chapter and pp. 64–66.

possibility for default, the expected yield on a security will be less than the promised one. To carry this reasoning one step further, if capital markets were perfect, the rate expected by investors at the margin would equal the rate on a default-free security. In other words, the difference between the promised rate and the expected rate on a security would correspond to the risk premium defined earlier. The implication of this notion is that the differential between the promised and default-free rates is equal to the expected default loss for investors at the margin.

To understand this notion better, consider the behavior of a prospective investor. It is assumed that at a particular moment in time he forms a subjective probability distribution of possible returns from holding a security. This distribution is not symmetrical but highly skewed to the left. For the typical fixed-income security, there is a high probability that the issuer will meet all principal and interest payments. However, no probability exists for the realized yield to exceed the promised yield, assuming the security is held to maturity.[2] The promised rate, then, represents the highest return possible from holding the security to maturity. However, if the issuer defaults in any of the principal or interest payments, the realized rate will be less than this promised rate.

Legally, an issuer defaults anytime he is unable to meet the terms of the contract. However, degrees of default vary from a simple extension all the way to liquidation involving legal procedures. An extension is nothing more than creditors extending the maturity of the obligation voluntarily or allowing the postponement of interest payments. Because of the time value of money, however, the realized yield will be less than the promised yield even in the case of an extension. To illustrate, suppose that the promised yield on a 20-year security at the time of issuing were $6\frac{1}{2}$ per cent, the market price $1,000, and the coupon rate $6\frac{1}{2}$ per cent. Suppose, however, that the issuer were unable to meet the annual interest payment at the end of the third year and that this payment were postponed until the end of the fourth year, at which time it was paid. Suppose further that the regular interest payment at the end of the fourth year as well as all other payments were met by the borrower. With annual interest payments,[3] the realized yield on the security would be found by solving the following equation for r:

$$1,000 = \frac{65}{(1+r)} + \frac{65}{(1+r)^2} + \frac{130}{(1+r)^4} + \frac{65}{(1+r)^5}$$
$$+ \ldots + \frac{65}{(1+r)^{20}} + \frac{1,000}{(1+r)^{20}} \tag{5-1}$$

---

[2] Again, maturity is held constant. Any selling of the security prior to maturity would be based upon considerations taken up in Chapter 4.

[3] For simplicity, we assume annual interest payments. The problem can be worked out for semiannual or quarterly payments with equation (3-3) in Chapter 3.

The yield realized in this case would be 6.47 per cent—only slightly less than the promised rate. With the liquidation of a corporate borrower, investors are likely to receive much less. To illustrate, suppose that the issuer of the security described above paid interest for the first three years but defaulted at the end of the fourth year because of inadequate liquidity. Suppose further that investors felt the borrower had no hope of turning the situation around and that liquidation was the only feasible alternative. Through bankruptcy proceedings, its assets are liquidated and investors receive an eventual settlement of 60c on the dollar at the end of the fifth year. In this case, the investors' cash outflow of $1,000 exceeds the total cash inflows they receive. As a result, the realized yield on the security will be negative. For negative yields, equation (5-1) is not appropriate; it computes smaller and smaller negative yields the further in the future that final settlement occurs. The implication is that it is more desirable to receive the $600 final settlement at the end of year 5 than it is at the end of year 3. Obviously, investors would like to receive final settlement as early as possible, all other things the same. To take account of the investor's opportunity cost, it is necessary to modify equation (5-1) when the realized yield is negative. To approximate the realized yield in an economic sense, we discount the final settlement amount back to the time of the last payment of interest on the security. The discount rate used is the initial promised yield on the security. If this yield is significantly out of line with prevailing yields in the market for the time span considered, however, an opportunity rate more closely in line with market rates of interest should be used. Using the promised rate, the realized yield for our example can be found by solving the following equation for r:

$$1,000 = \frac{65}{(1 + r)} + \frac{65}{(1 + r)^2} + \frac{65}{(1 + r)^3} + \frac{600/(1.065)^{5-3}}{(1 + r)^3} \quad (5\text{-}2)$$

When we solve for r, we find it to be -12.41 per cent. In a manner similar to that in equations (5-1) and (5-2), the realized yields for other possible default situations can be determined.

For each possibility, a probability should be attached and the possibilities ordered according to the magnitude of realized yield to form a probability distribution. An example of such a distribution is seen in Fig. 5-2. The figure illustrates that a relatively high probability exists for all interest and principal payments to be met by the borrower, resulting in the realized yield's equaling the promised one. However, the distribution is skewed to the left, indicating that a definite possibility exists for default. The further to the left in the figure, the higher the degree of default.

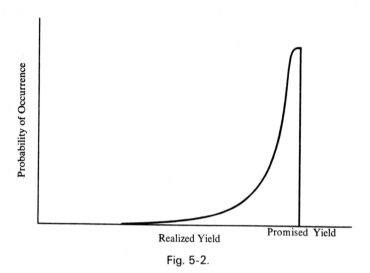

Fig. 5-2.

The *expected rate* for a security can be approximated by

$$ER = \sum_{x=1}^{n} Y_x P_x \tag{5-3}$$

where Y_x is the xth possible yield, P_x is the probability of occurrence of that yield, and n is the total number of possibilities. Suppose that an individual formulated the probability distribution of possible yields shown in Table 5-1. The expected yield for the security would be

$$
\begin{aligned}
ER =\ & (7)0.80 + (6)0.04 + (5)0.03 + (4)0.02 + (3)0.015 \\
& + (2)0.015 + (1)0.015 + (0)0.01 - (5)0.01 \\
& - (10)0.01 - (15)0.01 - (20)0.01 - (25)0.005 \\
& - (30)0.005 - (40)0.005 = 5.17 \text{ per cent}
\end{aligned}
\tag{5-4}
$$

Thus at time t the prospective investor expects an approximate return of 5.17 per cent on the security.

The *expected default loss* on the security is the difference between its promised and expected yields, or

$$7.00 - 5.17 = 1.83 \text{ per cent} \tag{5-5}$$

This percentage may or may not correspond to the *market risk premium*, defined as the differential between the promised yield and the actual yield on a comparable risk-free security. If the risk premium in the market

TABLE 5-1   Probability Distribution of
Possible Yields

Possible Yield	Probability
7 per cent (promised yield)	0.80
6	0.04
5	0.03
4	0.02
3	0.015
2	0.015
1	0.015
0	0.01
− 5	0.01
− 10	0.01
− 15	0.01
− 20	0.01
− 25	0.005
− 30	0.005
− 40	0.005

is more than the prospective investor's expected default loss, one rationale would suggest that he should invest in the security. He stands to benefit from an expected yield, adjusted for expected default loss, which is higher than that available on a risk-free security. By the same reasoning, if his subjectively formulated expected default loss exceeds the risk premium on the security, he should not invest. Here, the expected yield realized from the security would be less than that from a default-free one. If the expected default loss equaled the risk premium in the market, the investor should be willing simply to hold the security.

The action of all investors behaving in this manner will tend to raise or lower the differential between the promised and the default-free rates until it equals the default loss expected by investors at the margin.[4] Thus, the market risk premium would equal the expected default loss, and the expected rate would equal the default-free one. If the actual default-free rate in the example above were 5.17 per cent, the risk premium would be 1.83; and this premium would equal the default loss expected by investors at the margin.

The equilibrating process described above implies that the market is indifferent as to the variance and skewness of the probability distribution of possible realized yields; only the expected value of the distribution is important. However, it may well be that investors look with disfavor toward a distribution which is highly skewed to the left. Such a distribution means that there is a significant possibility of very unfavorable returns.

[4] In efficient markets, investors would be able to diversify in order to average out some default risk. However, a certain amount of risk of net default losses would remain. For example, in a depression, there are likely to be default losses. See Hickman, *Corporate Bond Quality and Investor Experience*, pp. 15–16. With diversification, the probability distributions in the above example would be formulated on the basis of nondiversifiable default losses.

To the extent that investors at the margin demand a higher return for dispersion and skewness, the risk premium in the market place would exceed the default loss expected by these investors. The greater the skewness to the left of the probability distribution of possible returns, the more the risk premium in the market would exceed the default loss expected by investors at the margin. The more risky the security, of course, the greater the expected default loss. Thus, over a long period of time, we would expect that the average promised rate for a large sample of bonds would exceed the average realized rate and that this differential would vary inversely with the quality of the security.

In summary, investors are assumed to form subjective probability distributions of possible realized returns for each security. Differences in these probability distributions will determine differences in risk premiums for the securities and, accordingly, will determine yield differentials between the securities. Figure 5-3 illustrates several of these distributions. The first probability distribution *a* represents the least risky security, while the last *c* is the most risky. On the basis of probability distributions of this sort, risk premiums are assumed to be determined in the market. However, these premiums may or may not conform to the expected default loss. We turn now to the empirical evidence.

Actual Risk Premiums

The most logical way to test the ideas discussed thus far is to compare actual realized yields on a large sample of securities with previous promised yields. The opportunity to test for default, however, depends upon a severe economic downturn. Only then are a significant number of issues likely to default. In other words, the probability of default on most securities is very small; it takes a sharp downturn to shake out those issuers possessing significant default risk. In this century, the depression of the 1930s provides the most valid test.

If risk premiums consistently equaled expected default losses by investors at the margin, we would expect that the average difference between the promised yield at time *t* and the realized yield at maturity would equal the average risk premium at time *t* for a large sample of bonds over a long period of time. The only comprehensive testing of this sort has been by Hickman, who investigated the default experience of fixed-income single-maturity corporate bonds over the period 1900–1943.[5] The sample consisted of all bonds over $5 million and a 10 per cent sample of smaller issues. For the sample, "life-span" default rates were computed depicting the proportion of bonds offered that defaulted between the offering date and extinguishment. In addition, loss rates representing the difference between promised and realized rates were computed.

Hickman's loss rate differed somewhat from the rate used earlier to

---

[5] *Corporate Bond Quality and Investor Experience.*

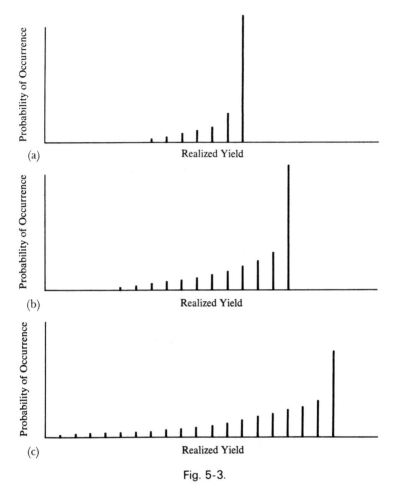

Fig. 5-3.

measure default loss. For one thing, the call feature was not held constant. If a bond were called, there was usually a capital gain because the call price was in excess of the par value of the bond. As a result, realized rates tended to be higher than they would otherwise have been. Additionally, there were a number of bonds outstanding at the end of the sample period, January 1, 1944. The realized rates computed for these bonds were based upon the market prices of the bonds at that date. Because of wartime controls on interest rates, however, yields were low and bond prices were relatively high at that time. This occurrence caused the realized rates on bonds outstanding at the end of the sample period to be artificially high. Both of these factors tended to bias the results in the direction of high realized rates in relation to promised ones. For all bonds, Hickman found that the weighted averages of both promised and realized rates were

5.6 per cent. Thus, the loss rate, as defined, was zero—an unusual phenomenon, explained primarily by the biases described. Capital gains
from calls and favorable conditions at the end of the sample period
simply offset the capital losses attributable to default.[6]

When he analyzed realized rates according to the quality of the bond
as described by its agency rating, Hickman found that these rates were
higher for low-grade bonds than for high-grade ones. Over the sample
period, the investor would have been better off on the average to have
invested in low-grade bonds. To be sure, the loss rates were higher, but
these rates were more than offset by the higher promised yields. Hickman
conjectured that this phenomenon was the result of institutional investors'
restricting their activity to higher-grade bonds. As these investors were
the ones who were able to diversify adequately, he reasoned that promised
yields on low-grade bonds must be relatively high to attract smaller investors unable to diversify adequately. However, the evidence also is consistent with the idea that the lower the grade of bond, the greater the
skewness to the left, and the greater the risk premium required in relation
to the expected value of default loss. As a result, the average realized rate
would be greater, the lower the grade of the security.

While Hickman's study contains a wealth of information, his aggregate
comparisons suffer from underlying movements in interest rates. As we
discussed, these movements biased the results in the direction of high
realized rates in relation to promised rates.

Harold G. Fraine and Robert H. Mills attempted to correct for these
biases by removing the effect of market influences on final liquidating
values from the estimates of realized yields and loss rates.[7] The authors
derived modified averages for large corporate bonds, using Hickman's
data for the 1900–1943 period. For bonds which did not default and whose
realized yield was in excess of the promised one, they substituted the
contractual yield for the realized yield. (The implication of this modification is that bonds called at premiums are assumed to run until maturity,
when they are redeemed at par. The same implication applies to unde-
faulted bonds outstanding at the end of the sample period.) After these
substitutions were made, modified realized yields were computed; these
yields are shown in Table 5-2. The results show that when realized yields
are modified for gains attributable to changes in interest rates, the realized
yield is less than the promised one. Still, the difference between the two
yields was somewhat smaller than the typical yield spread between cor-

---

[6]Over the sample period, different loss rates were experienced for the various sub-
periods. For bonds offered during 1900–1931 and extinguished during 1932–1943, the
average promised yield was 5.4 per cent and the average realized yield 4.6 per cent, the
average loss rate being 0.8 per cent. For securities both offered and extinguished during
the 1932–1943 period, the loss rate was more than offset by capital gains. The average
promised yield in this case was 4.9 per cent and the average realized yield 6.0 per cent.

[7]"Effects of Defaults and Credit Deterioration on Yields of Corporate Bonds," *Journal
of Finance*, XVI (September, 1961), 423–34.

TABLE 5-2   Promised vs. Modified Realized Yields 1900–1943

| Agency Rating | Weighted Mean Annual Rate | |
	Promised Yield	Modified Realized Yield
I	4.5 per cent	4.3 per cent
II	4.5	4.3
III	4.9	4.3
IV	5.4	4.5
I–III	4.7	4.3
I–IV	4.8	4.3

Source: Fraine and Mills, "Effects of Defaults and Credit Deterioration on Yields of Corporate Bonds," p. 428.

porate and government securities (the risk premium as defined) from 1920 to 1943.[8] Therefore, the results still would appear to be biased.

Agency Ratings

For the typical investor, risk is judged not by a subjectively formulated probability distribution but in terms of the quality rating assigned to the bond by investment agencies. The principal rating agencies are Moody's Investors Service and Standard and Poor's. These agencies evaluate the quality of bonds and give their opinion in the form of letter grades, which are published for the use of investors. In their ratings, the agencies attempt to rank issues according to the probability of default. A number of factors go into the analysis of an issue by an agency, including the cash-flow ability of the issuer to service debt, the amount and composition of existing debt, and the stability of cash flows. The highest grade bonds, whose risk of default is felt to be negligible, are rated triple A. The ratings used by the two agencies, as well as brief descriptions, are shown in Table 5-3. The first four grades in either case are considered to represent investment quality issues, whereas other rated bonds are considered speculative. The ratings by these two agencies are widely respected and are recognized by various government regulatory agencies as measures of default risk. In fact, many investors accept them without further investigation of the risk of default.

Hickman investigated the reliability of these ratings for corporate bonds over the period 1900–1943 and found a close correspondence between the rating category and the subsequent default experience.[9] The results of his investigation and the correspondence described are shown in Table 5-4. Hickman concluded that the record of the rating agencies over the sample period was remarkably good. Issues that were rated as high grade at the time of the offering generally had a much lower default rate than issues

[8] Prior to World War I, there were few U.S. Treasury securities outstanding. Because the market for government bonds was so thin, comparisons are not possible.

[9] *Corporate Bond Quality and Investor Experience*, p. 176.

TABLE 5-3   Ratings by Investment Agencies

Moody's	
Aaa	Best quality
Aa	High quality
A	Higher medium grade
Baa	Lower medium grade
Ba	Possess speculative elements
B	Generally lack characteristics of desirable investment
Caa	Poor standing; may be in default
Ca	Speculative in a high degree; often in default
C	Lowest grade

Standard & Poor's	
AAA	Highest grade
AA	High grade
A	Upper medium grade
BBB	Medium grade
BB	Lower medium grade
B	Speculative
CCC-CC	Outright speculation
C	Reserved for income bonds
DDD-D	In default, with rating indicating relative salvage value

rated in lower categories.[10] On the basis of this study, confidence would seem to be justified in the ability of the rating agencies to discriminate among issuers of bonds as to the probability of default. If so, these ratings can be used as measures of default risk in the study of differentials in yield in relation to differences in risk.

TABLE 5-4   Default Experience 1900–1943, per cent

	Rating					
	I	II	III	IV	V–IX	No Rating
Large issues (over $5 million)	5.9	6.0	13.4	19.1	42.4	28.6
Small issues (under $5 million)	10.2	15.5	9.9	25.2	32.6	27.0

Source: Hickman, *Corporate Bond Quality and Investor Experience*, p. 176.

---

[10] *Corporate Bond Quality and Investor Experience*, p. 141.

Regression Analysis

Another approach to the analysis of risk premiums involves the use of regression analysis. In an extensive study, Lawrence Fisher undertook a multiple regression analysis of five cross-sectional samples of corporate bonds for 1927, 1932, 1937, 1949, and 1953.[11] Using the risk premium (market yield less the corresponding default-free rate) as the dependent variable, he regressed this variable against four explanatory variables: the earnings variability of the company, the length of time the company has been solvent and creditors have not taken a loss, the equity/debt ratio, and the market value of all publicly traded bonds of the company. The first three variables relate to the risk of default while the last attempts to depict the marketability of the bond.

Fisher found that the four variables explained approximately 75 per cent of the variance in the logarithm of the risk premium. Moreover, the elasticity of the dependent variable with respect to these four variables was relatively stable over time. The regression coefficients for the explanatory variables all had the proper sign, and practically all were significant over the five dates. The sign for the first variable was positive, indicating that the greater the variability of earnings of the firm, the greater the default risk and the greater the risk premium embodied in the bond yield. The signs of the remaining three variables were negative. The second and third suggest that the greater the period of solvency and the greater the equity/debt ratio, the less the default risk and the lower the risk premium required. The sign for the last variable suggests that the greater the market value of total bonds outstanding, the greater the marketability of the issue to investors and the lower the risk premium. Overall, Fisher's study represents the first thorough and direct study of factors responsible for risk premiums. As such, it offers much insight into the bases for these premiums as well as the applicability of regression analysis as a tool for investigating them.

Cyclical Behavior of Risk Premiums

Another aspect of risk premiums is their cyclical behavior over time. A priori, we might expect risk premiums in the market for bonds to fluctuate in a systematic manner with the business cycle. During periods of economic downturn the risk premium might be expected to widen, while during periods of economic prosperity it might be expected to narrow. This pattern of behavior is attributable to investors' utility preferences for bonds changing with different states of nature. In a recession, their prime concern may be with safety. To invest in more risky bonds, the investor would have to be offered a substantial risk premium. On the

---

[11] "Determinants of Risk Premiums on Corporate Bonds," *Journal of Political Economy*, LXVII (June, 1959), 217–37.

other hand, during a period of prosperity, investors may be less concerned with safety and be willing to bear more risk of default. During such a time, there may be a tendency for them to seek out the highest yielding investments. A sufficient number of investors behaving in this manner would narrow risk premiums in periods of prosperity and widen them in times of recession.

The evidence since World War II has been partially consistent with this notion. In Fig. 5-4, yield differentials between long-term Treasury bonds and Aaa corporates and between Treasury bonds and Baa corporates are shown for the post-World War II period. The assumption underlying this type of analysis is that rating categories are consistent over time with respect to default risk. In the figure, we note that the yield differential between Treasury securities and Baa corporates did show a tendency to widen during the recessionary periods of 1949, 1954, 1957–1958, and 1960; this widening was evident particularly during the 1957–1958 recession. In recessions other than that, however, the widening was not nearly so distinctive. Moreover, during the 1950–1953 and 1955–1956 periods of prosperity, the differential narrowed only slightly. The most difficult pattern to explain is the 1961–1968 period of prosperity. The yield differential narrowed considerably during the period 1963–1965 but then increased sharply from 1966 through 1968. This latter behavior is not consistent with the pattern of behavior up to that time. Explanation of it comes not from an analysis of default risk premiums but from an analysis of the relative supply in the two markets. During this period, Treasury financing was confined mainly to short- and intermediate-term

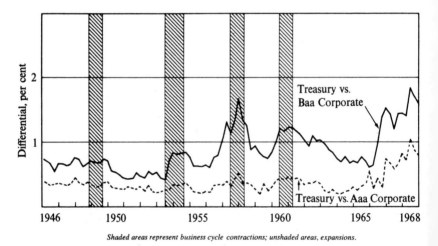

Shaded areas represent business cycle contractions; unshaded areas, expansions.

Fig. 5-4.   Yield differentials between Treasury bonds, Aaa corporate bonds, and Baa corporate bonds. Source: *Moody's Municipal & Government Manual* and *Moody's Industrial Manual*.

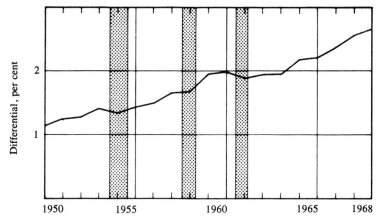

Shaded areas represent business cycle contractions; unshaded areas, expansions.

Fig. 5-5. Yield differential between long-term Treasury bonds and prime municipal bonds after taxes, 1950–1967, annual averages. Source: Solomon Brothers & Hutzler, *An Analytical Record of Yields and Yield Spreads.*

maturities, in part because of the $4\frac{1}{4}$ per cent coupon-rate ceiling on Treasury bonds imposed by Congress. On the other hand, corporate demands for long-term capital were at a historical high during the period. The logical result was that the yield differential widened.

The pattern for the yield differential between Treasuries and Aaa corporates is not nearly so distinctive as that for the differential between Treasuries and Baa corporates. This differential widened somewhat during the 1954, 1957–1958, and 1960 recessions; but the widening was not particularly sharp. The pattern for the 1963–1968 period was the same as that for the previous comparison. Because of negligible default risk for Aaa corporates, it is not surprising that the yield differential fluctuated within a relatively narrow range from 1946 through 1965. The sharp increase during the 1966–1968 period can be explained only in terms of the same supply forces as before.

It is interesting to consider also the yield differential for municipal securities. First, we consider the differential between Treasury securities and prime municipals after an adjustment has been made of the municipal yields for taxes. The differential over the period 1950–1968 is shown in Fig. 5-5. It is evident from the figure that there was little correspondence between the differential and the business cycle. However, the pattern of yield differential for different grades of municipal bonds shows evidence of a moderate relationship between the yield spread and the business cycle. Figure 5-6 shows the yield differential between Aaa municipals and Baa municipals over the period 1946–1968. As we see, the relationship pattern is somewhat less distinctive than that for corporate securities. The most

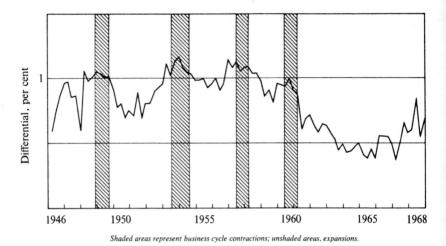

Shaded areas represent business cycle contractions; unshaded areas, expansions.

Fig. 5-6.   Yield differential between Aaa municipal bonds and Baa municipal bonds. Source: *Moody's Municipal & Government Manual.*

pronounced pattern is the narrowing of the yield spread in the 1961–1968 period of prosperity. Except for early 1968 the spread did not widen significantly for the 1966–1968 period as it did with corporate bonds. While the spread tended to be wide during the four recessions, it was only moderately wider than the yield spread on either side. At best, then, the evidence on municipals gives only moderate support to the notion that risk premiums widen during recessions and narrow during periods of prosperity.

For the earlier 1900–1943 period, Hickman found that when low-grade corporate bonds were purchased near the troughs of an investment cycle and sold during the peaks, the investor fared better than he did with similar purchases and sales of high-grade corporates. On the other hand, investors fared better with high-grade corporates bought near peaks and sold near troughs. He concluded that the market usually overpriced low-grade issues (and underestimated default risks) near the peaks of major investment cycles.[12] This behavior is consistent with risk premiums narrowing during periods of prosperity and widening during recessions.

In summary, for the yield differentials between corporate bonds and Treasuries and between different grades of municipals, there appears to be a tendency at times for risk premiums to vary with the business cycle. Certain evidence gives modest support to the notion that risk premiums narrow during periods of economic prosperity and widen during periods of economic downturn. Whether this phenomenon occurs because the utility of investors changes in keeping with changes in states of nature is problematical. The sharp widening of the yield differential between cor-

---

[12] *Corporate Bond Quality and Investor Experience,* p. 15.

porates and Treasuries during the period 1966–1968 clearly is inconsistent with previous behavior. Only time will tell whether this inconsistency continues or whether yield spreads return to their previous pattern of behavior.

Risk Structure and the Term Structure

With differences in both default risk and the length of time to maturity, yield curves may differ for different grades of securities. In other words, the default-risk premium is not necessarily a constant function of the length of time to maturity. If the default-risk premium were 1 per cent on a long-term bond, it does not follow that the premium on a short-term security of the same grade also would be 1 per cent. A priori, it might seem that the risk of default as perceived by investors for a particular grade of bond would vary directly with maturity. As the length of time to maturity grows shorter and the issuer does not default, a degree of uncertainty is resolved. With this resolution, investors may require a risk premium different from before, all other things remaining the same.

However, it is questionable whether all other things are the same. The problem is the grading category. For default-free securities, the yield-maturity relationship is internally consistent over various maturity points. However, for securities subject to default risk it is not necessarily consistent. For example, at 25 years to maturity, the observations used to determine the yield curve for a particular grade of corporate bond consist of a sample of bonds with that maturity. Ten years later, at time $t + 10$, these bonds will have 15 years until final maturity. However, the universe from which the sample observations are drawn is not the same. Only those bonds which have not defaulted, have not been called, or have not been upgraded or downgraded during the intervening period will remain in the universe. The point is that the bonds used to construct the yield curve for 15 years to maturity at time $t + 10$ will not be the same bonds as those used to construct the yield curve for 25 years to maturity at time t. Some bonds will have been dropped for the reasons cited, while others will have been added because they have been upgraded or downgraded from a previous rating category or because they are newly issued.

The rating agencies apply the same quality standards as before. However, with the passage of time the probability of default as perceived by investors for a particular rating category may lessen for the higher-grade categories. Accordingly, bonds of companies whose financial condition remained unchanged would need to be upgraded as the final maturity approached. This upgrading is not done; they are upgraded only if their financial condition improves. The problem is that we would like to study the yield-maturity relationship on bonds that have the same probability of default throughout all maturities. However, most investigations are limited to a particular rating category of bonds. For the higher-grade rating categories, the probability of default as perceived by investors would seem to lessen as maturity decreases and uncertainty is resolved.[13] Implied then is a bias toward an upward-sloping yield curve. However, the direction of the bias may differ for different rating categories. For those where the financial condition of the typical company is sufficient to service debt, the probability of default perceived by investors would seem to lessen as maturity approaches. However, for rating categories where the financial condition of the typical company is insufficient or marginal with respect to servicing debt and meeting the final redemption, the perceived probability of default may increase as maturity decreases.[14] Consequently, for lower-grade categories of bonds, the risk of default is unlikely to be an increasing function of maturity. For these grades, the probability of default may increase as the final redemption date grows nearer and the company is unable to improve its financial condition. Implied is a bias toward a downward-sloping yield curve.

Ramon E. Johnson defines the latter problem as "crisis-at-maturity."[15] This viewpoint, which arose during the depression, suggests that because of the difficulty of refinancing and meeting the final redemption payment during crisis periods, short maturities are more risky than long maturities. During periods of economic prosperity, crisis-at-maturity would be a factor only for lower quality bonds. The two types of bias are illustrated in Fig. 5-7. In both cases, the yield curve for default-free securities is assumed to be horizontal. The upper panel shows the pattern for high-grade securities, and the lower one the pattern for low-grade securities.

The most interesting part of Johnson's study was the construction of yield curves based upon empirical data for five grades of corporate securities and the comparison of these yield curves with Durand's basic corporate yield curves. Recall from the previous chapter that Durand's yield curves depict the yield-maturity relationship for corporate bonds of the lowest default risk. Johnson plotted yield curves for 1910 through 1944, although only 14 of them were shown in the article. Of particular interest were the yield curves which occurred during the depression. From 1933 on, the highest-grade issues tended to be upward sloping, as was Durand's basic yield curve, while lower-grade issues were downward sloping. Examples of yield curves for 1934 and 1938 are shown in Fig. 5-8. The line with the Bs refers to the basic yield curve, while the numbers 1 to 5 refer to different grading categories from high to low.

---

[13] Roland I. Robinson, in comparing the yield spread between Aaa and Baa municipal securities with the length of time to maturity, found that in most cases yield differentials were greater for long-term securities than they were for short-term ones. He concluded that default risk was an increasing function of maturity. *Postwar Market for State and Local Government Securities* (New York: National Bureau of Economic Research, 1960), pp. 184–88.

[14] In many cases, the redemption of a bond issue comes through refinancing with a new bond issue. As the ability to go to market with a new bond issue depends upon the financial condition of the company, the above argument holds regardless of the intended means for redemption.

[15] "Term Structures of Corporate Bond Yields as a Function of Risk of Default," *Journal of Finance*, XXII (May, 1967), 318–21.

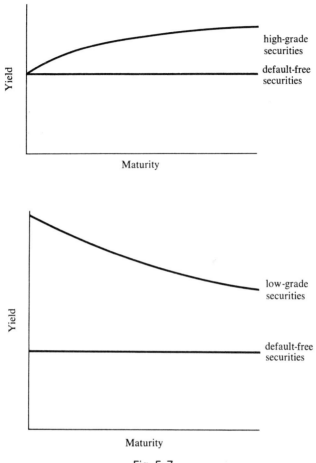

Fig. 5-7.

Johnson postulated that the downward-sloping yield curves for lower quality issues, seen particularly during the depression, were primarily the result of crisis-at-maturity considerations.[16] Upward-sloping yield curves for low-grade bonds occurred only when the prospect for crisis-at-maturity was slight. Moreover, Johnson contended that upward-sloping yield curves for high-grade securities were the result of risk premiums increasing with maturity. On the other hand, U-shaped curves were said to result from a combination of crisis-at-maturity considerations and expectations that default-risk premiums would increase in the future. Similarly, other shaped yield curves were explained in terms of risk

---

[16]"Term Structures of Corporate Bond Yields as a Function of the Risk of Default," pp. 340–45.

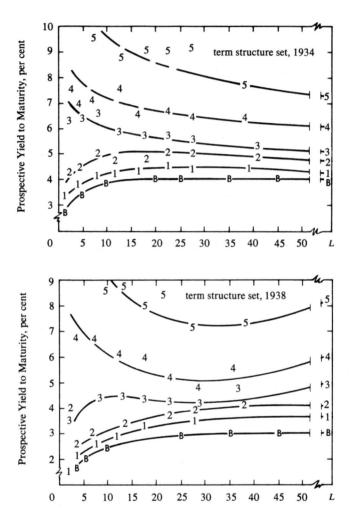

Fig. 5-8.   Source: Johnson, "Term Structure of Corporate Bond Yields as a Function of Risk of Default," pp. 337–38.

premiums increasing with maturity, crisis-at-maturity, and expectations of changing risk premiums.

While one may quarrel with Johnson's interpretations of the causes of various shaped yield curves, he provided much needed evidence on default risk and maturity. To be sure, the construction of his yield curves is subject to a number of technical and measurement problems.[17] Con-

---

[17]See David Durand, "Comment," *Journal of Finance*, XXII (May, 1967), 348–50, for a discussion of these problems.

sequently, it is inappropriate to make precise distinctions among various shaped yield curves over time. Nevertheless, the curves give general indication of yield-maturity relationships for various grades of bonds. The evidence tends to support the notion that measured risk premiums are an increasing function of maturity for high-grade securities and a decreasing function for low-grade ones. This finding is consistent with the idea that uncertainty is resolved for a particular grade of security as maturity grows shorter.

Marketability

Differences in yield for various financial instruments may also result from differences in marketability. The marketability of an asset means the ability of the owner to convert it to cash. There are two dimensions: the price realized and the amount of time required to sell the asset. The two are interrelated in that it is often possible to sell an asset in a short period of time if enough price concession is given. For financial instruments, marketability is judged in relation to the ability to sell a significant volume of securities in a short period of time without significant price concession.[18] As a part of the price concession, one must consider transactions costs. The more marketable the security, the greater the ability to execute a large transaction near the quoted price.

In general, the lower the marketability of a financial instrument, the greater the yield necessary to attract investors. Thus, the yield differential between different securities of the same maturity is caused not only by differences in default risk but also by differences in marketability. Recall from our discussion earlier that Fisher tested for the effect of marketability on yield spreads. Fisher called marketability "the risk associated with the difficulty of turning the bond into cash before it matures."[19] As a measure of marketability, he used the total market value of publicly traded bonds of the corporation, justifying its use by its positive association with transaction frequency. The fewer bonds that change hands, the thinner the market is said to be, and the more uncertain the market price. As we brought out before, Fisher found an inverse and significant relationship between yield spread and his marketability measure, holding constant the effect of the three variables dealing with default risk. This finding supports the notion that the greater the marketability of a bond, the lower the risk premium.

Summary

The relationship between yield and the risk of default, with other factors constant, is known as the *risk structure* of interest rates. This relationship usually is studied through the analysis of risk premiums, the difference between the yield on a security and the yield on a corresponding

---

[18] See Chapter 1 for additional discussion of marketability.
[19] "Determinants of Risk Premiums on Corporate Bonds," p. 130.

security which is free of default risk. The promised yield on a security is its *ex ante* yield at a moment in time. The expected yield, on the other hand, is the expected value of the probability distribution of possible realized yields. The distribution itself is highly skewed to the left. In perfect markets, the expected yield for investors at the margin should equal the risk-free rate. If this relationship held, the expected default loss on a security would equal the market-determined risk premium. However, to the extent that the market as a whole is adverse to dispersion and skewness to the left of the probability distribution, the risk premium will exceed the default loss expected by investors at the margin. Empirical tests have indicated that realized yields tend to be higher on lower-grade securities, a finding that is consistent with this idea.

Various investment agencies rate securities as to their probability of default. Available evidence suggests that these ratings are consistent with respect to default risk. By and large, the risk structure of interest rates is analyzed in relation to differences in ratings. Another method for analyzing yield differentials is regression analysis, and this method was examined. In addition, the cyclical behavior of risk premiums over time was studied. It was noted that there appears to be a slight tendency for risk premiums to narrow during periods of economic prosperity and to widen during periods of economic downturn.

The risk structure and the term structure of interest rates were examined jointly in an effort to explain differing shapes of yield curves for different risk categories of securities. The idea that uncertainty is resolved as maturity grows shorter implies a bias toward an upward-sloping yield curve for high-grade securities and a downward-sloping yield curve for lower-grade securities. Finally, yield differentials on securities may result from differences in marketability. We would expect that the lower the marketability of a financial instrument, the greater would be the yield demanded by investors, and the greater the risk premium.

Selected References

Boness, A. James, "A Pedogogic Note on the Cost of Capital," *Journal of Finance,* XIX (March, 1964), 99–106.

Fisher, Lawrence, "Determinants of Risk Premiums on Corporate Bonds," *Journal of Political Economy,* LXVII (June, 1959), 217–37.

Fraine, Harold G., and Robert H. Mills, "Effects of Defaults and Credit Deterioration on Yields of Corporate Bonds," *Journal of Finance,* XVI (September, 1961), 423–34.

Hickman, W. Braddock, *Corporate Bond Quality and Investor Experience.* New York: National Bureau of Economic Research, 1958.

Johnson, Ramon E., "Term Structures of Corporate Bond Yields as a Function of Risk of Default," *Journal of Finance,* XXII (May, 1967), 313–45.

Macaulay, Frederick R., *The Movement of Interest Rates, Bond Yields, and Stock Prices in the United States Since 1856.* New York: National Bureau of Economic Research, 1938.

Robichek, Alexander A., "The Impact of Risk on the Value of Securities." Unpublished research paper presented at the meeting of the Institute for Quantitative Research in Finance, October 10, 1968.

Robinson, Roland I., *Postwar Market for State and Local Government Securities.* New York: National Bureau of Economic Research, 1960.

Sloane, Peter E., "Determinants of Bond Yield Differentials—1954–1959," *Yale Economic Essays*, 3 (Spring, 1963), 3–56.

```
6666666666666666666666666666666666666666666666666666666666666666666666666666666666
6666666666666666666666666666666666666666666666666666666666666666666666666666666666
6666666666666666666666666666666    6666666666666    666    6666666666666666666666666666666
6666666666666666666666666666666    6666666666    6666    6666666666666666666666666666666
6666666666666666666666666666666    666666666    66666    6666666666666666666666666666666
6666666666666666666666666666666    6666666    666666    6666666666666666666666666666666
6666666666666666666666666666666    66666    6666666    6666666666666666666666666666666
6666666666666666666666666666666    666    66666666    6666666666666666666666666666666
6666666666666666666666666666666    6    666666666    6666666666666666666666666666666
6666666666666666666666666666666        6666666666    6666666666666666666666666666666
6666666666666666666666666666666    6666666666    6666666666666666666666666666666666
6666666666666666666666666666666666666666666666666666666666666666666666666666666666
6666666666666666666666666666666666666666666666666666666666666666666666666666666666
```

Callability, Taxability, and the
Structure of Long-term Yields

IN the preceding two chapters, maturity, default risk, and marketability were found to be important in explaining differences in yields on fixed-income securities. In this chapter, we consider two additional factors that account for the yield differentials we observe: callability and the impact of taxes on realized returns. Once these factors are studied, an examination of the structure of yields for fixed-income securities is possible. In the last section of this chapter, we study relative yields on Treasury securities, corporate bonds, municipal bonds, mortgages, and straight preferred stocks. These yields are analyzed in relation to factors which affect supply and demand functions in each of the markets.

The Call Feature

Many bonds do not have a single maturity but are callable at the option of the issuer prior to final maturity.[1] For example, most corporate bond and preferred stock issues provide for a call feature, and some Treasury securities are callable. Generally municipal securities are not callable. A call feature allows the issuer to buy back the issue at a stated

---

[1] Parts of this section are adapted from James C. Van Horne, *Financial Management and Policy* (Englewood Cliffs, N.J.: Prentice-Hall, Inc., 1968), pp. 245–47.

price before maturity. In the case of a corporate bond or preferred stock, the call price usually is above the face or par value of the security and decreases over time. For example, a 30-year bond issue might be callable at $106 ($1,060 per $1,000 face value bond) the first five years, $105 the second five years, and so on until the final five years, when it is callable at $101. Frequently the call price in the first year is established at one year's interest above the face value of the bond. If the coupon rate were 7 per cent, the initial call price might be $107 ($1,070 per $1,000 face value).

The call feature on a security modifies its maturity and thereby affects its relative yield. For corporate securities, there are two types of call provisions, specifying when the call can be exercised. For some issues, the call privilege can be exercised immediately after issuance; for other issues, it is deferred for a period of time. The most widely used deferred call periods are five years for public utility bonds and ten years for industrial bonds. During this deferment period, the investor is protected from a call by the issuer.

To the corporate borrower, the call provision gives it flexibility. Should interest rates decline significantly, the borrower can call the bonds and refund the issue at a lower interest cost. Thus, the company does not have to wait until final maturity to refinance. The optimal time for an issuer to call bonds is when the present value of the difference between the price at which the new, or refunding, bonds can be issued and the call price is greatest (holding constant the coupon rate and the final maturity).[2] In addition to flexibility, the call provision may be advantageous to the company with any protective covenants in its existing bond indenture unduly restrictive. By calling the bonds before maturity, the company can eliminate these restrictions.

The call privilege works to the benefit of the borrower but to the detriment of investors. If interest rates fall and the bond issue is called, they can invest in other bonds only at a sacrifice in yield to maturity. Consequently, the call privilege usually does not come free to the borrower. Its cost, or value, is measured by the difference in yield on the callable bond and the yield that would be necessary if the security were non-callable. This value is determined by supply and demand forces in the market for callable securities. In equilibrium, the value of the call feature will be just sufficient to bring the demand for callable securities by investors into balance with the supply of callable securities by borrowers. In the equilibrating process, both borrowers and investors are influenced by expectations as to the future course of interest rates.

When interest rates are high and expected to fall, the call feature is likely to have significant value. Investors are unwilling to invest in callable bonds unless such bonds yield more than bonds that are noncallable, all

[2] See Gordon Pye, "The Value of the Call Option on a Bond," *Journal of Political Economy*, LXXIV (April, 1966), 200–201.

other things the same. In other words, they must be compensated for assuming the risk that the bonds might be called. On the other hand, borrowers are willing to pay a premium in yield for the call privilege in the belief that yields will fall and that it will be advantageous to refund the bonds. In equilibrium, both the marginal borrower and the marginal investor will be indifferent as to whether the bond is callable or noncallable.[3]

When interest rates are low and expected to rise, the call privilege may have negligible value, in that the borrower might pay the same yield if there were no call privilege. For the privilege to have value, interest-rate expectations must be such that there is a possibility that the issue will be called. If interest rates are very low and are not expected to fall further, there is little probability that the bonds will be called. The key factor is that the borrower has to be able to refund the issue at a profit. For him to do so, interest rates have to drop significantly, since the issuer must pay the call price, which usually is at a premium above par value, as well as flotation costs involved in the refunding.[4] If there is no probability that the borrower can refund the issue profitably, the call feature is unlikely to have a value.

Because most corporate bonds have call features, an empirical study of the differential in yield between a noncallable bond and a callable one is not possible. However, it is possible to examine the yield differential between newly issued corporate bonds having an immediate call privilege and those of the same grade and maturity having a five-year deferred call. For the immediate call privilege to have a value over that of the deferred call, interest-rate expectations must be such that the bonds callable immediately might be called during the deferment period. If there is no probability of their being called during this period, the value of the immediate over the deferred call privilege will be zero.

An examination of the yield differential between the two types of call privilege for newly issued bonds reveals that the differential tends to increase in times of high interest rates and tight money and to decline in periods of easy money and low interest rates. The differential for Aa public utility bonds over the period 1958–1968 is shown in Fig. 6-1. For the 1959 and 1966–1968 periods of high interest rates, the differential exceeded 25 basis points, whereas during the 1963–1965 period an immediately callable bond offered no premium over a deferred callable bond. In addition to this evidence, Frank C. Jen and James E. Wert tested the offering yields of newly issued utility bonds over the 1960–1964 period and found a positive relationship between the yield differential and the level of the coupon rate. The yield differential was around zero when coupon rates were low and was positive when coupon rates were

---

[3] Pye, "The Value of the Call Option on a Bond," p. 203.

[4] For analysis of the profitability of refunding, see Oswald D. Bowlin, "The Refunding Decision: Another Special Case in Capital Budgeting," *Journal of Finance*, XXI (March, 1966), 55–68.

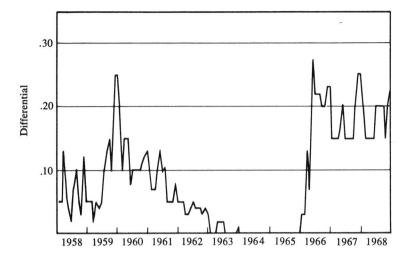

Fig. 6-1.   Yield differential between immediately callable and deferred callable Aa public utility bonds, 1958–1968. Source: Solomon Brothers & Hutzler, *An Analytical Record of Yields and Yield Spreads*.

high.[5] The evidence supports the notion that the call privilege has the most value and the most cost to the corporation when interest rates are high and are expected to fall. By the same token, it has the greatest potential benefit to the corporation at these times.

In contrast to those for corporate bonds, call provisions for Treasury bonds are geared to the final maturity date. About one-third of all Treasury bonds outstanding have a call feature, enabling the Treasury to call the bonds so many years prior to maturity. For example, the terms of the $4\frac{1}{4}$ per cent bonds of August 15, 1987–1992 enable the Treasury to call the bonds anytime between August 15, 1987 and final maturity five years later. The primary purpose of the call privilege is to give the Treasury flexibility in refinancing. Unlike that of many corporations, the debt of

---

[5] "The Value of the Deferred Call Privilege," *National Banking Review*, 3 (March, 1966), 369–78. In a second article, "The Deferred Call Provision and Corporate Bond Yields," *Journal of Financial and Quantitative Analysis*, III (June, 1968), 157–69, the authors computed modified realized returns on immediately callable bonds and deferred callable bonds. The test was based upon a sample of public utility bonds for the 1956–1961 period. Experience through June, 1966, was tested. They found that deferred callable bonds bought during periods of high interest rates showed a greater realized return, despite the lower initial yield, than freely callable bonds. They suggest that this evidence implies that issuers have underpriced the deferred call privilege in the period of high interest rates. While the evidence is interesting, the sample period is too short to represent the full span of cyclical behavior. It amounts to a case study for a particular period of time; generalizations on the basis of this period are problematical. In addition, the sample was relatively small; only seven out of the 107 issues were actually called.

the federal government is generally "rolled over" at maturity. The Treasury is primarily concerned with the tone of the market when it has to refinance its maturing obligations. By having five years in which to "roll over" the debt, the Treasury is flexible in the timing of its refinancing. Thus, the principal purpose of the call privilege is not to achieve a savings in interest, but to obtain flexibility in new financing near the final maturity of the existing obligation.[6]

Because the maturity of a Treasury bond can be shortened by only five years, the call privilege does not pose the same disadvantage to investors as does the call privilege for a corporate bond. Another protection to the investor is the $4\frac{1}{4}$ per cent coupon ceiling imposed by Congress. (The ceiling was in effect at the time this book was written.) This ceiling means that if interest rates rise above $4\frac{1}{4}$ per cent, Treasury bonds will sell at a discount. To call the bond, the Treasury would have to pay a premium over its market price; therefore, a call is unlikely. Thus, the interest-rate ceiling assures that the Treasury will not issue long-term debt in periods of high interest rates, when the call privilege might have value. For these reasons, the call privilege for Treasury securities has little discernible value even when interest rates are high.[7]

A form of call privilege exists on mortgages. Unless otherwise specified in the contract, the borrower may pay the loan off at any time. In other words, the loan is callable immediately. Frequently, however, lenders demand a prepayment penalty if the loan is paid off before a certain date. For example, insurance companies usually require a prepayment penalty on residential mortgages which is graduated downward through five years. After five years, the loan can be paid without penalty.

In contrast to corporate bonds, very few municipal securities are issued with a call provision. One reason for this may be the nature of political life. If a municipal security were made callable, the immediate interest cost to the municipality would rise. Pye suggests that the issuance of callable bonds would result in higher current taxes with the possibility of tax savings sometime in the future.[8] Because public officials may not be in office in the future, Pye reasons that they place a higher utility on lower taxes now than on possible savings in the future. Another reason for state and local governments to issue noncallable bonds is the difference between their borrowing and lending rates. Because interest on municipal securities is exempt from federal income taxes, the borrowing rate is lower than the lending rate; the latter rate might be the return on

---

[6] For a discussion of this point as of other aspects of the call privilege, see Willis J. Winn and Arleigh Hess, Jr., "The Value of the Call Privilege," *Journal of Finance* (1959), reprinted in James Van Horne, ed., *Foundations for Financial Management* (Homewood, Ill.: Richard D. Irwin, Inc. 1966), pp. 234–46.

[7] For callable Treasury bonds, yield to maturity is computed on the basis of final maturity when the market price of the bond is below par and on the basis of the earliest call date when its market price is above par. When it is below par, the implication is that the Treasury is unlikely to call the security.

[8] "The Value of the Call Option on a Bond," p. 304.

a Treasury or corporate bond. Richard R. West theorizes that public officials may discount possible future interest savings by the lending rather than the borrowing rate. If that were done, the present value of expected cash savings from the exercise of the call privilege usually would be less than the cost of the privilege, and thereby its attractiveness would be reduced considerably.[9]

Taxation

Another factor affecting observed differences in market yields is the differential impact of taxes. The most important tax we shall consider, of course, is the federal income tax. A differential impact on yields arises because interest income and dividends are taxed at the ordinary rate, while capital gains on securities held for more than six months are taxed at the more favorable capital-gains rate. Only one-half of a long-term capital gain is taxable; and the maximum rate for individuals on a taxable gain is 50 per cent.

The favorable tax treatment of capital gains has made this type of return very desirable and has contributed importantly to the popularity of common stocks. Fixed-income securities which sell at a discount because of a low coupon rate in relation to prevailing yields also are attractive to investors. The reason is that part of the yield to maturity is a capital gain. For example, a bond having a 4 per cent coupon and ten years to final maturity would sell at a price of $815 to yield 6.55 per cent to maturity. If the bond were held to maturity and redeemed at $1,000, the investor would realize a long-term capital gain of $185. Only one-half of this gain would be taxable; and the tax would not be paid until the maturity of the issue. The investor, of course, would pay normal income taxes on the $40 in interest received each year.

Because of the desirability of discount bonds, their yield to maturity tends to be lower than the yield on comparable bonds with higher coupon rates. The greater the discount, the greater the capital-gains attraction of the bond and the lower its yield relative to what it would be if the coupon rate were such that the bond sold at par.[10] In the analysis of market yields, it is important to account for the differential tax impact of ordinary income versus capital gains. Consider, for example, the term structure of interest rates. If the observations for a particular maturity range consisted only of bonds selling at a discount, while the observations for other ranges consisted of bonds selling around par, the fitted yield curve would be distorted. The discount bonds, particularly if the discounts are deep, are not comparable directly with bonds selling at par or above. In studying the relationship between yield and maturity, one would not hold the impact of taxation constant. It would be an explanatory variable.

[9]"On the Noncallability of State and Local Bonds: A Comment," *Journal of Political Economy*, 75 (February, 1967), 98–99.

[10]Another attraction of discount bonds is that they are unlikely to be called.

If we knew the typical tax bracket for investors in a particular security, it would be possible to calculate yield to maturity after taxes. This calculation would allow a direct comparison of yields. The difficulty, of course, is in estimating the applicable tax rate, particularly where individuals constitute a large portion of the ownership.[11] For this reason, Salomon Brothers & Hutzler and various other organizations publish separate yield data for low and high coupon bonds. With a rising trend in interest rates, bonds issued in the past sell at increasing discounts, and the need to take account of the differential tax effects becomes ever more important.

In addition to the federal income tax, the federal estate tax has a differential impact on the yields for Treasury securities. This tax is on the right of an individual to pass assets on to others at his death. Certain Treasury bonds, if owned by the deceased, are redeemable at par if the proceeds are used to pay federal estate taxes. To illustrate, suppose a qualifying bond selling at $80 were bought by an individual. Upon his death, this bond would be worth $100 if used in the settlement of estate taxes. For this reason, qualifying Treasury bonds selling at a deep discount are even more attractive than the capital-gains tax advantage alone would suggest. As a result, the yield to maturity on these bonds is lower than it would be if the bond were selling at par or above, holding constant the capital-gains tax advantage.

The interest income on all but one category of securities is taxable: Interest income from state and local government securities is tax exempt.[12] The impact of this feature on yields will be analyzed later in the chapter. Prior to 1941, the income of certain Treasury bonds was partially tax exempt; however, the income of all Treasury securities now outstanding is fully taxable.

Structure of Long-term Yields

In this chapter and the previous two, a number of factors were studied that affect relative yields on financial instruments. We considered interest-rate expectations and the term structure of interest rates, default risk, marketability, callability, and taxability. The demand and supply functions for securities are affected greatly by these factors; as a result, we can use them to explain yield differentials between various securities. In this section, we shall investigate further relative yields in relation to the markets for the following fixed-income, long-term securities: Treasury bonds, corporate bonds, municipal bonds, preferred stocks, and mortgages. Convertible securities and common stocks are taken up in the next chapter.

---

[11] Alexander A. Robichek and W. David Niebuhr have developed a method for estimating the tax rate implied by the market for various securities and for estimating tax-adjusted yields. "Tax-Induced Bias in Reported Treasury Yields," unpublished paper, Graduate School of Business, Stanford University, 1969.

[12] Capital gains on municipal securities are subject to federal income taxes.

In our study, we examine important demand and supply characteristics in each of the five markets as they pertain to relative yields. Because some of the reasons for yield differentials have been considered previously, portions of the discussion are purposely brief. As a basis for discussion, yields over the post-World War II period are shown in Fig. 6-2 for each of the five markets.

Treasury Securities

Because Treasury securities represent the heart of financial markets, it is appropriate to begin with their consideration. The U.S. Treasury is the largest single borrower in the world and is engaged in almost continuous borrowing and refinancing. Treasury securities are traded in a highly organized market; dealers are strong and have access to adequate financing.[13] Of all the fixed-income security markets, marketability is greatest for these securities. Even here, however, it is not possible to sell a large block of long-term bonds without some price concession. On the short end, however, Treasury securities possess considerable marketability owing to the large volume of transactions.

Because Treasury securities are free of default risk and are highly marketable, they command the lowest yields to maturity of all securities whose income is taxable. As with all fixed-income securities, interest-rate expectations are important in determining the level of interest rates for various maturities. Because of the rising secular trend in interest rates, particular since 1965, many existing long-term bonds are selling at sizable discounts. With the $4\frac{1}{4}$ per cent coupon-rate ceiling imposed by Congress, the Treasury has been precluded from selling long-term bonds; consequently, all such bonds have been selling at a discount in recent years. Because of the attractiveness of discount bonds, yields to maturity are lower than would be the case if the coupon rates corresponded to prevailing interest rates in the market.

The supply of Treasury securities is determined primarily by the magnitude of the U.S. Government surplus or deficit on a cash basis, i.e., its fiscal policy. The greater expenditures are in relation to receipts, the greater the increase in federal debt and in the amount of Treasury securities outstanding. The principal increases in the debt occurred during World War II and to a lesser extent during the depression of the thirties and during the period 1966–1968. The type of security used to finance a deficit and the resulting overall maturity composition of the debt are the responsibility of the Treasury. In turn, the debt-management activities of the Treasury are influenced by the level of interest rates, the $4\frac{1}{4}$ per cent coupon-rate ceiling on Treasury bonds imposed by Congress, and a

---

[13]For an analysis of the dealer market, see Allan H. Meltzer and Gert von der Linde, *A Study of the Dealer Market for Federal Securities*, Joint Economic Committee, 86th Cong., 2d sess. (Washington, D.C.: Government Printing Office, 1960).

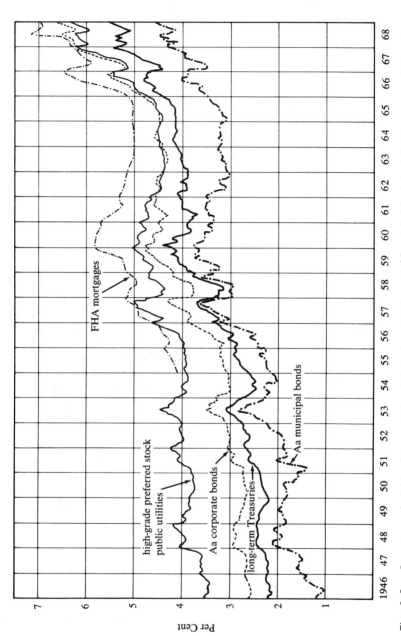

Fig. 6-2. Structure of yields. Source: *Moody's Industrial Manual, Moody's Municipal & Government Manual,* and Solomon Brothers & Hutzler, *An Analytical Record of Yields and Yield Spreads.* FHA mortgage rates are for the

130

desire to lengthen the debt to maintain stability and an orderly schedule of maturing obligations.[14] About two-thirds of the federal securities outstanding are marketable (consisting of bills, tax-anticipation bills, notes, and bonds); the other third is nonmarketable, comprised principally of savings bonds and special issues. The major private investors in Treasury securities are commercial banks and individuals. However, the Federal Reserve and government agency and trust funds, such as Social Security, also are large holders.

Because the U.S. Government security market is the largest fixed-income security market and because of its default-free nature, yields in this market serve as a point of reference for comparative purposes in analyzing other markets. In fact, the yield on very short-term Treasury bills is regarded as a close approximation of the risk-free rate—the base from which a structure of yields is built. By using yields in this market as our standard of comparison, we should gain a better understanding of the market for Treasury securities.[15] Consequently, we shall proceed by taking up the other markets.

Corporate Bonds

Corporate bonds are characterized by varying degrees of default risk, depending upon the issuer. In addition to default risk, these bonds are subject to the risk of being called; this factor is particularly important when interest rates are expected to decline. In general, corporate bonds are not nearly so marketable as are Treasury bonds. Because a high proportion of them are held to maturity, there are relatively few transactions in the secondary market. This market is rather inactive compared with that for Treasury securities. While some transactions occur on organized exchanges, particularly the New York Stock Exchange, the majority of transactions in the secondary market occur in the over-the-counter market. For reasons of default risk, call risk, and poorer marketability, yields on corporate bonds are consistently higher than those on Treasury securities. This relationship can be seen in Fig. 6-2.

It is important to recognize that the yield differential between these two securities is not constant over time; some of the causes for its variation were taken up in Chapter 5. Another cause is the $4\frac{1}{4}$ per cent coupon-rate ceiling on Treasury bonds. Because there is no coupon-rate ceiling on corporates, new long-term issues continually enter the market. Conse-

---

[14] For an analysis of debt management by the Treasury, see Tilford Gaines, *Techniques of Treasury Debt Management* (New York: The Free Press, 1962); and James C. Van Horne and David A. Bowers, "The Liquidity Impact of Debt Management," *The Southern Economic Journal*, XXXIV (April, 1968), 526–37.

[15] For a detailed examination of the market for Treasury securities, see Ira O. Scott, *The Government Securities Market* (New York: McGraw-Hill Book Company, 1965); and G. Walter Woodworth, *The Money Market and Monetary Management* (New York: Harper & Row, Publishers, 1965), Chapter 5.

quently, there are always some bonds outstanding that sell at around their par value. Because of the greater proportion of Treasury bonds selling at a discount, the differential in yield between corporate bonds and Treasury bonds will be greatest when interest rates are high, all other things being the same.

The principal factors affecting the supply of corporate securities are the level of capital expenditures by corporations, their profitability, and their dividend policies. When the economy is prosperous and capital expenditures are high, these expenditures must be financed internally or externally. The profitability of corporations together with their aggregate depreciation determine the total funds generated internally. From these funds must be subtracted total dividends to obtain the amount of internal financing. Capital expenditures and additions to working capital not financed internally, of course, must be financed externally; an important source for such financing is corporate bonds.

Although the supply of corporate bonds is believed to be more sensitive to the level of interest rates than is the supply of Treasury securities, it is still inelastic in many industries. Within a range, certain corporations appear to be willing to borrow for capital expenditures irrespective of the level of interest rates. This behavior would suggest that the expected profitability of the projects being undertaken is significantly higher than the interest rate on borrowings. Beyond a certain point, however, increases in interest rates would be expected to affect the level of capital expenditures at an increasing rate. Interest rates and the supply of corporate bonds then would be determined simultaneously.

The principal investors in corporate bonds are state and local retirement funds, life insurance companies, and private pension funds. In recent years, however, mutual savings banks have made sizable net purchases of corporate bonds. Both life insurance companies and savings banks recently have diverted funds away from home mortgages into corporate bonds where the net yields are considered more attractive. Where once individuals were large investors in corporates on a net basis, the market is now dominated by institutions, of which state and local retirement funds are the fastest growing element. These institutions essentially are long-term investors. Because many hold the bonds until maturity, transactions in the secondary market are small.

Besides the sale of bonds to the public, another major source of long-term funds for corporations is debt placed privately with institutional investors. A private, or direct, placement involves the sale of an entire issue of bonds to a single institutional investor or a small group of such investors. The borrower negotiates directly over the terms of the offering. Private placements increased rapidly during the early to middle 1960s and by 1964 accounted for about two-thirds of the total bond issues. However, with the large increase in corporate bond financing, the composition of financing then shifted toward public offerings, with private placements accounting for only about one-third of the total bond financing by corporations in the late 1960s. The variation in private placements relative to public offerings reflects, in part, the limited capacity of the private placement market to handle volume. When the total volume of corporate bond financing increases sharply, the capacity of institutional investors does not increase proportionately.[16]

There are two costs to consider in comparing a private placement of debt with a public offering: the initial cost and the interest cost. As negotiations usually are direct with a private placement, there are no underwriting or selling expenses. For this reason, the initial cost is less than that of a public offering. Evidence on the interest cost, however, suggests that it is significantly higher on a private than on a public offering. Thus, for a long-term debt issue, the total cost is somewhat higher for a private placement than for a public offering.[17]

Newly Issued Versus Seasoned Corporate Yields

When interest rates in the bond markets are relatively high, yields on newly issued corporate bonds are significantly higher than those on seasoned issues of the same grade and maturity. When interest rates move lower, the differential narrows appreciably. This behavior is illustrated in Fig. 6-3, where yields for newly issued and seasoned Aa Public Utility bonds with a current coupon are shown for the period 1958–1968. We see that during periods of peak interest rates, the differential has been in excess of 40 basis points, while during periods of relatively low interest rates, it has been zero or even slightly negative. As newly issued and seasoned corporates are essentially the same with respect to risk and maturity, we might expect arbitrage to eliminate the differential. Since this is not the case, we must look for the reasons the differential exists.

The most important reasons for the yield differential are the differential impact of taxation and the likelihood of callability. In times of high interest rates, seasoned issues tend to have a lower coupon rate than newly issued corporates; as a result, they sell at a discount. As we know, discount bonds are attractive to investors because of the capital-gains tax and the lower likelihood of their ever being called. For these reasons, seasoned bonds tend to sell at a lower yield to maturity than newly issued bonds do when interest rates are high.

Another cause for the differential in times of rising interest rates is the aversion of security dealers to declining bond prices. Because of the fear of a "frozen" inventory, dealers may be willing to accept smaller profits in order to encourage the quick sale of an issue to investors. More specifically, dealers are said to "sweeten" the yield on new issues to move

---

[16] See Henry Kaufman, *The Changing Dimensions of the Corporate Bond Market* (New York: Salomon Brothers & Hutzler, 1967), p. 11.

[17] See Avery B. Cohan, *Yields on Corporate Debt Directly Placed* (New York: National Bureau of Economic Research, 1967), Chapter 6.

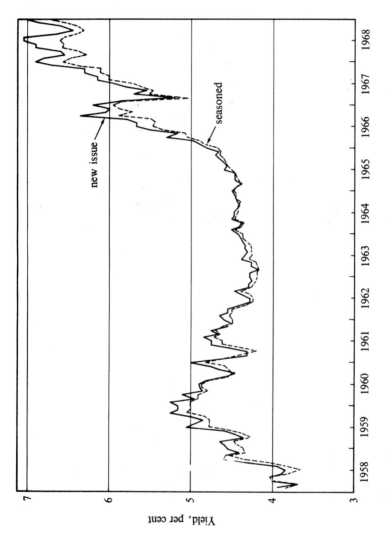

Fig. 6-3. Yields on new issue, callable Aa public utility bonds versus yields on seasoned Aa public utility bonds with current coupon. Source: Solomon Brothers & Hutzler, *An Analytical Record of Yields and Yield Spreads.*

the issue out quickly.[18] With rising interest rates, dealers will suffer considerable loss if an issue is not sold. In addition, the cost of dealer financing to carry inventories of securities is high. Therefore, considerable incentive to sell the issue exists, even if profits must suffer. Moreover, during these times, dealers are reluctant to bid aggressively for new issues. They would rather miss buying an issue than risk unnecessarily pricing the issue at too high a price to the public. Cautious bidding, of course, will result in lower prices and higher yields.[19] Thus, the behavior of dealers also may contribute to the tendency for new issues to provide higher yields than do seasoned bonds when interest rates are rising.

Conard and Freudenthal tested for the influence of dealer behavior on the yield differential for Aa corporate bonds over the period 1951–1960. For the dependent variable, they corrected the yield differential between newly issued and seasoned bonds for the coupon effect. For explanatory variables, they employed lagged changes in yields, the recent volume of new issues, and the current Treasury bill rate. Using multiple regression analysis, they found all of the variables to be positive and significant, suggesting that when interest rates are high and rising and when volume is heavy, the differential in yield between seasoned bonds and new issues widens. This evidence is consistent with dealers' sweetening the yield to investors and bidding lower prices when there is fear of capital loss.[20] However, the predominant factor affecting the yield differential is the differential impact of taxation.

Municipal Securities

The distinguishing feature of municipal securities is their tax-exempt status. For this reason, yields are lower than those on other securities; this relationship is shown in Fig. 6-2. Because of the tax-exempt feature, municipals are of interest mainly to individuals in high tax brackets and to corporations paying taxes at the full corporate tax rate. A nonprofit organization, which pays no taxes, would have little reason to invest in municipal securities, considering that yields on default-free Treasury securities are higher. Similarly, life insurance companies, which pay only a limited tax, are able to take only partial advantage of the tax-exempt feature.

There are two principal types of municipal securities: general credit obligations and revenue bonds. General obligation bonds are backed by the "full faith and credit" of the municipality—i.e., its full taxing power. Revenue bonds, however, are backed only by the revenue of the specific project and not by the taxing power of the municipality. An example

---

[18]See Joseph W. Conard, *The Behavior of Interest Rates* (New York: National Bureau of Economic Research, 1966), pp. 113–15.

[19]See Andrew F. Brimmer, "Credit Conditions and Price Determination in the Corporate Bond Market," *Journal of Finance*, XV (September, 1960), 440–43.

[20]Conard, *The Behavior of Interest Rates*, pp. 109–16.

of a revenue-bond issue is one to build a toll road. Because of the greater risk of revenue bonds, they must provide higher yields to maturity. Two other types of securities that fall under the classification of municipal securities are obligations of local public housing authorities, which are guaranteed by the Public Housing Administration, and industrial aid bonds. The latter have been used by municipalities in the past to encourage new industry. A municipality would finance the construction of new facilities for a company by issuing revenue bonds and then lease the facilities to the company. Because the borrower was a municipality, interest on the bonds was tax exempt to investors. Thus, the municipality was able to borrow at an interest rate lower than that which the company would have had to pay; and these savings were passed on to the company in the form of lower lease payments. Although industrial aid bonds helped municipalities attract industry, by the late 1960s the volume had grown so that it placed quite a strain on the municipal market. The marginal result was higher interest costs for the construction of schools and other noncorporate facilities. In 1968, Congress revoked the tax-exempt privilege of industrial aid bonds, and it is doubtful that it ever will be restored.

Municipal securities, like corporates, are subject to default risk and are rated by Moody's and Standard and Poor's as to their probability of default. Factors considered include the municipality's taxing base, existing debt in relation to this base, and the variability of tax revenues. As discussed earlier in this chapter, relatively few municipal securities have a call feature, so the investor is seldom subjected to call risk. Moreover, a reasonable secondary market exists for municipal securities. While this market is not so strong as that for Treasury securities, it is more viable than that for corporates. Unlike corporates, a small proportion of long-term municipal bonds are held to final maturity; as a result, there are more transactions in the secondary market.

The supply of municipal securities is the result of expenditures by state and local governments in excess of their tax revenues. Since World War II, the debt of these governments has increased steadily and rapidly. There is indication, however, that municipalities are more sensitive to the level of interest rates than either the Treasury or corporations. As a result, the supply of securities is affected by interest rates, the two being determined simultaneously. Some municipalities actually have statutes specifying the maximum interest rate that can be paid. They are forced to postpone bond issues if market rates are above that maximum.

As a result of the tax-exempt feature, the demand for municipal securities is relatively segmented. The market consists mainly of commercial banks, wealthy individuals, and fire and casualty companies. Since the early 1960s, however, the market has been dominated by commercial banks, which have accounted for over two-thirds of the net purchases. Because of this dominance, the behavior of commercial banks is very important in explaining differentials in yields between municipals and other securities. When banks experience a period of tight money and high loan demand, their relative commitment to municipal securities declines. As a result, investment in new issues must be filled by other investors, primarily individuals. The consequence of this action is that municipal yields tend to rise relative to interest rates in other markets. This was evident in both the 1966 and the 1969 periods of tight money. The narrow market for municipal securities, the fluctuating behavior of commercial banks, and the heavy demand for funds by municipalities make yields subject to more variation than is true in other markets. This variation is somewhat evident in Fig. 6-2. The dominance of commercial banks on the demand side also affects the term structure of interest rates for municipal securities. Because of the nature of their deposit liabilities, banks are interested primarily in the shorter maturities. Very seldom will a bank purchase a long-term municipal. As a result, there is greater relative demand for short-term securities than for long-term securities. Accordingly, the yield curve for municipals is almost always upward sloping. Only for a few months during 1966 when interest rates were at then historical highs was it horizontal. The term structure for municipal securities appears to be influenced by market segmentation— an influence that has not received strong support as an explanation for the term structure for Treasury securities.[21]

In the past and to a lesser extent recently, there has been evidence of monopsony in the underwriting and distribution of municipal securities.[22] In many cases, only one bid is received for an issue, with the result that the state or local government does not receive the benefits possible with competitive bids. In testing the effect of the number of bidders on the interest cost to the issuer, Richard West found that those municipal issuers which received only one bid paid higher net interest costs than issuers which received multiple bids. On the basis of this study, it would appear advantageous for state and local governments to encourage multiple bidding, thereby realizing a lower interest cost. While small issuers may be unsuccessful in this regard, other issuers may be able to attract multiple bids where before only single bids were received.

One of the interesting features of the municipal market is the value placed on tax exemption. By and large, this exemption is not fully priced in the market place. If we assume a marginal tax rate of 50 per cent for the typical investor in the market (and this rate may be reasonable), the average yield on Aaa municipals for 1965, 1966, 1967, and 1968 on a before-tax basis would be 6.32 per cent, 7.34 per cent, 7.48 per cent, and 8.40 per cent, respectively. These adjusted yields are considerably in excess of the average yields on Aaa corporates of 4.49 per cent, 5.13 per cent,

---

[21] See Roland I. Robinson, *Postwar Market for State and Local Government Securities* (New York: National Bureau of Economic Research, 1960), pp. 180–88.

[22] See Richard West, "New Issue Concessions on Municipal Bonds: A Case of Monopsony Pricing," *Journal of Business*, XXXVIII (April, 1965), 135–48; and West, "More on the Effects of Municipal Bond Monopsony," *Journal of Business*, XXXIX (April, 1966), 305–8.

5.51 per cent, and 6.18 per cent, respectively, for the period 1965–1968. If Aaa-grade municipals and corporates are roughly comparable with respect to other qualities, this suggests that municipalities are not obtaining the full benefit from the tax-exemption feature. A substantial portion of it goes to investors.

The reason for this occurrence is that a limited number of investors are able to take advantage of the feature, resulting in a narrow market. State and local governments might be better off with a direct subsidy from the federal government and the sale of bonds without the tax-exemption feature. (The federal government foregoes substantial tax revenues in order to aid these governments.) If the interest income on municipal securities were taxed fully and the federal government provided municipalities with the taxes it received from investors, the municipalities might receive greater benefits than they presently do. To be sure, municipalities would pay a higher interest cost, but they would be appealing to a broader market. The higher interest cost would likely be more than offset by the subsidy.[23] However, since it is unclear what the marginal tax bracket of the typical investor in taxable municipal securities would be, a definitive statement as to whether municipalities would be better off is not possible.

The portion of the tax-exempt feature going to investors varies over time depending upon the differential in yield between municipal and other securities. When interest rates on municipals are high relative to other rates, the investors' portion increases; when municipal rates are relatively low, the investors' portion narrows. In all cases in recent years, however, municipalities have received less than the full value of the tax-exempt feature. Robinson maintains that to market the increasing volume of municipals, new investors have to be found who place a lower marginal value on the tax-exempt feature.[24] As a result, the investors' portion of the tax-exempt feature has risen in the overall post-World War II period.

Preferred Stock

Preferred stock is a hybrid form of security, combining most of the features of debt with some of those of common stock. In the event of liquidation, the preferred stockholders' claim on assets comes before that of common stockholders. Although preferred stock carries a stipulated dividend rate, the actual payment of a dividend is a discretionary rather than a fixed obligation of the company. The omission of a dividend will not result in a default of the obligation as will the nonpayment of interest or principal on a debt contract. Consequently, the risk of nonpayment of income on an issue of preferred stock is greater than that on the bonds of the same company. As practically all preferred stocks are callable, the investor is subject to this type of risk.

---

[23] For a further analysis of this point, see Robinson, *Postwar Market for State and Local Government Securities*, Chapter 6.

[24] Robinson, *Postwar Market for State and Local Government Securities*, p. 159.

Because the maximum return to preferred stockholders usually is limited to the specified dividend and these stockholders do not share in the residual earnings of the company, we treat preferred stock as a fixed-income security rather than as an equity security. For corporate income-tax purposes, preferred stock dividends are not considered an expense, as are interest payments on debt. Hence preferred stock is little used as a method of financing. During the period 1960–1968, it accounted for only about 4 per cent of the total external long-term financing by corporations; and a substantial portion of this percentage was comprised of convertible issues. The marketability of most preferred stocks is quite good, as many are traded on a major stock exchange.

Because of the lower claim on assets and the dividends being a discretionary rather than a contractual obligation of the corporation, we would expect preferred stocks to yield more than bonds of the same risk class. Through the early 1960s this relationship held, as shown in Fig. 6-2. However, by the middle of the decade, the differential had narrowed so that preferred stocks sometimes yielded less. The cause for this narrowing can be attributed to the increasing popularity of preferred stocks as investments for corporations. This popularity is due to a special tax feature: For the corporate investor, 85 per cent of dividends received are exempt from federal income taxes. As a result, preferred stocks are attractive investments for corporations relative to other fixed-income securities. Despite the greater risk, we therefore have seen yields on them at lower levels than those on corporate bonds.

Mortgages

Of all the fixed-income securities examined in this chapter, the mortgage market is the least perfect. Only in recent years has it taken on the status of a national market; previously, it was largely an aggregation of local markets. Except for the Treasury security market, however, it is by far the largest market. The major portion of the market (about three-quarters) is comprised of residential mortgages, including apartments. Other classes include mortgages on commercial and industrial buildings and farm mortgages. Residential mortgages are of two types: insured (or guaranteed) and conventional. In the first category, the Federal Housing Administration (FHA) insures the lender against loss on mortgages meeting its specifications. For this insurance, a fee of $\frac{1}{2}$ per cent is charged; and the FHA sets ceilings on the coupon rate that can be charged. In addition to the FHA, the Veterans Administration (VA) guarantees mortgage loans made to veterans who purchase homes. Interest-rate ceilings are set for these too, but no fee is charged for the guarantee. The coupon-rate ceilings on FHA and VA mortgages have resulted in their selling at discounts when market rates of interest are high. Because of political pressure to make mortgage financing available to home owners on attractive terms, the FHA and VA frequently have been reluctant to raise their ceilings to market levels. These ceilings and the discounts which result have probably hampered the flow of funds into mortgages, tending to increase rather than to decrease rates.

A conventional mortgage is one where the lender assumes the full risk of default, there being no insurance or guarantee. Of all residential mortgages, over three-quarters are conventional. The default risk on a conventional mortgage loan varies according to the credit worthiness of the borrower, his ability to service debt, the ratio of the loan to the value of the property, economic conditions in the community, and economic conditions generally. In a portfolio of conventional mortgages there are bound to be some delinquencies and default losses. Just how many there are will depend upon the quality standards of the lender at the time of purchase, the diversification achieved, and subsequent economic conditions.[25] FHA-insured and VA-guaranteed mortgages ensure that the lender eventually will get his money back. However, there is considerable red tape and delay involved in foreclosure and final settlement, all of which involve an opportunity cost.

Mortgages do not have a specific call feature as such; the borrower is able to pay off the loan at any time. The lender, however, can impose a prepayment penalty on payment before a certain time has elapsed. Prepayment penalties occur more frequently when interest rates are high and mortgage funds are scarce; the lender, accordingly, is in a strong bargaining position. Although the original length of a typical mortgage is over 20 years, its actual duration is much shorter. The periodic sale of existing homes means that many mortgages are paid off before financial maturity. Other mortgages are paid off for the purpose of refinancing at lower rates. Thus, a lender constantly must make new mortgage loans simply to maintain his portfolio at a given level. Because the size of the typical mortgage is small relative to other types of investment, a certain nuisance factor is involved for the investor.

The supply of mortgages is dependent upon building activity and upon interest rates. There is little question that supply is extremely sensitive to the level of rates. When mortgage rates rise sharply, potential home buyers tend to postpone purchases, and builders curtail their construction activity. Probably more than in any other market, the supply of mortgages is very dependent on interest rates.

The principal investors in this market are savings and loan associations, commercial banks, savings banks, and life insurance companies. In recent years, life insurance companies have largely withdrawn from home mortgages on a net basis in favor of corporate bonds and other investments considered more attractive in yield. However, insurance companies are still active in commercial mortgages. The other major investors depend upon the savings flows they receive. In turn, these flows are affected by the

---

[25] For a detailed evaluation of the mortgage market, see Saul B. Klaman, *The Postwar Residential Mortgage Market* (New York: National Bureau of Economic Research, 1961); and Sherman J. Maisel, *Financing Real Estate* (New York: McGraw-Hill Book Company, 1965).

regulated rates that they are able to offer savers. Savings and loan associations and savings banks, in particular, usually suffer from reduced flows of savings when interest rates rise sharply in relation to the rates that they are able to pay. As a result, the flow of funds available for mortgage financing is reduced. When this effect, known as *disintermediation*, occurs, there is evidence that these institutions ration funds for mortgage loans on a basis other than price. In other words, the mortgage rate does not rise sufficiently to clear the market. It might well be argued that if interest rates were allowed to seek their own level, more funds would flow into this market, particularly from life insurance companies and savings banks.

There is a significant cost to servicing a mortgage, unlike the other securities we have studied. The initial, or closing, costs involve a title search, appraising the property, preparing the mortgage papers, and filing the lien. These costs usually are charged to the borrower at the time the loan is made. In addition, however, there are regular costs incurred in collecting mortgage payments (usually monthly), maintaining records, keeping track of insurance and tax payments, and making periodic inspections of the property to make sure it is being maintained properly. To determine the rate of return on a mortgage, it is necessary to deduct the cost of servicing the mortgage from the contract rate. Therefore, the mortgage rates shown in Fig. 6-2 are net of estimated servicing costs of $\frac{1}{2}$ per cent.

A lender does not have to service the mortgage himself. Mortgage bankers exist in local areas throughout the country; and they are in business to originate mortgages in that area, locate lenders, and service the mortgages after a lender is found. Life insurance companies and savings banks frequently purchase mortgages outside of their own area through mortgage bankers. The mortgage banker will service the mortgage after it is sold, thereby representing the lender throughout the duration of the loan. The lender benefits from this arrangement by not having to maintain local offices to originate and service mortgages. The typical service fee is $\frac{3}{8}$ to $\frac{1}{2}$ of 1 per cent per year. Savings and loan associations almost always originate and service their own mortgages in their local areas, while commercial banks sometimes work through mortgage bankers and purchase mortgages outside their area.

The secondary market for mortgages is relatively weak, although existing mortgages can be sold. The sale of them usually is negotiated either directly by the buyer and the seller or through a mortgage broker. With FHA and VA loans, a degree of uniformity exists in the quality of home as well as in the terms of the mortgage. This uniformity facilitates the sale of existing mortgages. The Federal National Mortgage Association (Fanny May) was started in the late 1930s to provide a secondary market for FHA mortgages. The FNMA does this by issuing its own debt instruments and purchasing mortgages. However, the organization has not lived up to its original expectations; it has tended to support the market by purchasing mortgages in times of tight money but has done little to make a viable secondary market. While the secondary market for mortgages has improved significantly, it is still small; and geographical differentials in rates continue to exist. Little in the way of a secondary market exists in rates continue to exist. Little in the way of a secondary market exists for conventional mortgages. The majority of mortgages never change hands between the time of origin and the time of final payment.[26] Overall, then, the marketability of mortgages can be considered only fair.

Yields on mortgages typically have been significantly higher than yields on other fixed-income securities, as seen in Fig. 6-2. This differential has been attributed to the relatively poor marketability of the instrument, the specialized nature of investment, and the general lack of call protection to the investor. Because most lenders raise or lower their rates by $\frac{1}{4}$, or even $\frac{1}{2}$, per cent at discrete intervals, mortgage rates tend to be less volatile than rates on other fixed-income securities. In general, they tend to lag behind. Moreover, there is a tendency for the yield differential between mortgages and rates on other securities to be widest when interest rates are relatively low and for it to narrow appreciably as interest rates rise. This behavior results not only from the lag in adjustment but also from a seeming upper resistance in mortgage rates.

The resistance is caused by interest-rate ceilings established by the FHA and VA, an aversion to discount these mortgages, regulatory limits on rates paid on savings (which place implied limits of sorts on the differential between mortgage rates and savings rates), efforts by the Federal Home Loan Bank to make funds available to savings and loan associations during periods of tight money, and social and political pressure against high mortgage rates. These factors have caused institutions to ration mortgage funds in times of high interest rates by increasing down-payment requirements and tightening other credit standards rather than by raising interest rates.

We see in Fig. 6-2 that the differential between mortgage rates (net of the $\frac{1}{2}$ per cent service fee) and corporate bond rates narrowed during 1967 and 1968 to the point where corporates were yielding more at times. This phenomenon can be attributed to the lag in adjustment of mortgage rates to other rates and to the upper resistance in mortgage rates. However, in mid-1968, mortgage rates rose sharply and kept well above corporate rates for the remainder of the year. There was some indication that home buyers had become accustomed to the higher level of interest rates on mortgages. In addition, life insurance companies and savings banks had turned away from residential mortgages for more attractive investment outlets. With their withdrawal and the growing acceptance of higher rates by potential borrowers, rates on mortgages reached new highs.

[26]Raymond W. Goldsmith, *The Flow of Capital Funds in the Postwar Economy* (New York: National Bureau of Economic Research, 1965), p. 278.

Summary

Additional factors that influence relative yields in the market place are callability and taxability. While the call feature gives the borrower flexibility in refinancing, it works to the disadvantage of the investor. If a security is called, the investor usually suffers an opportunity loss because he can invest in other bonds only at a sacrifice in yield. For this reason, the call feature usually has value when interest rates are relatively high. By value, we mean that there is a differential between what the callable bond yields and what it would yield if it were noncallable. The call feature usually has value as long as there is a probability that the issue might be called. In turn, this probability depends upon interest-rate expectations. The call feature may provide for either an immediate call at the discretion of the issuer or a deferred call, which is a call permitted only after a specified deferment period. Empirical evidence on immediately callable and deferred callable bonds is consistent with the call feature's having the most value when interest rates are relatively high and little or no value when they are low. Practically all corporate-bond and preferred-stock issues have call features, whereas municipal securities seldom do. Treasury bonds sometimes provide for callability several years before final maturity, but there the purpose is somewhat different than in the case of a corporation.

The differential impact of taxation also results in differentials in yields between different securities. When a security sells at a discount from its par value because of a coupon rate lower than prevailing yields, part of the yield to maturity is a capital gain. The favorable tax treatment of capital gains makes discount bonds attractive to investors. In addition, the federal estate tax makes certain Treasury bonds selling at a discount attractive because they can be redeemed at par in settlement of the tax. These factors result in upward pressure on prices and downward pressure on yields for the discount bonds relative to bonds selling closer to their par values. When interest rates are relatively high, seasoned corporate bonds sell at a lower yield than do newly issued bonds. The principal explanation for this difference is coupon-rate effect, since seasoned bonds tend to sell at a discount. Also, the cautiousness of dealers when interest rates are rising contributes to the differential.

Finally, the structure of yields and the markets for various long-term fixed-income securities were examined. The securities studied were Treasury bonds, corporate bonds, municipal bonds, preferred stock, and mortgages. Yield differentials for these securities were evaluated in relation to their default risk, marketability, maturity, callability, and taxability. These factors were examined in relation to the supply and demand forces in each of the markets. The important characteristics of each market were evaluated in relation to observed interest rates.

Selected References

Brimmer, Andrew J., "Credit Conditions and Price Determination in the Corporate Bond Market," *Journal of Finance*, XV (September, 1960), 353–70.

Cohan, Avery B., *Yields on Corporate Debt Directly Placed*. New York: National Bureau of Economic Research, 1967.

Conard, Joseph W., *The Behavior of Interest Rates*. New York: National Bureau of Economic Research, 1966.

Homer, Sidney, *A History of Interest Rates*. New Brunswick, N.J.: Rutgers University Press, 1963.

Jen, Frank C., and James E. Wert, "The Value of the Deferred Call Privilege," *National Banking Review*, 3 (March, 1966), 369–78.

———, "The Deferred Call Provision and Corporate Bond Yields," *Journal of Financial and Quantitative Analysis*, III (June, 1968), 157–69.

Kaufman, Henry, *The Changing Dimensions of the Corporate Bond Market*. New York: Salomon Brothers & Hutzler, 1967.

Klaman, Saul B., *The Postwar Residential Mortgage Market*. New York: National Bureau of Economic Research, 1961.

Maisel, Sherman J., *Financing Real Estate*. New York: McGraw-Hill Book Company, 1965.

Pye, Gordon, "The Value of the Call Option on a Bond," *Journal of Political Economy*, LXXIV (April, 1966), 200–205.

———, "The Value of Call Deferment on a Bond: Some Empirical Results," *Journal of Finance*, XXII (December, 1967), 623–36.

Robinson, Roland I., *The Postwar Market for State and Local Government Securities*. New York: National Bureau of Economic Research, 1960.

Scott, Ira O., *The Government Securities Market*. New York: McGraw-Hill Book Company, 1965.

Winn, Willis J., and Arleigh Hess, Jr., "The Value of the Call Privilege," *Journal of Finance* (1959), reprinted on pp. 234–46 in James Van Horne, ed., *Foundations for Financial Management*. Homewood, Ill.: Richard D. Irwin, Inc., 1966.

Woodworth, G. Walter, *The Money Market and Monetary Management*, Chapter 5. New York: Harper & Row, Publishers, 1965.

Equity Securities

So far, our examination of returns has been confined to fixed-income securities. Because of the special nature of common stock and securities convertible into common stock, discussion of them was postponed purposely. In this chapter, we consider supply and demand conditions in the market for common stocks, the problems involved in measuring returns, the rationality of the pricing mechanism, and finally, the valuation of, and the calculation of expected returns for, convertible securities.

Supply and Demand

In recent years, the most notable feature of the market for common stocks has been the small amount of net new issues and the heavy demand for equity securities. Since World War II, corporations have relied predominantly upon internal financing and increases in their debt to finance expansion. In Table 7-1, one sees that equity issues accounted for a very small proportion of their total financing. This lack of equity financing is surprising in view of the sharp rise in stock prices during the last 15 to 20 years. A number of reasons can be offered for the inelasticity of supply, most of which are subjective. To place them in proper perspective, however, we first must investigate when a firm should issue stock from a theoretical standpoint.

TABLE 7-1   Financing of Nonfinancial Corporations
1956–1968, billions of dollars

	Total Sources	Internal Sources	Undistributed Profits	External Sources	Stocks	Bonds
1956	47.2	28.9	13.2	18.3	2.3	3.6
1957	42.0	30.6	11.8	11.4	2.4	6.3
1958	42.2	29.5	8.3	12.7	2.1	5.7
1959	55.5	35.0	12.6	20.5	2.2	3.0
1960	47.3	34.4	10.0	12.9	1.6	3.5
1961	54.7	35.6	10.2	19.1	2.5	4.6
1962	63.3	41.8	12.4	21.5	0.6	4.6
1963	65.9	43.9	13.6	22.0	0.3	3.9
1964	70.2	50.5	18.3	19.7	1.4	4.0
1965	89.3	56.6	23.1	32.7	—	5.4
1966	99.1	61.1	24.4	38.0	1.2	10.2
1967	94.0	61.5	20.7	32.5	2.3	15.1
1968	109.1	63.8	21.3	45.3	0.2	13.4

Source: *Economic Report of the President*, 1969.

Negligible Supply

If a company has an investment opportunity that provides a return equal to or in excess of the opportunity cost of funds employed in the project, it should accept the project. If we assume an objective of maximizing the value of the firm to its shareholders, this opportunity cost should be the rate of return on the project that will leave unchanged the market price of the firm's stock. Thus, if the acceptance of an investment project is expected to result in a higher market price, the project should be accepted, and the firm should raise capital to finance it. As long as investment projects are expected to provide a return greater than that required by investors at the margin, the firm is justified in undertaking the projects and financing them.[1]

A firm should issue common stock as a part of its total financing if it is advantageous for it to do so. Although common-stock financing will result in a temporary dilution in earnings per share, this dilution should at least be offset by the expected future returns from the project. This does not suggest that new common stock necessarily need be issued. To the extent that the number of investment opportunities is limited, it may be possible to finance growth through the retention of earnings and the debt that the increased equity base will support. Earnings retention has several advantages over common-stock financing. For one thing, the sale of stock is "lumpy" and is best suited to raising large blocks of capital at one time, while the retention of earnings is steadier over time and therefore is

[1] The rationale for the normative behavior described above is taken up in James C. Van Horne, *Financial Management and Policy* (Englewood Cliffs, N.J.: Prentice-Hall, Inc., 1968), Chapters 1–9.

better suited to financing a steady stream of capital expenditures. In addition, flotation costs and the underpricing of a new issue of stock make it a more expensive method of financing. Finally, the differential tax rate between dividend income and capital gains creates a bias in favor of the retention of earnings. Thus, the retention of earnings has several advantages over the sale of common stock.

However, retention represents dividends foregone by stockholders; therefore, investors' preferences must be considered. If investors have a systematic preference for current dividends over capital gains, this preference may partially or wholly offset the advantage of earnings retention.[2] Overall, however, there may be theoretical justification for retaining earnings rather than selling common stock. Firms without reasonably abundant investment opportunities simply may have no occasion to sell common stock. Earnings retention, the debt that these retained earnings will support, and funds provided through depreciation may be sufficient to finance all acceptable investment opportunities.

However, there is sufficient evidence to believe that some companies simply avoid the sale of common stock no matter how attractive their investment opportunities are. In some of these situations, the sale of common stock as part of a total mix of financing used to finance worthwhile investments would be in the best interests of common stockholders. In essence, these companies engage in capital rationing, for they place a constraint on the funds to be invested during a specific period of time. Investment opportunities may be foregone that would enhance the market price of the company's stock; as a result, capital is less than efficiently allocated.

One reason for the reluctance of management to sell common stock is the immediate dilution that results. Upon announcement of the offering (or before, if rumors are out), the market price of the stock usually drops. In the long run, however, this initial dilution in the earnings per share would be expected to be more than offset by the expected gains from the investment projects undertaken. Otherwise, common stock should not be sold. Another reason for the reluctance to sell common stock is the inconvenience. A great deal of work is necessary to prepare papers, register the issue with the Securities and Exchange Commission, negotiate with underwriters, etc. In an interview study of a number of large companies, Gordon Donaldson discovered an almost complete avoidance of common-stock financing.[3] Reasons for this avoidance included the fear of dilution, the risk of having to maintain cash dividends on the additional shares issued, and the feeling that retained earnings had no cost. In many of the financial executives interviewed Donaldson found an attitude of "playing

---

[2] For an analysis of this point, together with the Modigliani-Miller argument for the irrelevance of dividends (i.e., investors are indifferent between dividends and the retention of earnings), see Van Horne, *Financial Management and Policy*, Chapter 8.

[3] *Corporate Debt Capacity* (Boston: Division of Research, Harvard Business School, 1961), Chapter 3.

it safe" and an unwillingness to subject themselves to possible criticism from outside suppliers of capital. A few executives even stated that they would not sell stock under any circumstances. In summary, it seems clear that certain companies avoid the use of common-stock financing even when it might be in their best interest.

To compound the problem of supply, a growing number of companies are repurchasing their own stock. Repurchase of stock can be justified theoretically when there is a lack of acceptable investment opportunities and the firm wishes to distribute excess funds. When stock is repurchased with the full intention of retiring it, the transaction can be treated as an alternative to paying cash dividends.[4] Although they were once greatly reluctant to repurchase their own stock, companies are doing so increasingly. Thus, we see a continuation of the reluctance by some companies to employ equity financing, while other companies, justifiably, are reducing the number of shares outstanding through repurchase. The result is that there is little net increase in common stock outstanding. As evident in Table 7-1, common-stock financing has declined as a proportion of the total source of funds for nonfinancial corporations. The supply of securities, then, is relatively inelastic.

Vigorous Demand

On the other side of the supply-demand scissors, all indications point to a great increase in underlying demand for common stocks. With inflation and the differential tax treatment favoring capital gains over ordinary income, common stocks have proven to be an extremely popular store of value since the early 1950s. Moreover, the composition of holdings has shifted toward greater ownership by institutional investors and less by individuals. For stocks on the New York Stock Exchange, the percentage of total market value held by institutions increased from 12.7 per cent in 1949 to 22.4 per cent in 1968. If bank-administered funds are added to those of the institutions, the proportion came to about one-third in 1968.[5]

Since 1945, there has been a sharp growth in the net purchase of common stocks by mutual funds. This growth resulted from an intensive sales effort and from an ever-increasing emphasis upon performance. While the greater portion of the money invested in mutual funds would have flowed directly into the market if mutual funds had not existed, a significant portion probably would not have. Thus, the growth in mutual funds would seem to have resulted in a net injection of funds into the stock market.[6] Moreover, an increasing percentage of the portfolios of other institutional investors is being invested in common stocks. The

---

[4] See Van Horne, *Financial Management and Policy*, pp. 208–11.

[5] *New York Stock Exchange Fact Book*, 1969, p. 45.

[6] Irwin Friend, F. E. Brown, Edward S. Herman, and Douglas Vickers, *A Study of Mutual Funds*, Report of the Committee on Inter-state and Foreign Commerce, 87th Cong., 2d sess., August 28, 1962, p. 359.

result of these factors is that individuals increasingly are becoming indirect rather than direct owners of common stocks. As long as this pattern of behavior continues, prices of common stocks will be bid up by institutions purchasing stocks on a net basis from individuals. The total number of investors in publicly held common stocks has increased greatly since World War II, from about 5 million in 1950 to over 26 million in 1969.[7] Thus, concurrent with the increase in ownership of common stocks by institutions has been a decline in the average number of shares owned by individuals.

In recent years, institutional investors have become very performance oriented. As Edmund A. Mennis points out in his evaluation of these investors, the word "performance" is construed to mean appreciation in capital, to the exclusion of almost everything else.[8] Moreover, it is not capital appreciation over the long run that is important, but very short-term changes in portfolio value. In fact, institutions are judged on their daily capital appreciation. This obsession with very short-run capital appreciation has relegated risk (as depicted by the stability of stock-price movements about a trend) and dividend income to very secondary roles.

With short-term capital appreciation as the primary goal, there has been an understandable and discernible change in the investment behavior of institutions. They have tended to invest more heavily in risky stocks where the prospect for short-run capital appreciation is greatest. This behavior has occurred particularly in mutual funds, but it is evident also on the part of other institutional investors. Institutions must show performance to make a favorable impression on savers who place funds in their stewardship. However, the total number of stocks meeting the performance criterion is limited. Moreover, larger institutions are unable to invest effectively in issues when the number of shares outstanding is small. An investment in such a stock would have only a modest effect on their total portfolio. In addition, institutions seek stocks that are marketable. They do not want to have a large position in a stock for which the market is so limited that if they want to sell, they will have to make a large price concession. Marketability is extremely important, for few institutions want to be left "holding the bag."

Seeking marketable stocks with good prospects for short-term capital appreciation reduces greatly the number of stocks available for potential investment. Consequently, there tends to be concentration in the stock holdings of institutional investors.[9] Many institutions are interested in the same stocks. When a particular stock is favored, it may show considerable capital appreciation because of the concentration of buying. However, stocks and industries come into favor and go out. When a stock goes out of favor, the concentration of ownership works in reverse. Here, institu-

---

[7] *New York Exchange Fact Book*, 1969, p. 43.

[8] "New Trends in Institutional Investing," *Financial Analysts Journal*, 24 (July–August, 1968), 133–38.

[9] Mennis, "New Trends in Institutional Investing," p. 135.

tions getting out unload their stock on individual investors, with a depressing influence on price. The problem is not that an institution is able to sell a stock; indeed, a free market demands it. Rather, the problem is in the concentration of selling. News travels very fast among institutional investors, particularly among mutual funds. As soon as several appear to be selling a particular stock, others may join in, not wanting to be left holding a stock that is no longer in favor.

To the extent that the purchase or sale of stocks is based upon a "band wagon" effect of doing what others are doing, the increasing importance of institutional investors in the market makes it inherently more volatile. Certain institutional investors may gear their activity to what they believe others will do and to market psychology rather than to any appraisal of underlying value. They can be likened to the competitors in Keynes' famous beauty contest, where the winner is the one who picks the face that most closely corresponds to the average preferences of all competitors:

> . . . so each competitor has to pick, not those faces which he himself finds prettiest, but those which he thinks likeliest to catch the fancy of the other competitors, all of whom are looking at the problem from the same point of view.[10]

The concern with performance relative to one's competitors has made certain institutional investors quick to join any change in sentiment toward a stock or toward a group of stocks. While the notion of increased volatility in stock prices because of the concentration of buying and selling power has not been tested empirically,[11] we do know that the transactions activity of institutional investors has increased. For example, the activity ratio of stocks on the New York Stock Exchange held by mutual funds increased from about 20 per cent in 1965 to well over 40 per cent in 1968.[12] The activity ratios for pension funds and life insurance companies also have increased; however, they are considerably lower than those for mutual funds.

Although it has been said that institutional investors contribute to the stability of the market, such a statement today would be naïve. All indications point to certain stock prices' being more volatile as a result of the concentration of ownership. The concentration of wealth in institutions, the limited number of stocks in which they can invest, their objective of short-term capital appreciation, and the ready availability of information about each other's activities make this increased volatility almost inevitable. The smaller, less-informed investor may well be hurt by sharp changes in price. Whether or not he is placed at an unfair disadvantage,

---

[10] John Maynard Keynes, *The General Theory of Employment Interest and Money* (New York: Harcourt, Brace & World, Inc., 1936), p. 156.

[11] The Securities and Exchange Commission currently is conducting a study to test this notion.

[12] *New York Stock Exchange Fact Book*, 1969, p. 46.

however, is unclear. The concentration of buying and selling power in the hands of institutional investors may have little or no effect upon long-run equilibrium prices of common stocks. The adjustment in prices toward equilibrium simply may be more volatile. Discussion of the random-walk theory later in this chapter will cast additional light on whether stock prices rationally portray the true value of ownership of a corporation.

Price Trends

Since World War II, common stocks have shown appreciation in price far in excess of that for goods and services. From 1945 through 1968, the Standard & Poor's 500 stock index increased six-fold. During this same period of time, consumer prices and wholesale prices doubled, as shown in Table 7-2. We note that from the beginning of 1950, when stocks first

TABLE 7-2   Wholesale, Consumer, and
Stock Price Indexes (1940–1968)

	Wholesale Price Index	Consumer Price Index	Standard & Poor's 500 Stock Index
1940	43.0	48.8	11.02
1941	47.8	51.3	9.82
1942	54.0	56.8	8.67
1943	56.5	60.3	11.50
1944	56.9	61.3	12.47
1945	57.9	62.7	15.16
1946	66.1	68.0	17.08
1947	81.2	77.8	15.17
1948	87.9	83.8	15.53
1949	83.5	83.0	15.23
1950	86.8	83.8	18.40
1951	96.7	90.5	22.34
1952	94.0	92.5	24.50
1953	92.7	93.2	24.73
1954	92.9	93.6	29.69
1955	93.2	93.3	40.49
1956	96.2	94.7	46.62
1957	99.0	98.0	44.38
1958	100.4	100.7	46.24
1959	100.6	101.5	57.38
1960	100.7	103.1	55.85
1961	100.3	104.2	66.27
1962	100.6	105.4	62.38
1963	100.3	106.7	69.87
1964	100.5	108.1	81.37
1965	102.5	109.9	88.17
1966	105.9	113.1	85.26
1967	106.1	116.3	91.93
1968	108.7	120.9	98.70

Source: *Economic Report of the President*, 1969.

began to increase significantly in value, through 1968, the increase in stock prices relative to other price indexes was even more pronounced. Thus, common stocks have been an extremely effective hedge against inflation; this has been one of their principal attractions. In the postwar period, investors have come to regard purchasing-power risk as more insidious than default risk. One reason for this feeling has been the prolonged period of economic prosperity, with only short-lived recessions. As a result, investors' fear of default, which prevailed earlier in this century, has diminished in importance. As long as common-stock prices increase relative to other prices in the economy, they attract increased interest, which in turn further enhances market prices.

As a result of the relatively fixed supply of common stock and the increasing demand for stocks as investments, there has been a sharp increase in trading activity as well as in the market values of stocks. The market itself is dominated by the exchange of existing securities in the secondary market. The average daily volume of shares traded on the New York Stock Exchange rose from about $3\frac{1}{2}$ million in 1961–1962 to 10 million in 1967, and this trend shows signs of continuing. Moreover, market values have risen in the post-World War II period, particularly since 1950, as shown in Table 7-2. With other financial instruments, the increase in total value of securities outstanding is primarily the result of the creation of new financial assets. Relatively little increase can be attributed to transactions involving existing securities in the secondary market. In fact, with the trend of increasing interest rates since World War II, the market value of existing fixed-income securities has declined steadily. It is only the infusion of new issues that has produced an increase in the total market value of issues outstanding. The opposite is true for common stocks, whose increase in market value is attributable almost exclusively to transactions involving existing securities in the secondary market.

Returns on Common Stock

Because of the potential for capital appreciation, the return on a common stock differs somewhat from that on a fixed-income security. Under most circumstances, this return consists of more than the dividend yield—i.e., the ratio of the current dividend per share to the market price per share of the stock. In theory, the rate of return that can be expected on a common stock is the rate of discount that equates the present value of the expected future stream of income to the investor with the present market price of the stock. At time 0, it is

$$P_0 = \frac{D_1}{(1+k)} + \frac{D_2}{(1+k)^2} + ... + \frac{D_\infty}{(1+k)^\infty}$$

$$P_0 = \sum_{t=0}^{\infty} \frac{D_t}{(1+k)^t}$$

(7-1)

where P_0 is the market price per share of the stock at time 0, D_t is the dividend per share expected to be paid in period t, and k is the discount rate, which represents the expected return as defined.

We assume that investors may be analyzed as though they formulate subjective probability distributions of possible dividends per share to be paid in each future period. For the individual investor, the D_t in equation (7-1) are the expected values, or means, of these probability distributions. For the market as a whole, the D_t represent the expected values for investors at the margin. Here k is the market discount factor, which represents the implied required rate of return by the market.

If dividends per share in every future period were expected to be the same as the current dividend, we would have a perpetuity where

$$P_0 = \sum_{t=0}^{\infty} \frac{D_0}{(1 + k)^t} \qquad (7\text{-}2)$$

For a perpetuity, where a steady dividend is expected forever, the rate of discount which equates the present value of the expected dividend stream with the current market price of the stock is

$$k = \frac{D_0}{P_0} \qquad (7\text{-}3)$$

Thus, the expected return on the common-stock investment is equivalent to the current dividend yield.[13] If future dividends are expected to either increase or decrease, however, this equation does not hold. With an increase, the expected return will be higher than the current dividend yield; with a decrease, lower. Suppose that dividends per share were expected to grow at a 15 per cent compound rate for five periods, followed by a 10 per cent growth rate through the tenth period, and a 5 per cent growth rate thereafter. We then would have

$$P_0 = \sum_{t=1}^{5} \frac{D_0(1.15)^t}{(1 + k)^t} + \sum_{t=6}^{10} \frac{D_5(1.10)^{t-5}}{(1 + k)^t} + \sum_{t=11}^{\infty} \frac{D_{10}(1.05)^{t-10}}{(1 + k)^t} \qquad (7\text{-}4)$$

It is clear that with rising dividends in the numerator, the rate of discount necessary to equate the present value of the expected future dividends with P_0 will be higher than it was in equation (7-2)—that is, higher than the dividend yield.

Because common stock has no maturity, the measurement of expected return, in theory, depends upon expected dividends to infinity. One could argue, of course, that few investors ever intend to hold a stock forever; at some time in the future they will want to sell it. Under these circum-

---

[13] See Van Horne, *Financial Management and Policy*, pp. 49–51, for the proof.

stances, the return will be comprised not only of the dividends received but also of the capital gain or loss that arises from the sale of the stock at the end of the holding period. The expected holding-period yield, or return, is the rate of discount that equates the present value of expected future dividends and the present value of the expected market price at the end of the holding period with the current market price of the stock. To determine this return, we would solve the following equation for k:

$$P_0 = \sum_{t=0}^{n} \frac{D_t}{(1 + k)^t} + \frac{P_n}{(1 + k)^n} \tag{7-5}$$

where P_n is the market price at which the investor expects to be able to sell the stock at the end of his holding period.

Thus, the expected return consists of both dividends and capital gains or losses. However, the expected market price at the end of period n will depend upon expected future dividends beyond that point. Accordingly,

$$P_n = \sum_{t=n+1}^{\infty} \frac{D_t}{(1 + k)^{t-n}} \tag{7-6}$$

Substituting this equation into equation (7-5), we obtain

$$P_0 = \sum_{t=0}^{\infty} \frac{D_t}{(1 + k)^t} \tag{7-7}$$

which is the same as our original equation, (7-1). In theory, then, the expected return from a common stock is the rate of discount that equates the present value of the expected future dividend stream with the present market price of the stock. It encompasses both expected dividends and the expected market price at the end of an investor's holding period.

The above discussion does not imply that the company that pays no dividend has no value. Investors in such stocks purchase them with the expectation of being able to sell them in the future at a price greater than what they paid for them. Instead of dividend income plus terminal value, they rely only upon terminal value. However, the terminal value will depend upon the expectations of other investors at the end of the holding period. The ultimate expectation is that the company someday will pay dividends, whether regular or liquidating, and that investors will receive a cash return. Because cash dividends are all that stockholders as a whole receive from their investment, they are the foundation for valuation. These dividends, of course, are closely tied to the prospective earnings performance of the company.

The appropriate *ex post* measure of return on investment in a common stock is the discount rate that equates the present value of actual dividends received, as well as the present value of the price realized on the sale of the

stock, with the original price paid for it. If the stock were purchased at
time 0, the return for a holding period of n periods could be found by
solving the following equation for k:

$$P_0 = \sum_{t=0}^{n} \frac{D_t^*}{(1 + k)^t} + \frac{P_n^*}{(1 + k)^n} \tag{7-8}$$

where D_t^* is the actual dividend per share at the end of period t, and P_n^*
is the actual market price per share of the stock at the end of the holding
period.

Bond Versus Stock Yields

When studying the returns on common stock, we clearly cannot
restrict our analysis to dividend yields over time. The return that is
important is comprised of dividends received plus the capital gain or
loss that arises from the sale of the stock at the end of a holding period.
We saw earlier that as long as dividends are expected to rise, the expected
return on investment will exceed the dividend yield. Therefore, it is not
appropriate to compare dividend yields on common stocks with the yields
on other financial instruments. Common stocks do not have a contractual
redemption value to be paid at maturity; they represent perpetual
investments. While it has been popular in the past, and may still be,
to compare common-stock dividend yields with yields on bonds over
time, these comparisons are not valid. The current dividend accounts
for only one aspect of the return for stocks.

An example of a comparison between bond yields and stock yields
since 1871 is shown in Fig. 7-1. In the period from 1900 to the mid-1950s,
stock yields generally were substantially in excess of bond yields. The
popular reasoning for this spread was that stocks had to yield more than
bonds because of their greater risk. In a rough sense, the yield spread
between the two was thought to represent the risk premium necessary
to attract investors into common stocks. However, we know that this
type of analysis of risk premiums is based upon an inappropriate measure
of the return on common stocks. Differences in yields between stocks and
bonds cannot be compared in the same manner as yield spreads on
different grades of fixed-income securities. The comparison must account
for prospective changes in the market price of stocks.

A number of market analysts have employed the type of evidence in
Fig. 7-1 to predict turning points in stock prices.[14] It was reasoned that
whenever the yield spread in either direction became large, a reversal
was in order. In particular, when stock yields moved below bond yields,

---

[14] For an excellent analysis of these attempts and the conditions that gave rise to them,
see Nicholas Molodovsky, "The Many Aspects of Yields," *Financial Analysts Journal*, 18
(March-April, 1962), 49–62, 77–86.

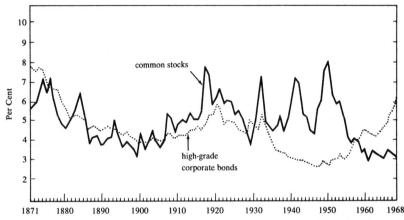

Fig. 7-1.   Bond versus stock yields, 1871–1968. Source: Molodovsky, "The Many Aspects of Yields," p. 86; and *The Federal Reserve Bulletin*.

it was inferred that market prices of common stocks had risen to excessive heights. On the basis of this comparison, predictions were made that stock prices would subsequently fall. In 1929, stock yields were below bond yields, and this occurrence supposedly portended the disastrous market downturn which followed. On the other hand, during the thirties and forties, there was a wide spread in favor of stock yields. Bond yields were very low because of the depression and the "pegging" of rates at low levels during World War II and through 1951. Stock yields, on the other hand, fluctuated freely at their previous higher levels.[15] During this time, stocks were not looked upon favorably as investments, with the result that dividend yields remained high.

After 1949, stock prices began to rise as corporate earnings increased rather dramatically. Dividends also rose, but not at nearly so fast a rate as stock prices. Consequently, dividend yields dropped sharply and only began to level off around 1960. When the stock-yield line crossed the bond-yield line in the mid-1950s, there were many forecasts of disaster for the stock market. A number of reputable analysts attributed this crossing to excessive speculation in stocks—an excess that was sure to be corrected.[16] These predictions continued throughout the 1960s, but the "disparity" continued and, in fact, widened. The continuing differential in favor of bond yields has tended to quiet the once dominant view of corrections between bond and stock yields, as well as to negate the belief that turning points in stock prices can be predicted on the

[15] Molodovsky, "The Many Aspects of Yields," pp. 49–55.

[16] For a presentation of a number of notable quotations in this regard, see Molodovsky, "The Many Aspects of Yields."

basis of a comparison of bond and stock yields. The fallacy of the approach can be attributed to the faulty measure of return on investment in common stocks. That return encompasses both dividends and market-price appreciation is becoming increasingly accepted.

Empirical Evidence

The comparison of returns for stocks with those for investments in other securities must allow for prospective capital gains. Ideally, the implied discount rate in equation (7-1) for stocks would be compared with the expected yields on fixed-income securities. However, the implied rate of return required by investors at the margin is not directly observable. Estimating it is extremely difficult because of the difficulty of evaluating expectations of future income by investors at the margin. Instead of *ex ante* returns, it is more fruitful to employ *ex post* measures of what the returns on common-stock investments have been over various periods of time.

Perhaps the most comprehensive series of *ex post* returns is that prepared by Lawrence Fisher and James H. Lorie of the University of Chicago Center for Research in Security Prices.[17] They computed returns for portfolios of all common stocks listed on the New York Stock Exchange during the period 1926–1965. Equal initial investments in each of these stocks were assumed, and compound annual rates of return for all possible annual holding periods to the end of 1965 were computed. In other words, for an assumed investment at the beginning of 1926, the compound annual rate of return on the portfolio was computed for a holding period of one year (to the end of 1926), for two years (to the end of 1927), for three years (to the end of 1928), and so forth for 40 years (to the end of 1965). Similarly, compound annual rates of return for portfolios starting at each of the other 39 years were computed.

These rates were calculated (1) assuming reinvestment of dividends, (2) assuming no such reinvestment, and (3) ignoring dividends. In the last category, returns were computed on the basis of capital appreciation alone, whereas in the first two, dividends were a part of the measure. In categories (1) and (3), the rate of return is simply the discount rate that equates the present value of terminal value of the portfolio with its initial value. In category (1), dividends are assumed to be reinvested in the stock at the time paid. For category (2), the rate of return is the discount rate that equates the present value of terminal value plus the present value of all dividends received during the time span with the initial value of the portfolio. For each of these cases, three variations with respect to taxes were employed: (1) no taxes; (2) a low tax bracket, applicable to individuals with incomes of $10,000 in 1960; and (3) a

---

[17]"Rates of Return on Investments in Common Stock: The Year-by-Year Record, 1926–65," *Journal of Business*, 41 (July, 1968), 291–316.

high tax bracket, applicable to individuals with incomes of $50,000 in 1960. In all, nine series of rates of return were computed.

The major shortcoming of the Fisher-Lorie data is the assumption of equal investment in all stocks on the New York Stock Exchange. Stocks with small amounts of shares outstanding are weighted the same as stocks with a large number of shares outstanding. Because the amounts of stock actually outstanding differ greatly, investors as a whole are not able to have such a portfolio. Therefore, the rates of return calculated do not measure the exact return on investment for all stocks on the New York Stock Exchange. Although a portfolio of stocks weighted according to the amounts outstanding would be more suitable, it would add considerable complexity to the job of data collection. Despite this shortcoming, the data offer considerable insight into realized returns on investment in common stocks over time.

The average annual compound rates of return over the 40-year period were the following for the nine categories, on a cash to cash basis:

	No Taxes	Low Tax Rate	High Tax Rate
Reinvestment of dividends	9.3 per cent	8.5 per cent	7.1 per cent
Without reinvestment	7.3	6.9	6.1
Ignoring dividends	4.6	4.3	4.1

We see that the return on investment in common stocks for a 1926–1965 holding period was higher than that for bonds over the same period. The *ex ante* promised yield on a long-term, high-grade corporate bond in 1926 was only $4\frac{1}{2}$ per cent; and the typical realized yield was even less. When taxation is considered, the differential in after-tax return would be even greater, because capital appreciation on common stocks is taxable at the lower capital-gains tax rate. The rather wide difference in realized yields between corporate bonds and stocks is consistent with the greater risk inherent in a stock investment.

The base period used for initial investment was characterized by high stock prices. For all periods beginning after 1929, the average rate of return to 1965 was higher than for the full 1926–1965 period. These returns are shown in Table 7-3, under the assumptions of reinvestment of dividends and no taxes. Because of the volatility of stock prices over time, the annual rates of return for short holding periods such as one year fluctuated greatly. This variation is shown in Table 7-4, again under the assumptions of reinvestment of dividends and no taxes. As the holding period is lengthened, however, the annual rates of return tend to show more stability. Still, the actual return depends upon when stocks are bought and sold. Although the expected returns on common-stock invest-

TABLE 7-3   Rates of Returns on Common Stocks
Held Through 1965
(Reinvestment of Dividends, No Taxes)
(Cash to Cash)

Initial Investment (End of Year)	Return	Initial Investment	Return
January 1926	9.3 per cent	December 1945	12.6 per cent
December 1926	9.5	1946	14.1
1927	9.0	1947	14.8
1928	8.2	1948	15.9
1929	9.9	1949	15.7
1930	12.0	1950	14.4
1931	14.9	1951	14.3
1932	15.8	1952	14.6
1933	13.9	1953	16.2
1934	14.0	1954	13.0
1935	12.6	1955	12.4
1936	11.5	1956	13.5
1937	14.6	1957	17.5
1938	14.2	1958	12.5
1939	14.9	1959	12.3
1940	16.0	1960	15.7
1941	17.5	1961	12.6
1942	16.9	1962	22.2
1943	15.3	1963	22.7
1944	14.4	1964	26.9

Source: Fisher and Lorie, "Rates of Return on Investments in Common Stock."

ments defy precise measurement, *ex post* data on realized returns give considerable insight into the magnitude of and general relationship to expected returns on other financial instruments.

This *ex post* information suggests that the expected return on common stock is significantly higher than that on bonds. The evidence is consistent with the idea that investors require a higher expected return to invest in common stocks than they do to invest in bonds because of the greater risk associated with fluctuations in market price as well as the lower residual claim on assets. An additional study, using Center for Research in Security Prices (Chicago) data, indicated that lower grades of common stocks provide higher realized returns than do high-grade stocks. For the period 1931–1960, Shannon Pratt graded all stocks in the sample according to their relative variation of past prices. The greater the relative variation, the greater the risk of the stock and the lower the grade assigned to it. The average return for all stocks in a particular grading category then was calculated for various holding periods. Pratt found that in general the lower the grade of stock and the greater the risk, the higher the

TABLE 7-4   One-Year Rates of Return
on Common Stocks 1926–1965
(Reinvestment of Dividends, No Taxes)
(Cash to Cash)

Terminal Period (End of Year)	Return	Terminal Period (End of Year)	Return
1926	− 2.2 per cent	1946	−10.6 per cent
1927	29.3	1947	− 1.5
1928	44.9	1948	− 4.0
1929	−30.4	1949	18.0
1930	−37.7	1950	34.5
1931	−48.7	1951	13.8
1932	−12.9	1952	7.8
1933	105.7	1953	− 4.3
1934	12.5	1954	53.2
1935	49.0	1955	17.8
1936	62.8	1956	5.4
1937	−46.6	1957	−13.9
1938	29.3	1958	56.1
1939	− 4.4	1959	13.2
1940	−10.9	1960	− 3.1
1941	−11.4	1961	26.2
1942	29.0	1962	−14.4
1943	54.7	1963	16.3
1944	36.8	1964	15.0
1945	58.7	1965	26.9

Source: Fisher and Lorie, "Rates of Return on Investments in Common Stock."

average realized return.[18] Pratt's findings, together with a straight comparison of realized returns on bonds and stocks, are consistent with the notion of financial risk premiums in the market for common stocks. The greater the risk, the greater the expected return necessary to compensate for the risk.

Valuation and Speculation

Much attention has been directed recently to whether stock prices reflect adequately the true value of ownership of a corporation. On the one hand are those who believe that the market and its pricing mechanism are fairly rational. Not only is the market price of a share of stock based upon best estimates of the future earnings potential of the company, but this earnings potential is discounted at a rate appropriate to the risk involved. The greater the dispersion in possible earnings available to stockholders, the higher the market discount rate and the lower the market price of the stock, all other things being the same. Thus, stock

---

[18] "Relationship Between Risk and Rate of Return for Common Stocks" (Ph.D. dissertation, Indiana University, 1966).

prices are said to portray rationally the value of a corporation with respect to its expected future earnings and the risk associated with those earnings. If the stock market is to be effective in allocating resources in society, William J. Baumol suggests that a necessary condition is that market prices be rational—i.e., they conform to the earnings potential and risk of the company involved.[19] Otherwise, funds will not be channeled to the most productive investment opportunities. A company with inferior investment opportunities may have the same success in attracting equity capital as the firm with quite promising opportunities. This reasoning must be qualified for the relatively small supply of new issues of common stocks. It is new equity financing that is important in the allocation process, not the exchange of existing securities.

On the other side of the coin is the argument that stock prices are not rational; that they do not depict the value of a corporation. Rather, the stock market is said to be subject to considerable emotion, with the result that certain stocks are valued on the basis of rumor and whim alone. As a result they fluctuate sharply in price. The argument is that stocks are priced according to the vagaries of the market and not according to any underlying value based upon potential earnings and risk.[20]

It is important to recognize that sharp fluctuations in stock prices are not necessarily in conflict with a rational system of pricing. To illustrate, consider the dividend valuation model in equation (7-1). Assume also that the dividend-payout ratio of the company—the ratio of current dividends to current earnings—is held constant. The model is

$$P^* = \sum_{t=0}^{\infty} \frac{D_t}{(1 + k)^t} \qquad (7\text{-}9)$$

where P^* is the market price justified by a stream of expected future dividends D_t, discounted at a required rate of return k. The greater the expected future growth in earnings and resulting growth in D_t, the more sensitive is the market price of the stock to changes in these expectations.[21] To illustrate, consider two stocks at a particular point in time. Suppose that the current market price of one were $44 per share, that it paid a current dividend of one dollar per share, and that this dividend were expected by investors at the margin to grow at a 20 per cent annual rate for ten years, a 10 per cent annual rate for the next ten years, and a 5 per cent annual rate thereafter. Thus, growth is expected to taper off in the future; the company is not expected to grow at an above-normal

[19] *The Stock Market and Economic Efficiency* (New York: Fordham University Press, 1965), Chapter 3.

[20] These conflicting views are the same as those described by Baumol.

[21] See Burton G. Malkiel, "Equity Yields and the Structure of Share Prices," *American Economic Review*, LIIV (December, 1963), 1004–31; and Charles C. Holt, "The Influence of Growth Duration on Share Prices," *Journal of Finance*, XVII (September, 1962), 465–75.

rate forever. Suppose further that the market rate of discount for this stock were 15 per cent. The valuation equation becomes

$$\$44 = \sum_{t=1}^{10} \frac{1.00(1.20)^t}{(1.15)^t} + \sum_{t=11}^{20} \frac{D_{10}(1.10)^{t-10}}{(1.15)^t}$$

$$+ \sum_{t=21}^{\infty} \frac{D_{20}(1.05)^{t-20}}{(1.15)^t} \qquad (7\text{-}10)$$

Suppose that the other stock paid a current dividend of two dollars per share, that this dividend were expected to grow at a 5 per cent rate forever, and that the current market price of the stock were $40 per share. Because of the lower risk on this stock, however, suppose that the market discount rate k was only 10 per cent. The valuation equation would be

$$\$40 = \sum_{t=1}^{\infty} \frac{2.00(1.05)^t}{(1.10)^t} \qquad (7\text{-}11)$$

Assume now that the economy is in for a mild recession and that investors revise downward their estimates of growth in dividends per share by 20 per cent for all future periods for both companies. Suppose that the two market discount rates, or required rates of return, do not change; only the market's estimate of expected future growth changes. The new market prices of the stocks become

$$P^*1 = \sum_{t=1}^{10} \frac{1.00(1.16)^t}{(1.15)^t} + \sum_{t=1}^{20} \frac{D_{10}(1.08)^{t-10}}{(1.15)^t}$$

$$+ \sum_{t=21}^{\infty} \frac{D_{20}(1.04)^{t-20}}{(1.15)^t} = \$21.20 \qquad (7\text{-}12)$$

$$P^*2 = \sum_{t=1}^{\infty} \frac{2.00(1.04)^t}{(1.10)^t} = \$33.33 \qquad (7\text{-}13)$$

Given a percentage change in expected future growth, the value of the growth stock, # 1, declines by a greater percentage than does that of stock # 2. Thus, with a change in expected future growth, growth stocks tend to fluctuate sharply in price. If there is also a change in perceived risk such that the required rate of return k changes, the fluctuation in value may be even more pronounced. This illustration implies that sharp fluctuations in market prices of certain stocks are not necessarily inconsistent with rational pricing.

The greater the perceived growth of a stock, the more likely it is to fluctuate in market price. It is not surprising then that for stocks whose earnings are nominal or even nonexistent but whose prospects for growth are great, the price fluctuates considerably. In these cases, the market price of the stock is based almost entirely upon expectations of future growth, and these expectations are subject to considerable variation over a period of time. New information can have a marked influence upon expectations and result in a sharp change in the market price of the stock. Although the pricing mechanism may appear to be irrational, in view of the uncertain future of many of these companies, it may in fact be rational. This is not to say that the pricing mechanism is rational on all occasions, only that observed sharp variations in stock prices are not necessarily inconsistent with rationality. Additional insight into the question is gained by examining the random-walk theory of stock-price behavior.

The Random-Walk Theory

The random-walk theory, as applied to the stock market, implies that past stock-price movements cannot be used to predict future stock prices in such a manner as to "profit" from the predictions.[22] Profit here does not mean absolute profit but profit above an opportunity cost. Usually this opportunity cost is taken to be the profit that would result from a simple buy-and-hold investment strategy. The random-walk theory implies that a stock price fluctuates randomly about its "intrinsic" value, which is determined by a fundamental analysis of its expected future earnings and risk. According to the random-walk theory, the actual market price of a stock at a moment in time represents the market's best estimate of its intrinsic value, based upon all available information. The current price of a stock then embodies all available information. Any discrepancies between actual and intrinsic values would be random— in other words, there would be no systematic fluctuations in stock prices.

The intrinsic value of a stock can change in response to new information, however. When this occurs, the random-walk theory implies that actual market prices adjust instantaneously to the change. If the adjustment in market price to new information were "sticky," stock-price movements would be systematic in their adjustment to changes in intrinsic value, and a random-walk would not exist. Thus, the theory implies that the market for stocks is efficient. With information freely available, there should be no systematic over- or under-valuations of stocks. The market price of a stock could then be taken as the market's best estimate of its

---

[22]For a discussion of the random-walk theory, see Eugene F. Fama, "The Behavior of Stock Market Prices," *Journal of Business*, XXXVIII (January, 1965), 34–105; Eugene F. Fama, "Random Walks in Stock Market Prices," *Financial Analysts Journal*, 21 (September–October, 1965), 55–69; Paul H. Cootner, ed., *The Random Character of Stock Market Prices* (Cambridge, Mass.: The M.I.T. Press, 1964); Paul A. Samuelson, "Proof That Properly Anticipated Prices Fluctuate Randomly," *Industrial Management Review*, VI (Spring, 1965), 41–49; and James C. Van Horne and George G. C. Parker, "The Random-Walk Theory: An Empircal Test," *Financial Analysts Journal*, 24 (November–December, 1967), 87–92.

intrinsic value. If, for some reason, the fluctuation of actual market prices of a stock about its intrinsic value were to become systematic, a number of market participants would recognize the recurring pattern of price movements and would exploit them. The arbitrage action of these market participants would tend to drive out all nonrandom fluctuations in price and bring the stock-price series back to a random walk. Proponents of the random-walk theory suggest that there are simply too many market participants with sufficient resources competing against each other for a profit to exist. Consequently, any nonrandom fluctuations in stock prices are so small that they cannot be exploited profitably.

In addition to an efficient market, the theory maintains that series of stock-price changes are independent over time. As a result, a trader could not hope to predict future prices on the basis solely of past prices so as to profit from his predictions. Thus, the random-walk theory denies the benefits of purely technical trading rules. It implies that the "technician" or "chartist" would be as well off with a buy-and-hold strategy as he would be with mechanical decision rules based upon past stock-price movements.

Empirical testing of the random-walk theory has involved two approaches. The first and once predominant method has been the testing of the independence of stock-price changes over time. With runs tests and tests of serial correlation, the evidence has mostly supported the notion of independence in stock-price changes.[23] However, these tests look at the stock-price series as a whole and place equal weight on each observation. The trader is not interested in the entire price series but only in small segments of it in which there may be short-swing dependencies, or "bursts," in stock prices. What dependence was present during these changes would be overwhelmed by the great majority of data which do not exhibit statistical dependence.

For this reason, a second approach to empirical testing has arisen, which involves the use of mechanical trading rules similar to those employed by technicians or chartists. This approach takes account of short-swing dependencies in the price series. If stock-price changes are independent, trading rules should not show a return greater than that which results from a buy-and-hold strategy. The evidence in this second category of tests is somewhat mixed. While certain trading rules seem to be "profitable," when transaction costs are considered and certain biases eliminated, either the results are not convincing or they tend to support the random-walk theory.[24]

---

[23]See Fama, "The Behavior of Stock Market Prices"; M. G. Kendall, "The Analysis of Economic Time-Series," in Cootner, *The Random Character of Stock Market Prices* (Cambridge, Mass.: The M.I.T. Press, 1964), pp. 85–89; Arnold B. Moore, "Some Characteristics of Changes in Common Stock Prices," in Cootner, pp. 139–61; and C. W. J. Granger and O. Morgenstern, "Spectral Analysis of New York Stock Market Prices," in Cootner, pp. 162–88.

[24]Sidney S. Alexander applied various filter rules to industrial stocks and initially found the rules to result in gains substantially greater than those from a buy-and-hold strategy. In his second paper, corrected for certain biases, the gains were less. "Price Movements

In testing various mechanical trading rules over the 1960–1966 period on a random sample of 30 stocks on the New York Stock Exchange, we found the evidence to support rather convincingly the random-walk theory.[25] These tests were based upon daily closing market prices for each of the 30 stocks over the sample period. A number of tests were performed. The first group involved arithmetic moving averages of 100, 150, and 200 days for each security. Buy and sell signals were given on the basis of whether the actual price of the stock penetrated the moving average of stock prices. If it penetrated it from below, a buy signal was given; if from above, a sell signal was given. To lessen the number of transactions triggered by fluctuations around the moving average, various thresholds were employed. With a 5 per cent threshold, for example, a buy signal was given only when the market price of the stock rose more than 5 per cent above the moving average, and a sell signal was given when it fell more than 5 per cent below the average. Thresholds of 0, 2, 5, 10, and 15 per cent were employed; decision rules were tested for the investor who took only a long position in the market and for the investor who took both long and short positions. With the latter, it was assumed that a short position was undertaken anytime a long position was liquidated.

To supplement the arithmetic moving averages, various exponentially smoothed, weighted moving averages were employed. With these averages, more significance is attached to recent past prices than to distant past prices in the calculation of the moving average. In addition to decision rules based upon weighted and unweighted moving averages, a quadratic predictive model was employed that examined stock prices sequentially in time. The coefficients of the model were updated daily by adaptive exponential smoothing; transaction signals were given on the basis of whether or not the cumulative sum of forecasting errors was statistically significant.

in Speculative Markets: Trends or Random Walks, Parts 1 and 2," *Industrial Management Review* (1961 and 1964), in Cootner, *The Random Character of Stock Market Prices*, pp. 199–218 and 338–72. Eugene F. Fama and Marshall E. Blume, "Filter Rules and Stock-Market Trading," *Journal of Business*, XXXIX (January, 1966), 226–41, tested various filter rules of Alexander using 1956–1962 data and found them to do significantly worse than a buy-and-hold strategy. Robert A. Levy, "Random Walks: Reality or Myth," *Financial Analysts Journal*, 23 (November–December, 1967), 69–77, develops a portfolio upgrading model and presents evidence which allegedly disproves the random-walk theory. In a comment to the article, Michael C. Jensen, "Random Walks: A Comment," *Financial Analysts Journal*, 23 (November–December, 1967), 77–85, points out certain biases in Levy's work which detract from the validity of his conclusions. Paul H. Cootner, "Stock Prices: Random vs. Systematic Changes," *Industrial Management Review* (1962), reprinted in Cootner, pp. 231–52, finds that while certain technical trading rules show a "profit" on a gross bases, they do not when transaction costs are deducted.

[25] Van Horne and Parker, "The Random-Walk Theory: An Empirical Test," *Financial Analysts Journal*, 23 (November–December, 1967), 87–92; Van Horne and Parker, "Technical Trading Rules: A Comment," *Financial Analysts Journal*, 24 (July–August, 1968), 128–32; and Alan Seelenfreund, George G. C. Parker, and James C. Van Horne, "Stock Price Behavior and Trading," *Journal of Financial and Quantitative Analysis*, III (September, 1968), 263–81.

The decision rules were tested with and without brokerage commissions. The results of all of the tests were found to be consistent with the random-walk theory of stock-price behavior. The average profits for the trading rules tested were considerably less than those achieved with a simple buy-and-hold strategy. In most circumstances, profits were even less when transaction costs were ignored. This evidence supports the notion that there is not a meaningful degree of dependence in a series of stock-price changes and that fluctuations in stock prices about their intrinsic values essentially are random.

As discussed earlier, the implication of the random-walk theory is that the market for common stocks is efficient and that market prices adjust very quickly to new information. If the theory holds, it follows that the actual market price of a stock represents the market's best estimate of the intrinsic value of that stock, based upon all available information about earnings potential and risk. The further implication of the theory is that stock prices are reasonably rational. The greater the random fluctuation of stock prices about their intrinsic values, the less this statement would hold. Even with sharp fluctuations, however, stock prices would still bear a definite relationship to the "true" value of ownership in a corporation, as depicted by its earnings potential and risk. In the market as a whole, support of the random-walk theory supports also the notion of rational pricing.[26] This is not to say that all stocks are priced rationally all of the time. We simply do not have sufficient empirical evidence to test this statement. However, in view of the uncertainty associated with most stocks, it appears that the pricing mechanism is reasonably rational.[27]

Convertible Securities[28]

We have purposely postponed the consideration of convertible securities until this chapter because they resemble common stock more closely than they do fixed-income securities. A convertible security is defined as a bond or preferred stock that can be converted at the option of the holder into the common stock of the same corporation. The value of this type of security to an investor depends on (1) its value as a bond or preferred stock and (2) its potential value as common stock. Because the latter

---

[26]This conclusion conflicts with that of Baumol, *The Stock Market and Economic Efficiency*, pp. 39–52.

[27]In general, the growth in stock prices has somewhat paralleled the growth in the economy as measured by the gross national product. This evidence would give rough support to the idea that stock prices are rational and that they reflect intrinsic values. Ezra Solomon, "Economic Growth and Common-Stock Value," *Journal of Business*, XXVIII (July, 1955), 213–21, compared the growth in GNP with that for the Standard & Poor's stock price index for the 1874–1954 period. Both series were deflated by a price index, and Solomon found the real growth in stock prices to be about two-thirds of the rate of growth in GNP.

[28]The first part of this section is adapted from Van Horne, *Financial Management and Policy*, pp. 290–303.

factor tends to be the distinctive characteristic of the security and because it usually is dominant in the valuation of convertibles, the instrument generally is treated as delayed equity financing by corporations. Companies that issue convertible securities expect them to be converted in the future.

An investor in a convertible security obtains a hedge. If the market price of the stock rises, the value of his investment rises also. However, if the market price of the stock turns down, he still holds a fixed-income security, whose value provides a floor below which the price of the convertible is unlikely to fall. Because the principles of valuation of a convertible bond and a convertible preferred stock are nearly the same, our subsequent discussion will be in terms of convertible bonds. The bond value of a convertible is the price of a straight bond of the same company in the open market. If we assume annual interest payments, it can be determined by solving the following equation for B:

$$B = \sum_{t=1}^{n} \frac{I}{(1 + i)^t} + \frac{F}{(1 + i)^n} \qquad (7\text{-}14)$$

where B = straight bond value of the convertible
I = annual interest payments, determined by the coupon rate
F = face value of the convertible
n = years to final maturity
i = market yield to maturity on a straight bond of the same company

The bond-value floor of a convertible is not constant over time. It varies with (1) interest movements in financial markets and (2) changes in the financial risk of the company. If interest rates in general rise, for example, the bond-value floor of the convertible declines. Moreover, if for some reason the credit rating of the company deteriorates over time, the bond value of the convertible also will decline. Unfortunately for the investor, when the market price of the stock falls because of poor earnings, the company may find itself in financial difficulty, in which case its credit standing will suffer. As a result, the straight bond value of the convertible may decline along with the decline in its value as a stock, giving the investor less downside protection than he might have expected originally.

The value of a convertible security as a stock is expressed in terms of its *conversion value*. The conversion value is the number of shares into which the security is convertible times the current market price per share. For example, if a bond is convertible into 20 shares of common stock and the market price of the common is $62 a share, the conversion value of the bond is $20 \times 62 = \$1,240$.

Convertible securities usually sell at premiums over both their bond value and their conversion value. The fact that the security provides the investor with a degree of downside protection usually results in its selling at a market price somewhat higher than its conversion value. How much higher will depend upon the probability that the conversion value of the security will fall below its bond value. The difference between the market price of the convertible and its conversion value is known as the *premium-over-conversion* value. In addition to this premium, a convertible security usually will sell at a market price higher than its straight bond value because of the conversion feature. The higher the market price of the common, the greater the conversion value of the bond and the greater the premium over its straight bond value. The bond value and the conversion value provide floors below which the market price of the convertible will not go.

There is a tradeoff between these two premiums, as illustrated in Fig. 7-2, which shows an inverse relationship between them. At relatively high levels of common-stock prices, the value of the convertible as a bond is negligible. Consequently, its premium over bond value is high, while its premium over conversion value is slight. The security sells mainly for its stock equivalent. For several reasons, investors are unwilling to pay a significant premium over conversion value. First and foremost, the greater the premium of market price of the convertible over its bond value, the less valuable the bond-value protection to the investor. If the bond-value floor of a convertible bond is $900, for example, there is considerably more downside protection if the market price of the convertible is $1,000 than if it is $2,000. Second, when the conversion value is high, the convertible may be called. If it is, the investor will want to convert rather than redeem the bond for the call price. Upon conversion, of course, the bond is worth only its conversion value. Finally, as the market value of the convertible rises, the current yield of the security declines. If the company pays a dividend on its common stock, the current yield on the convertible may decline relative to the yield available on the stock equivalent. This decline also contributes to a narrowing of the premium as the conversion value of the security increases.[29]

On the other hand, when the market value of a convertible is close to its straight bond value, the conversion feature has little value. At this level, the convertible security is valued primarily as a straight bond. Here, its market price is likely to exceed its conversion value by a substantial premium. In addition to a convertible security's unique appeal as both a bond and a common stock, other features contribute to the premium in market price over both its conversion value and its straight bond value. For one thing, a convertible security is attractive to speculators who operate on margin. As the margin requirement on stock currently is somewhat higher than that on convertible securities, speculators are able to borrow more for investment in convertibles than they are able to do for stock. Another influence that may raise premiums is that certain

---

[29] See Eugene F. Brigham, "An Analysis of Convertible Debentures: Theory and Some Empirical Evidence," *Journal of Finance*, XXI (March, 1966), 37.

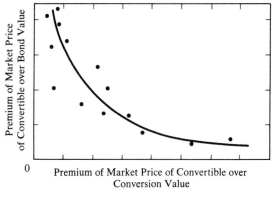

Fig. 7-2.

institutional investors are restricted in the portion of their portfolio they can invest in common stocks. By investing in convertibles, they gain the benefits of common stock but circumvent the restrictions.

Return on Convertibles

The return on a convertible security is complicated in that it derives its value from being both a bond and a common stock. If the individual prospective investor has a fixed investment horizon, the expected return might be found by solving the following equation for k_c.[30]

$$P_0 = \sum_{t=1}^{n} \frac{I_t}{(1 + k_c)^t} + \frac{P_n}{(1 + k_c)^n} \qquad (7\text{-}14)$$

where P_0 = market price of security at time 0

I_t = contractual interest payment at the end of period t

n = investor's horizon period

P_n = expected market price of the convertible at the end of period n

For simplicity, we assume that there is no risk of default on the contractual payment of interest.

The expected market value at the end of the horizon period, P_n, represents the mean of a subjective probability distribution. This distribution usually is skewed to the right because of the bond-value floor of the security. To illustrate, suppose that the investor at time 0 formulated the probability distribution of possible conversion values at the end of period n shown in Fig. 7-3. However, he knows that if the conversion value falls below the bond-value floor of the security, the market price

---

[30] Again, we assume that interest payments are annual.

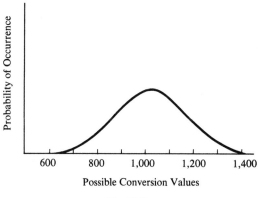

Fig. 7-3.

of the security will not drop below that. If a bond value of $900 is assumed, the modified probability distribution can be shown in Fig. 7-4. Over most of the probability distribution, however, the market price of the convertible security is likely to sell at a premium over both its bond value and its conversion value. Consequently, the probability distribution of conversion values in Fig. 7-4 must be modified to take account of these premiums. By comparing the two premiums for a sample of convertible securities of similar companies, an investor can gauge the size of the premiums. On the basis of this information, the probability distribution in Fig. 7-4 can be modified to reflect the addition of the premiums. An example of the modification appears in Fig. 7-5.

Given a probability distribution of possible market prices at the end of period n similar to Fig. 7-5, the expected value of the distribution can

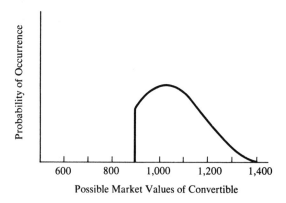

Fig. 7-4.

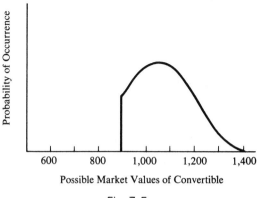

Fig. 7-5.

be determined. With P_n in equation (7-14) thus determined, the expected return to the investor can be found by solving the equation for k_c.[31] Whether the expected return is attractive to the prospective investor will depend upon his opportunity rate of return for investment in other securities of the same risk. The perceived risk of the convertible to the investor is determined mainly by the shape and dispersion of the probability distribution of possible market values at time n; this distribution was illustrated in Fig. 7-5.[32] If the computed expected return is higher than the investor's opportunity rate, he will purchase the convertible security; if it is lower, he will not. The action of all investors behaving in this manner should result in an equilibrium market rate of discount which is consistent with the risk-return tradeoff for all financial instruments.

The realized return on investment in a convertible security can be determined in the same manner as that for common-stock investments. For a given holding period, it would be the rate of discount that equates the present value of interest payments plus terminal value with the initial market price of the security. This realized rate then could be used for comparative purposes with rates of return on common stocks and returns on other financial instruments. Unfortunately, average rates of return for holding convertible securities are not available. Consequently, the analysis of returns tends to be confined to the evaluation of individual convertible securities.

---

[31] For a similar approach to valuation, see William J. Baumol, Burton G. Malkiel, and Richard E. Quandt, "The Valuation of Convertible Securities," *Quarterly Journal of Economics*, LXXX (February, 1966), 48–59.

[32] If the interest payments and bond value are assumed to be subjective random variables, the opportunity rate, or required return, of the investor also would depend upon these distributions. Figure 7-5 would have to be modified further to allow for possible variations in the straight bond value of the convertible.

Summary

Because of the residual-ownership characteristic of equity securities, they are best considered separate from other financial instruments. The most striking characteristics of the market in recent years have been the lack of new issues and the increasing demand for common stocks. As a result, almost all transactions are in the secondary market, where the volume of transactions and market prices have risen more or less steadily since World War II. The lack of new issues is attributable to a reluctance by most corporations to employ equity financing and to their increasing repurchase of existing stock. The growing interest of institutional investors in common stocks has resulted in individuals' increasingly becoming indirect owners of common stocks. Because of the performance orientation of these institutions, many analysts contend that the concentration of ownership by institutions has led to a stock market inherently less stable than before. Since World War II, stocks have been a good inflation hedge. They have shown an appreciation in price far in excess of that of other prices, which in part explains their popularity.

The return on investment in a common stock must include capital appreciation as well as dividends. The expected return on a stock is greater than its dividend yield, if future growth in earnings and dividends is expected. For this reason, it is inappropriate to compare the dividend yield on common stocks with the yield on other financial instruments. While this comparison was once popular for predicting over- and under-valued situations, it has become increasingly clear that the return measure for common stocks must allow for growth in market price. Data are available on average realized returns on common stocks that include both dividends and changes in market price.

There is concern over whether stock prices are rational in relation to the earnings potential and risk of the corporation. Many maintain that stock prices are primarily an emotional phenomenon and bear little relation to "true" value. This argument was examined in relation to a valuation model. It was found that sharp fluctuations in market price for certain stocks are not necessarily inconsistent with a rational pricing mechanism. In addition, the random-walk theory was examined. The theory and the empirical testing of the theory were found to be consistent with the notion that stock prices are rational.

Finally, convertible securities were examined. A convertible security derives its value both as a fixed-income security and as a common stock. Generally, the convertible sells at a premium above its bond value and above its stock equivalent. The tradeoff between these two factors was examined. The return on a convertible security can be measured as the discount rate that equates the present value of interest payments and expected terminal value at the end of a horizon period with the current market price of the security. The estimation of possible terminal values is complicated because the security is both a fixed-income security and common stock.

Selected References

Baumol, William J., *The Stock Market and Economic Efficiency*. New York: Fordham University Press, 1965.

——, Burton G. Malkiel, and Richard E. Quandt, "The Valuation of Convertible Securities," *Quarterly Journal of Economics*, LXXX (February, 1966), 48–59.

Brigham, Eugene F., "An Analysis of Convertible Debentures: Theory and Some Empirical Evidence," *Journal of Finance*, XXI (March, 1966), 35–64.

Cootner, Paul H., *The Random Character of Stock Market Prices*. Cambridge, Mass.: The M.I.T. Press, 1964.

Donaldson, Gordon, *Corporate Debt Capacity*. Boston: Division of Research, Harvard Business School, 1961.

Fama, Eugene F., "The Behavior of Stock Market Prices," *Journal of Business*, 38 (January, 1965), 34–105.

Fisher, Lawrence, and James H. Lorie, "Rates of Return on Investments in Common Stocks: The Year-by-Year Record, 1926–65," *Journal of Business*, 41 (July, 1968), 291–316.

Goldsmith, Raymond C., *The Flow of Capital Funds in the Postwar Economy*, Chapter 9. New York: National Bureau of Economic Research, 1965.

Mennis, Edmund A., "New Trends in Institutional Investment," *Financial Analysts Journal*, 24 (July–August, 1968), 133–38.

Molodovsky, Nicholas, "The Many Aspects of Yields." *Financial Analysts Journal*, 18 (March–April, 1962), 49–62, 77–86.

Seelenfreund, Alan, George G. C. Parker, and James C. Van Horne, "Stock Price Behavior and Trading," *Journal of Financial and Quantitative Analysis*, III (September, 1968), 263–82.

Soldofsky, Robert M., "Yield-Risk Performance Measurements," *Financial Analysts Journal*, 24 (September–October, 1968), 130–39.

Van Horne, James C., *Financial Management and Policy*, Chapters 1–9, 14. Englewood Cliffs, N.J.: Prentice-Hall, Inc., 1968.

——, and George G. C. Parker, "The Random Walk Theory: An Empirical Test," *Financial Analysts Journal*, 23 (November–December, 1967), 87–92.

——, "Technical Trading Rules: A Comment," *Financial Analysts Journal*, 24 (July–August, 1968), 128–32.

Weil, Roman L., Jr., Joel E. Segall, and David Green, Jr., "Premiums on Convertible Bonds," *Journal of Finance*, XXIII (June, 1968), 445–64.

Index